ANNUAL '96

NON FICTION

Membri della Commissione Internazionale di Selezione 1996

Members of the 1996 International Selection Committee

Jacques Binsztok
Seuil Jeunesse
Paris, France

Cristina Drago
Istituto Geografico
De Agostini
Novara, Italy

K.T. Hao
Grimm Press
Taipei, China

Christoph Goldlin
Schule fuer Gestaltung
Zürich, *Switzerland*

John Vernon Lord
School of Design,
University of Brighton
Great Britain

JACQUES BINSZTOK. Schivo e ironico, Binsztok affida a poche righe gli avvenimenti della sua vita degni di passare alla storia: "Nato sotto il segno del Topo, è sotto il segno del Topo che viene invitato a partecipare alla Giuria della Mostra Illustratori per il 1996.
Compiuta una brillante carriera scolastica nel miglior ambiente laico della capitale francese, intraprende studi superiori aleatori che lo conducono non a grandi cose per diversi anni.
Il caso e un certo interesse lo portano a scoprire il mondo dell'editoria e, dopo aver contribuito a far fallire diverse piccole imprese, si ferma per alcuni anni presso Albin Michel.
La vicinanza con la Senna lo spinge a stabilirsi alle edizioni Le Seuil dove fa la felicità dei piccoli e dei grandi dal 1992".

JACQUES BINSZTOK. Reserved and ironic, Binsztok sums up in a few lines the events in his life that are worth recording: "Born under the sign of the Rat, it is under the sign of the Rat that he was invited to join the 1996 Illustrators Exhibition jury. After concluding a brilliant school career in the very best secular environment of the French capital, he embarked on an uncertain course of higher education that did not lead to much for several years. Chance and a certain degree of interest led him to discover the world of publishing and, after helping a number of small businesses go bust, he stayed for several years at Albin Michel. Proximity to the Seine prompted him to settle at Editions Le Seuil, where he has been making children and grown-ups happy since 1992".

CRISTINA DRAGO lavora nella casa editrice di famiglia, l'Istituto Geografico De Agostini. Dal 1994 si occupa della produzione per bambini e ragazzi, come responsabile del coordinamento editoriale.
Con un centinaio di società, la De Agostini è presente in ventisei Paesi ed opera in diversi settori: dai libri illustrati per adulti e ragazzi ai testi di scolastica e parascolastica, dalle dispense per l'edicola ad una prestigiosa produzione cartografica. In rapido sviluppo anche l'area multimediale, che offre una vasta gamma di prodotti.

CRISTINA DRAGO works at the family publishing house Istituto Geografico De Agostini. Since 1994 she has been the publishing coordination manager in charge of products for children and young adults. Comprising one hundred or so companies, De Agostini is active in twenty-six countries and operates in a variety of fields, ranging from illustrated books for adults and children to text and extra-curricular books, and from serialised magazines to a high-profile map-production business. De Agostini is also growing rapidly in the multimedia sector and offers a vast range of products.

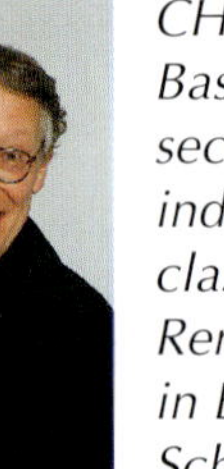

CHRISTOPH GOLDLIN è nato nel 1942 a Basilea. Dopo gli studi di base, ha frequentato i corsi di preparazione e la scuola di pittura di Martin A.Christ e René Acht. Sempre a Basilea, ha proseguito i suoi studi con il pittore Hans R. Schiess.
La sua formazione di disegnatore scientifico ha avuto inizio nel 1968 presso l'antica Ecole des Arts et Mètiers di Zurigo.

CHRISTOPH GOLDLIN was born in Basle in 1942. After finishing secondary school, he attended induction courses and the painting classes given by Martin A. Christ and René Acht. He continued his studies in Basle with the artist Hans R. Schiess. He began training as an illustrator of non-fiction subjects in 1968 at the old-established Ecole des Arts et Métiers

Ha lavorato come freelance per alcuni anni e dal 1972 insegna disegno e illustrazione scientifica presso l'Ecole d'Arts di Zurigo.

in Zurich. He worked as a freelance for several years and since 1972 has been teaching non-fiction drawing and illustration at the Ecole d'Arts in Zurich.

K.T. HAO è nato il 3 aprile 1961 a Taipei dove, nel 1983, si è laureato presso la National Cheng-Chin University. Dopo diverse esperienze nel mondo dell'editoria, dal 1992 è direttore editoriale della Grimm Press. Il suo incontro più o meno casuale con questo mondo gli ha permesso di riscoprire una sua antica passione. il disegno. La Fiera del Libro di Bologna è sempre stata per lui un'occasione preziosa, un luogo unico di incontro e scambio di idee e progetti. A Bologna ha conosciuto i grandi artisti, che invidia per la loro bravura, ed ha imparato molto dagli altri editori; in particolare ha scoperto che un bel libro è frutto di un lungo e complesso lavoro. Questo lavoro lo affascina e vuole farlo bene perché i bambini possano avvicinarsi sempre più ai libri e alla lettura.

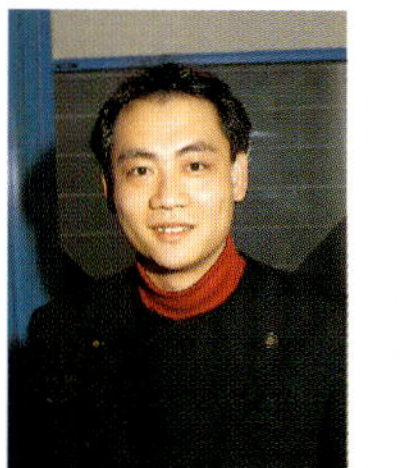

K.T. HAO was born on 3rd April 1961 in Taipei where, in 1983, he graduated from the National Cheng-Chin University. After a variety of experiences in publishing, he joined Grimm Press as publishing director in 1992. His quite accidental entry into this world enabled him to rediscover one of his earliest passions: drawing. For him the Bologna Book Fair has always been a very special occasion, a unique forum for meeting people and swapping ideas and projects. In Bologna he has met great artists, whose abilities arouse his envy, and he has also learned a great deal from other publishers. In particular, he has found that a beautiful book is the result of long and complex process. The work fascinates him and he wants to do it well so that more and more children will be encouraged to discover books and reading for themselves.

JOHN VERNON LORD ha studiato a Salford e al Central College of Arts and Craft di Londra. Autore e illustratore di libri per bambini, insegna illustrazione presso l'Università di Brighton. Il suo libro "The Giant Jam Sandwich", pubblicato per 25 anni e tradotto in diverse lingue, è diventato un classico. Le sue più recenti "Aesop's Fables" hanno ricevuto il prestigioso premio "W.H.Smith Illustration Award" nel 1990 in Inghilterra; di non minor prestigio i premi ricevuti dalle sue 330 illustrazioni per "The Nonsense Verse of Edward Lear". Tiene diversi corsi presso l'Università di Brighton, una istituzione di grande prestigio per lo studio dell'illustrazione.

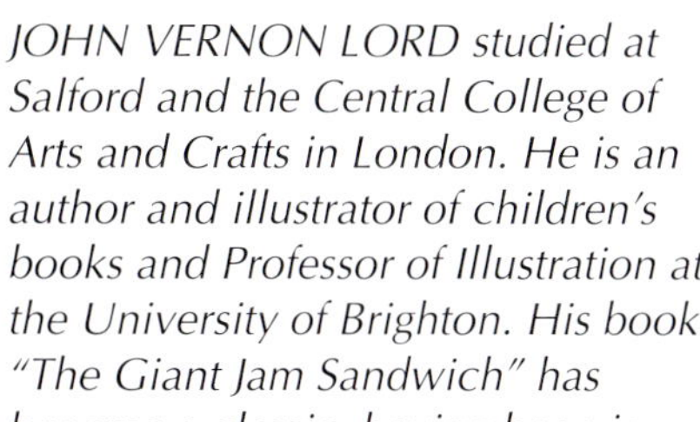

JOHN VERNON LORD studied at Salford and the Central College of Arts and Crafts in London. He is an author and illustrator of children's books and Professor of Illustration at the University of Brighton. His book "The Giant Jam Sandwich" has become a classic, having been in print for over 25 years and translated worlwide. His more recent "Aesop's Fables" won the prestigious "W.H. Smith Illustration Award" in the UK in 1990 and his 330 illustrations for the "The Nonsense Verse of Edward Lear"also won awards. He teaches on the BA and MA courses at the University of Brighton which is a highly regarded institution for the study of illustration.

MIROIR, MIROIR DIS-MOI........

Cinq personnes, cinq cultures, cinq sensibilités enfermés deux jours durant avec/contre 8000 images.

Le résultat..... ce livre!

Un autre jury aurait fait un autre livre: meilleur ou pire?
C'est notre choix, notre goût et ses imperfections en sont la saveur.

Artistes confirmés ou débutants talentueux, nous avons été également injustes. Nous avons été plus réceptifs aux talents originaux, même avec leurs faiblesses, plutôt qu'à la perfection formelle de l'imitation.

Nous avons essayé de déceler les talents de demain sans négliger ceux qui nous font rêver depuis longtemps.

Nous avons été sensibles à la qualité des images, à la technique, à l'inventivité mais avant tout nous avons été émus, bouleversés!
Les couleurs de la création nous ont fait oublier le gris du quotidien.

C'est grâce à Francesca Ferrari et à l'equipe de la Foire de Bologne que nous avons vécu cette expérience passionnante qui nous a beaucoup appris. Merci!

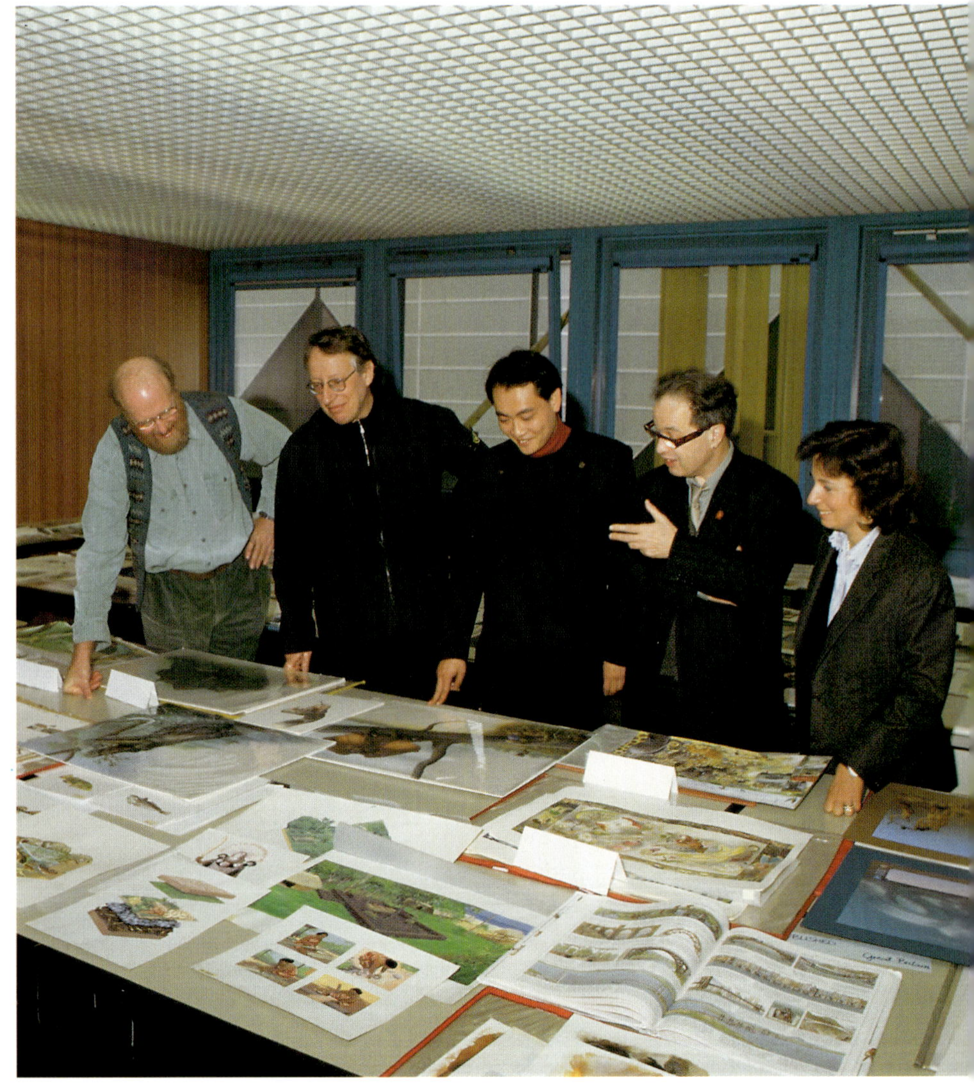

SPECCHIO. SPECCHIO DELLE MIE BRAME...

Cinque persone, cinque culture, cinque sensibilità, si sono confrontate e..... scontrate - per due interi giorni - con 8000 immagini.

Il risultato...... questo libro!

Un'altra Giuria avrebbe realizzato un altro libro: migliore o peggiore?
Questo è l'immagine delle nostre scelte, del nostro gusto e proprio le sue imperfezioni ne determinano il sapore.

Artisti affermati o debuttanti di talento, con tutti siamo stati ugualmente ingiusti.
Più sensibili ai talenti originali, con tutti i loro difetti, piuttosto che alla perfezione formale dell'imitazione.

Abbiamo scelto di mettere in evidenza i talenti di domani pur senza trascurare quelli che da tanto tempo ci fanno sognare.

Siamo stati affascinati dalla qualità delle immagini, dalla tecnica, dall'inventiva ma, soprattutto ci siamo commossi, emozionati.
I colori della fantasia ci hanno fatto dimenticare il grigio di tutti i giorni.

Ed è grazie a Francesca Ferrari e all'equipe della Fiera di Bologna che abbiamo vissuto questa esperienza appassionante, che ci ha arricchito. Grazie

MIRROR, MIRROR ON THE WALL.....

Five individuals, each from a different culture and each with their own sensitivities and perceptions, came together and spent two whole days discussing and arguing over the merits of 8000 illustrations.

The result of our confabulations is this book.

Another jury would have compiled a different book, maybe better, maybe worse.
This catalogue reflects our choices and our tastes and its very imperfections are what gives the book its own unique character.

Established artists and talented newcomers - we were equally unjust to both camps.
We were more sensitive to original talent, with all its defects, rather than to the formal perfection of imitation.

It was our decision to give prominence to youngsters of promise, though without neglecting those artists who have always fired our imagination.

We were much taken with the quality of the images, with the technique and the invention; but most of all, we were thrilled and moved to be cast adrift in a colourful sea of imaginative fancy that made us forget the greyness of the world outside.

And it is thanks to Francesca Ferrari and her team at the Bologna Book Fair that we enjoyed such a stimulating experience - and one which has left us all the richer. Thank you.

Illustratori

Selezionati

Selected

Illustrators

A

Michele Artusi 10/*135*

B

Nancy Benjamin 12/*135*
Charles Benoit 14/*135*
Jean Louis Besson 16/*136*
Pierre Bon 20/*136*
Susanne Bräunig-Harald Vorbrugg 22/*136*
Laura Bruni 24/*137*

C

Giovanni Caselli 26/*137*
Matteo Chesi 30/*137*
M. Gabriella Colombo 32/*138*
Isabelle Courmont 34/*138*

D

Brian Delf 36/*138*
Myriam Deru 40/*139*
François Desbordes 42/*139*
Stephane Dessaint 44/*139*
Marina Durante 46/*140*

E

Christer Eriksson 48/*140*

F

Carlo Ferrantini 52/*140*
Elisabetta Ferrero 54/*141*
Giona Fiocchi 56/*141*
Concetta Flore Harris 58/*141*

G

Henri Galeron 60/*142*
Jean-Marie Guillou 62/*142*

H

Matthias Haab 64/*142*
Andrea Hebrock 68/*143*

I

Istvan 70/*143*

K

Jean Michel Kacédan 72/*143*

L

Marc Lagarde 74/*144*
Doris Lecher 76/*144*

M

Sabrina Marconi 78/*144*
G. Marfurt - M.G. Di Bernardo 80/*145*
Gabriele Maschietti 82/*145*
Maria Grazia Masoni 86/*145*
Stefano Maugeri 88/*146*
Alessandra Micheletti 90/*146*
Philippe Munch 92/*146*

N

Simona Nepa 96/*147*

O

Monica Ottelli 98/*147*

P

Jean Marc Pau 100/*147*
Daniela Perani 102/*148*
Sylvaine Perols 104/*148*
Maurice Pommier 108/*148*
James Prunier 110/*149*

R

Pascal Robin 114/*149*

S

Frank Scímia 116/*149*
Valérie Stetten 118/*150*
Gabor Szittya 120/*150*

W

Nicolas Winz 122/*150*

Z

Marek Zawadzki 124/*151*
Mona Zimen 126/*151*

Michele Artusi

Vietnam

Title of Work
Ancient Rome

Technique
Tempera and gouache

Legend
. *Warships: the trireme*

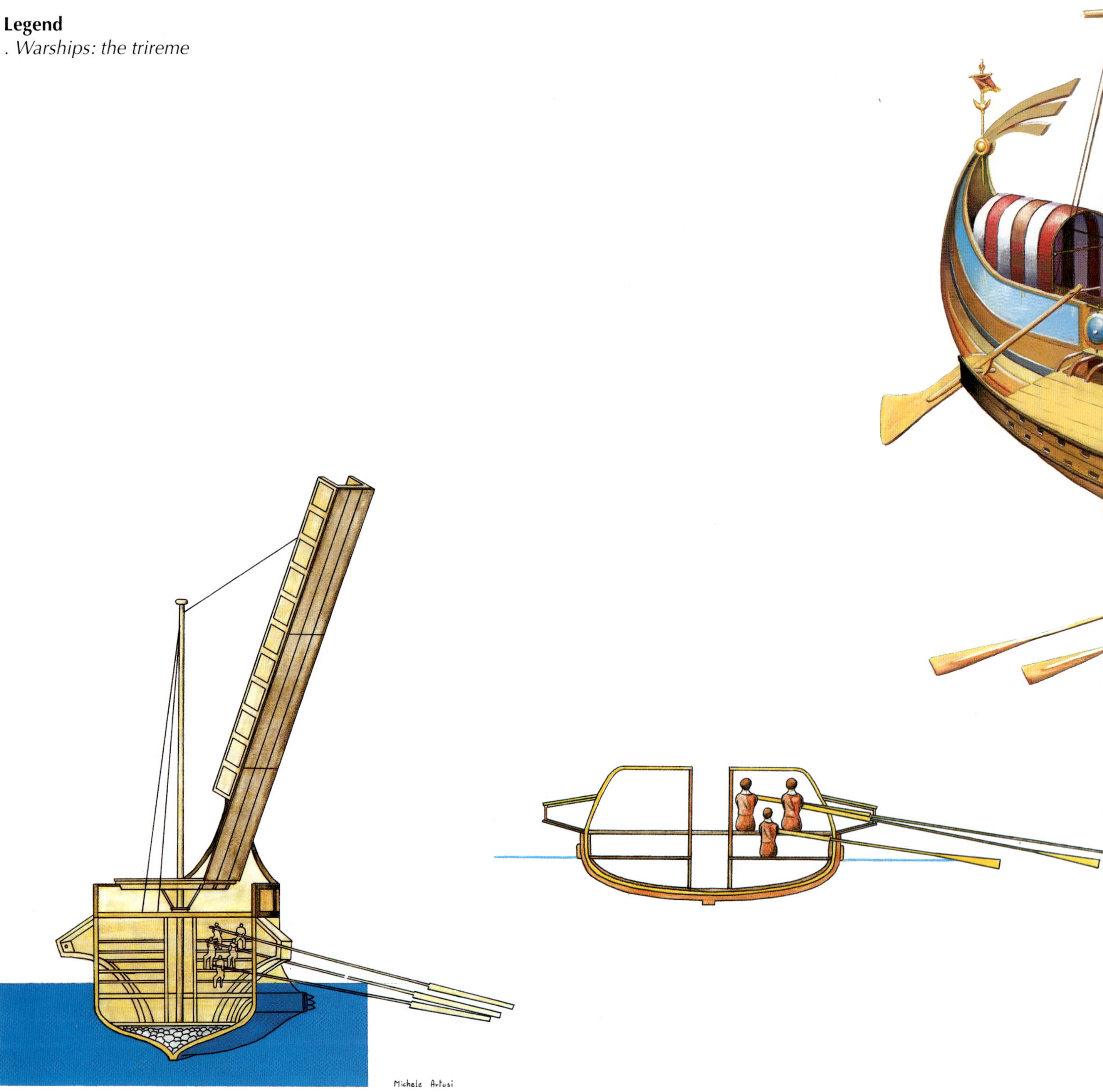

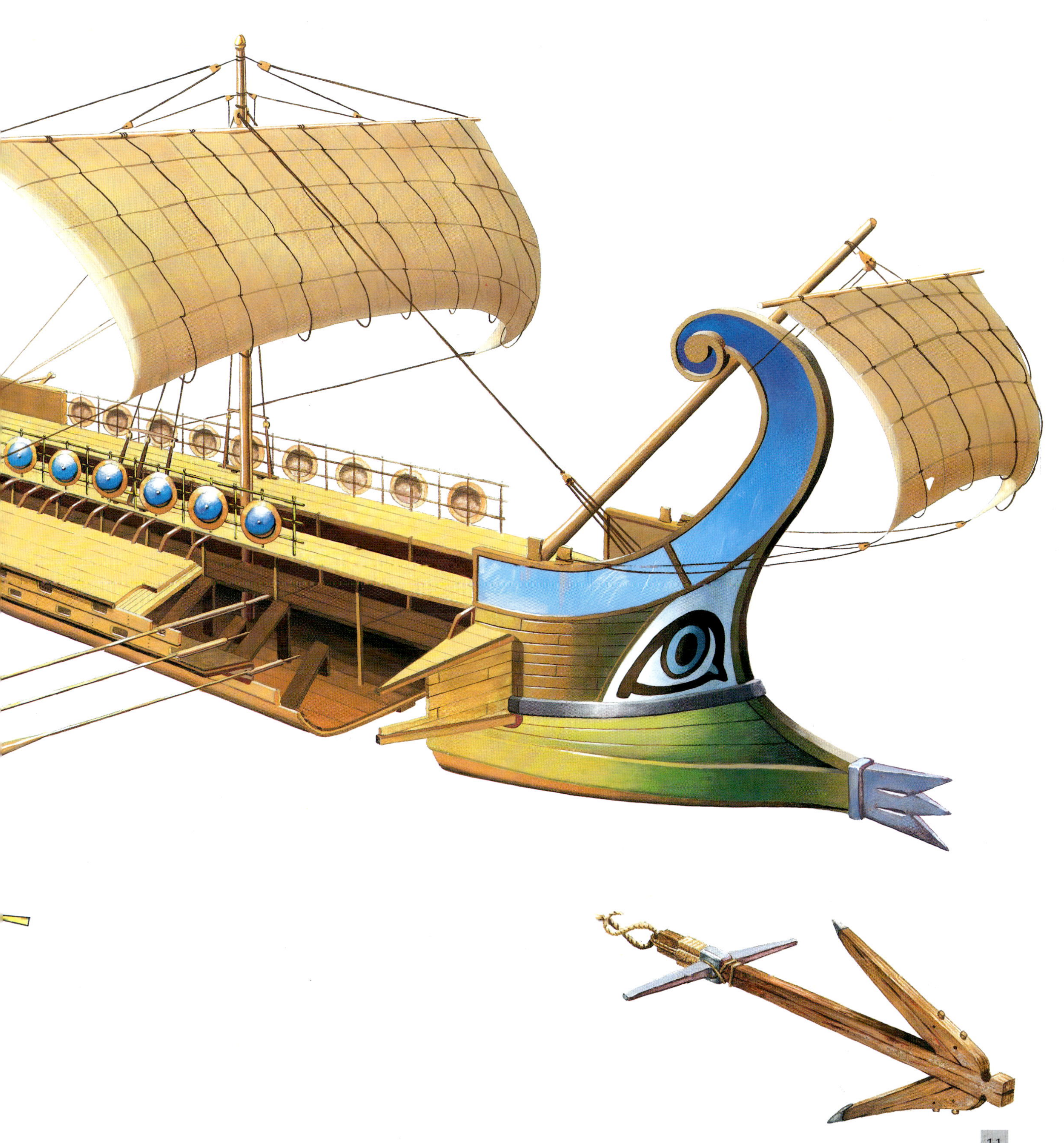

Nancy Benjamin

Italy

Technique
Coloured pencil and tempera

Legend
. *Red eye roach*
. *Appennine roach*
. *Artichokes*

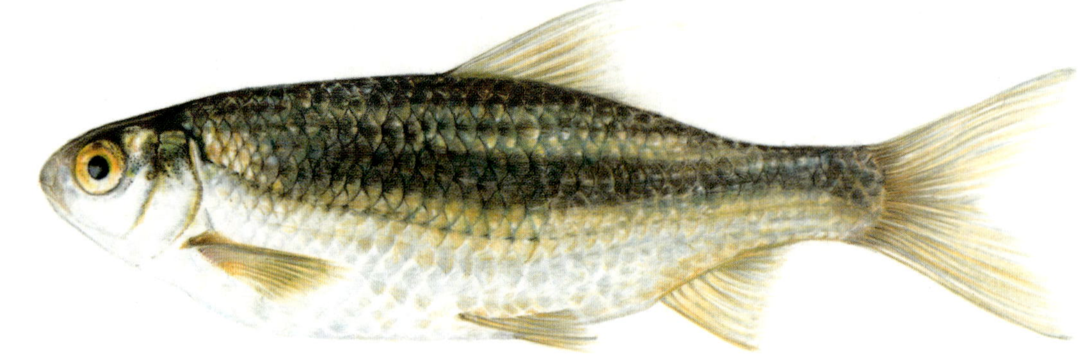

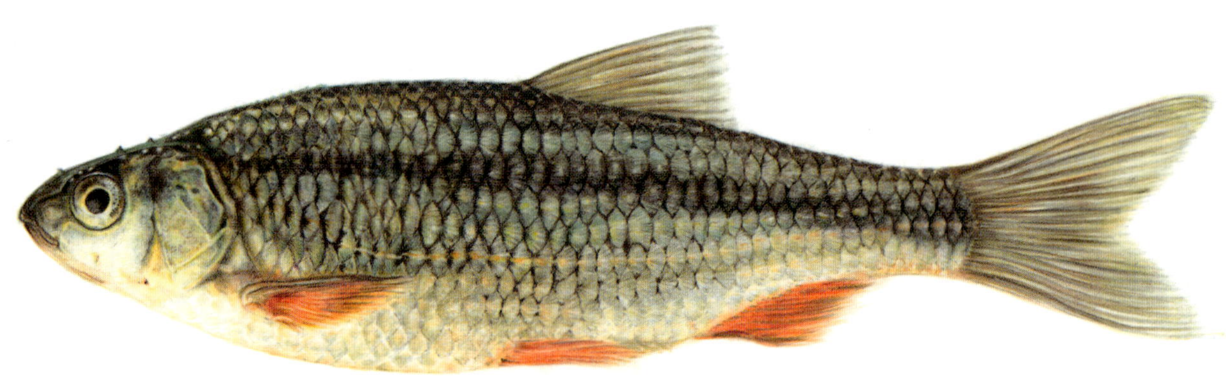

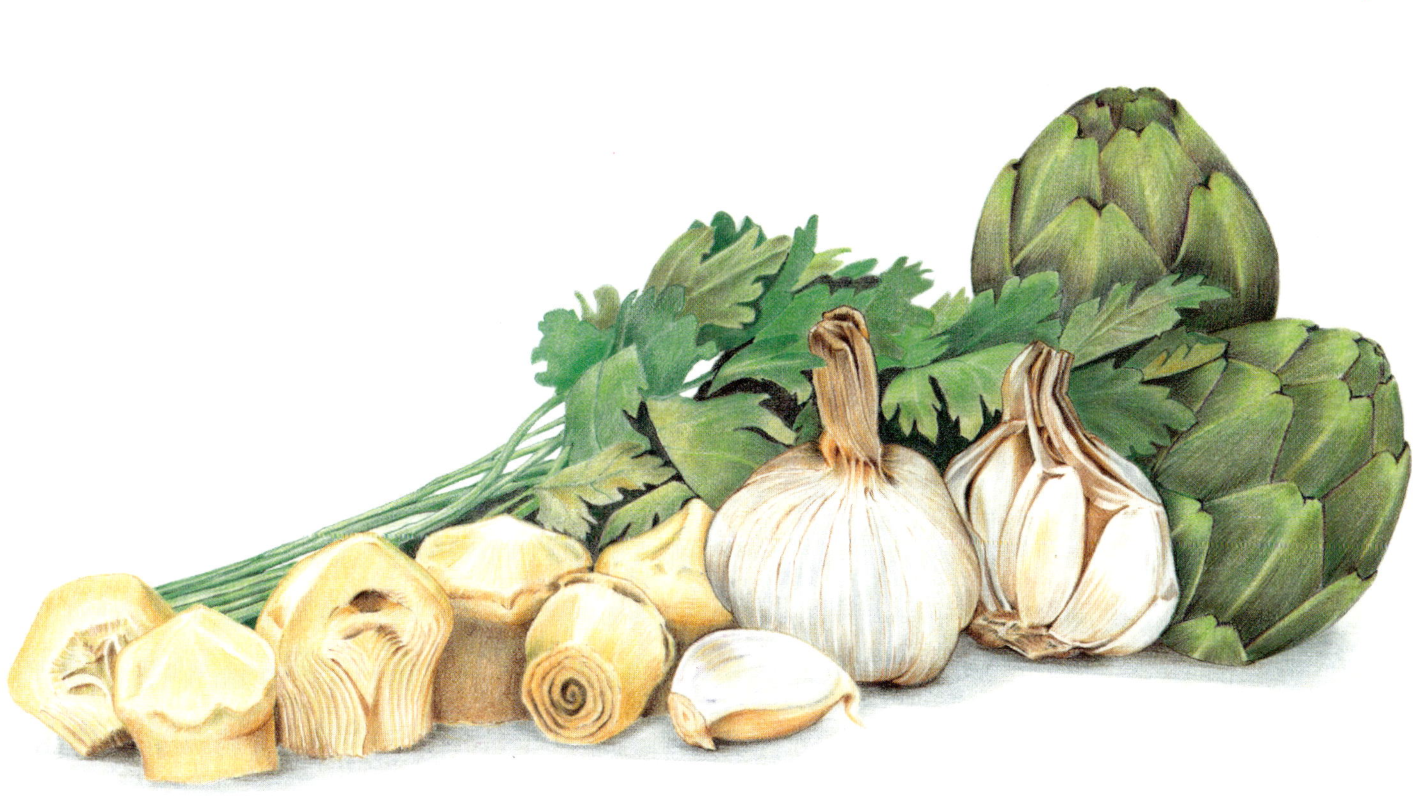

Charles Benoit

France

Title of Work
Woodland animals

Technique
Mixed

Legend
. Boar

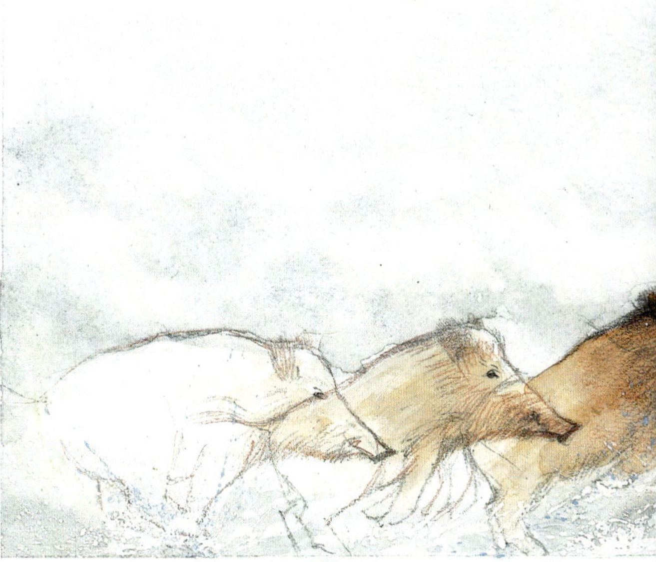

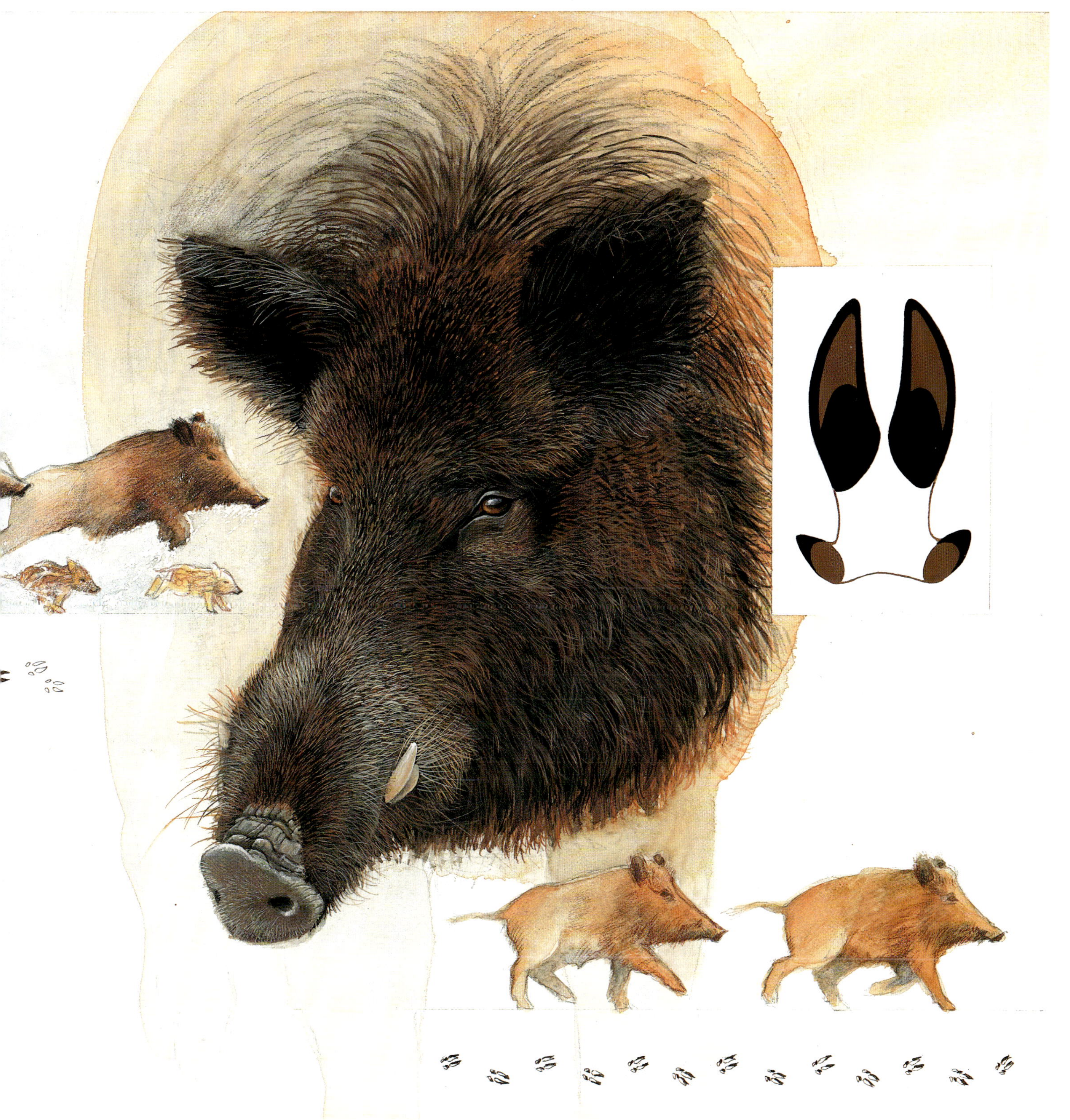

Jean Louis Besson

France

Title of Work
October 45 - Childhood memories of the war

Original Publisher and Date of Publication
The Creative Company,
October 1995
ISBN 0-15-200955-8

Technique
Watercolour and coloured pencil

Legend
. The Jourdain metro station during a night-time air-raid
. June 1940: the German army enters Vitré in Brittany

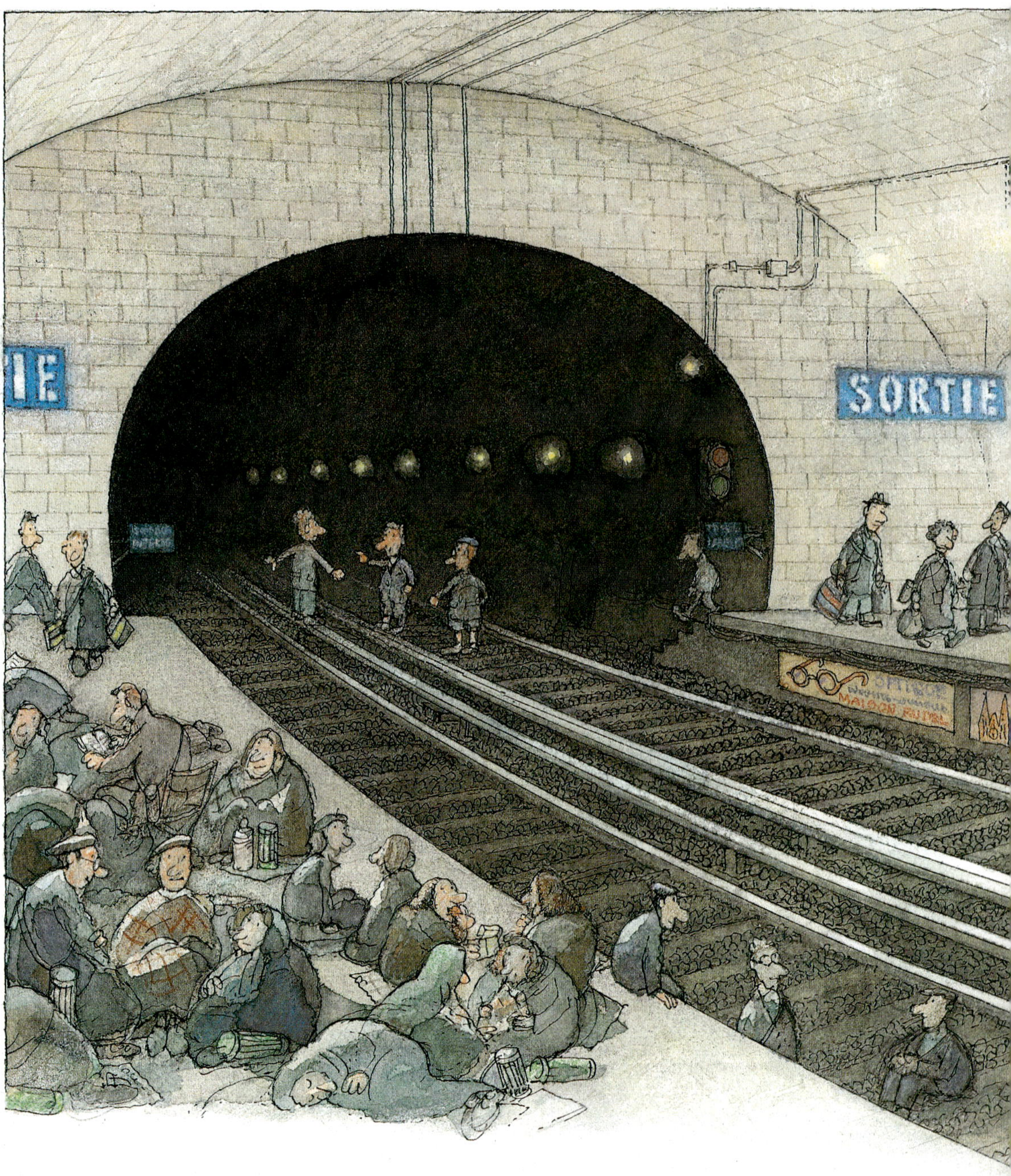

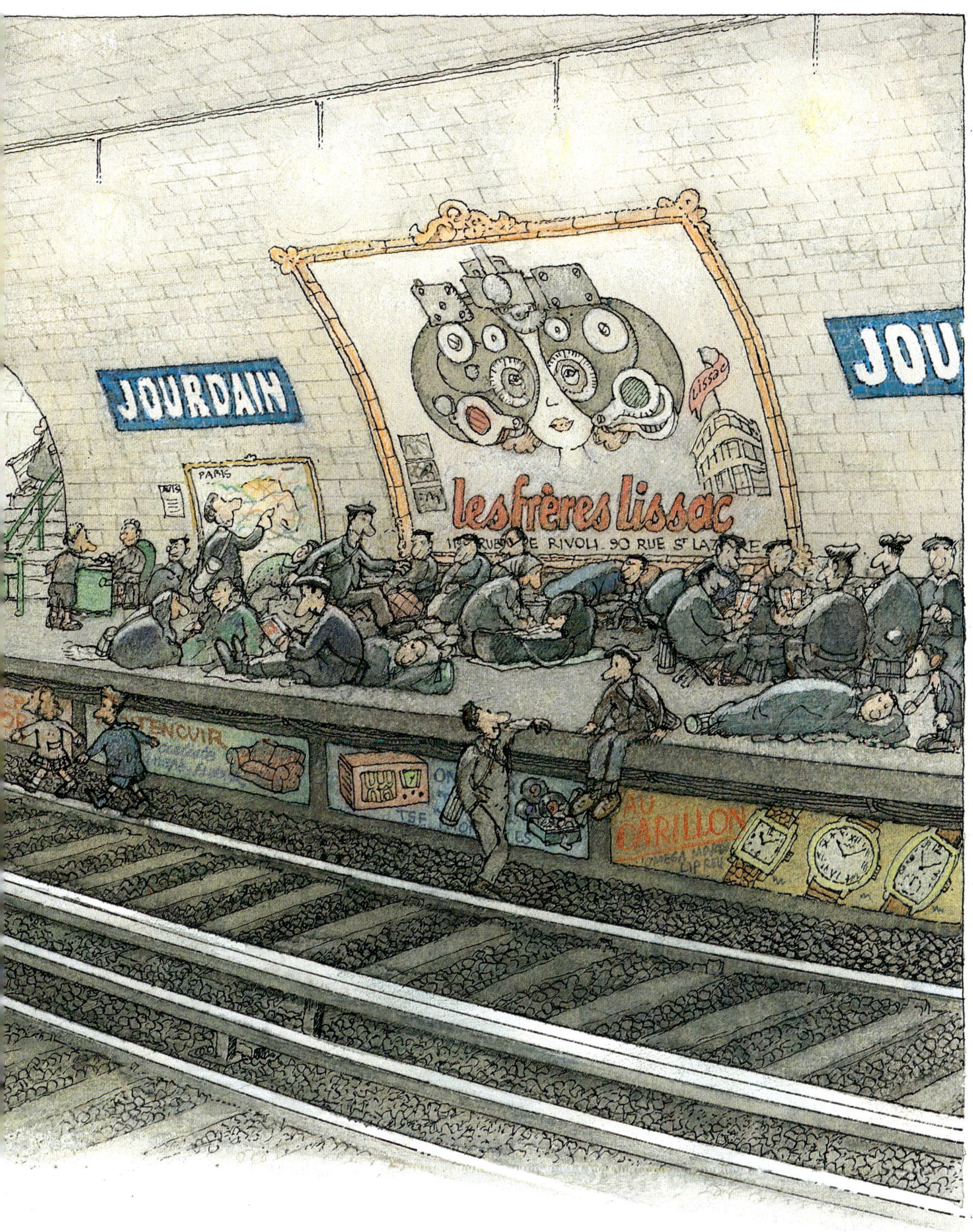
JOURDAIN
JOU
LISSAC
PARIS
les frères lissac
AU CARILLON
TSF

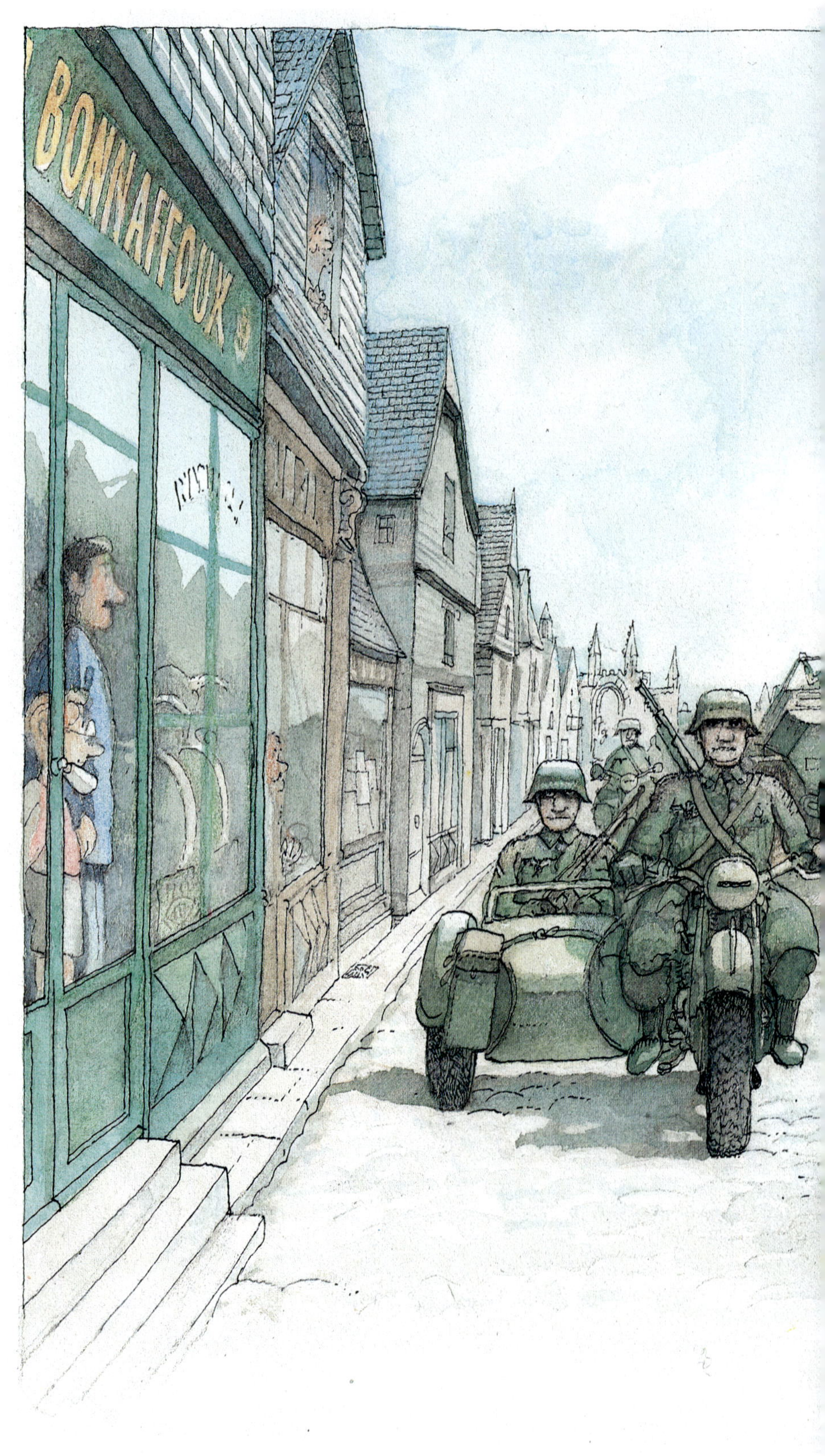
BONNAFFOUX

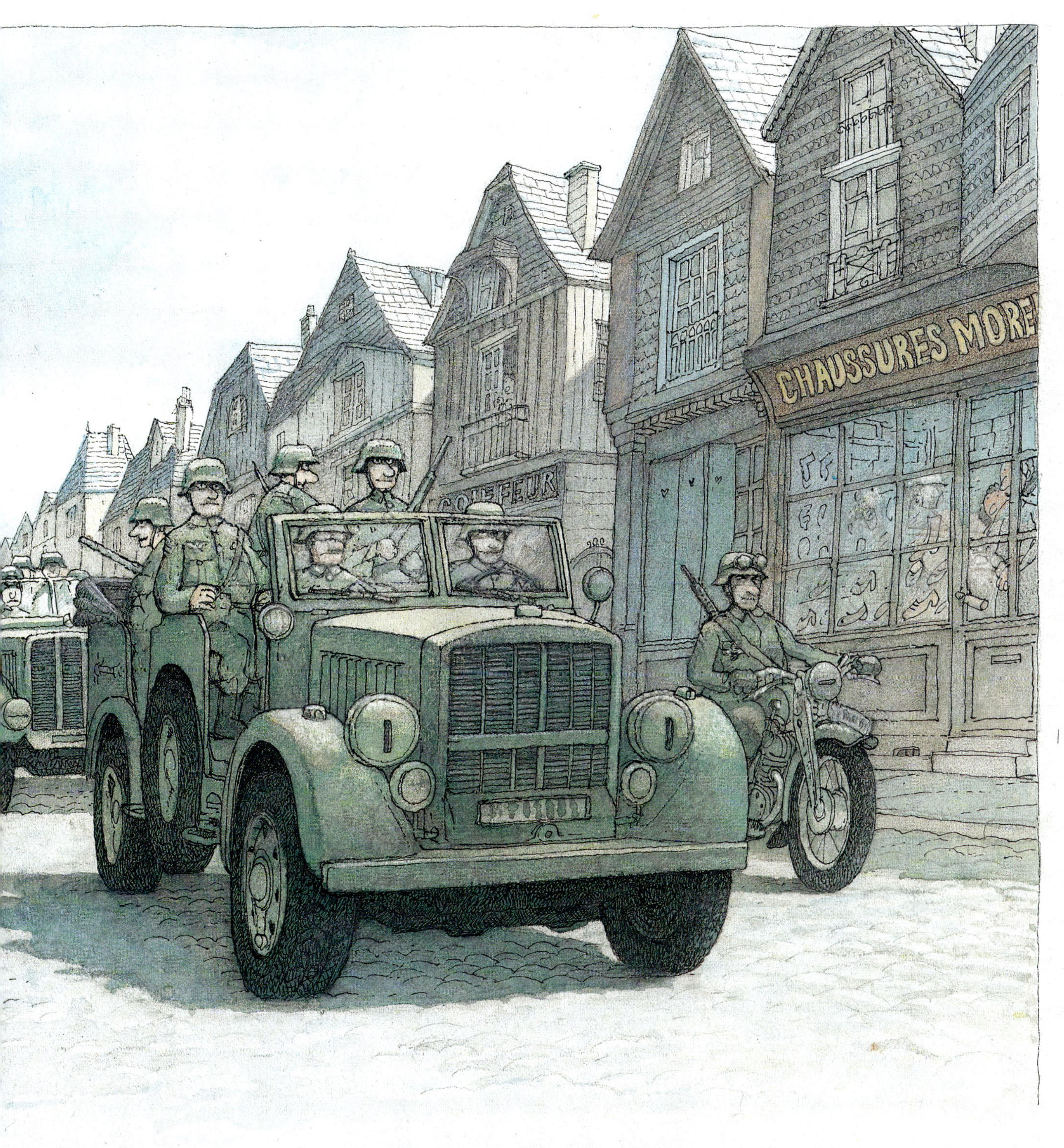
CHAUSSURES MORE

Pierre Bon

France

Title of Work
L'encyclopédie des jeunes: The Universe

Original Publisher and Date of Publication
Larousse S.A., 1995
ISBN 2-03-652401-X

Technique
Ink

Legend
. Stages in star formation
. Old age and death of a star

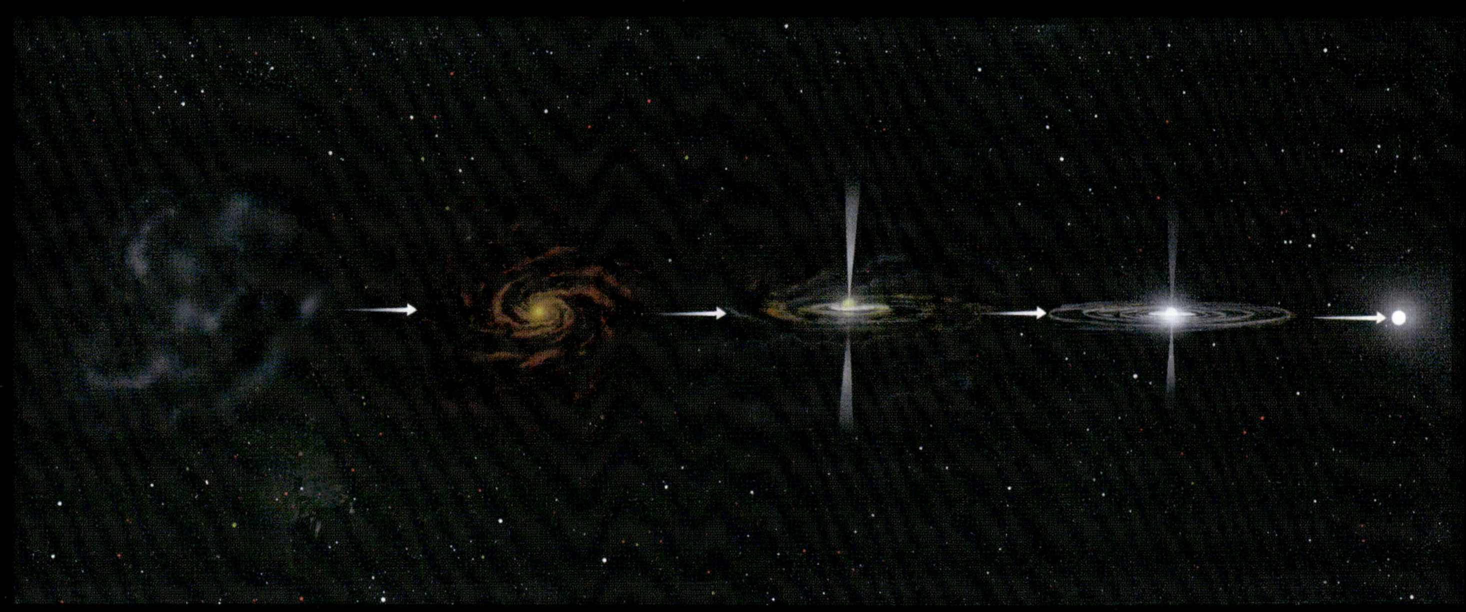

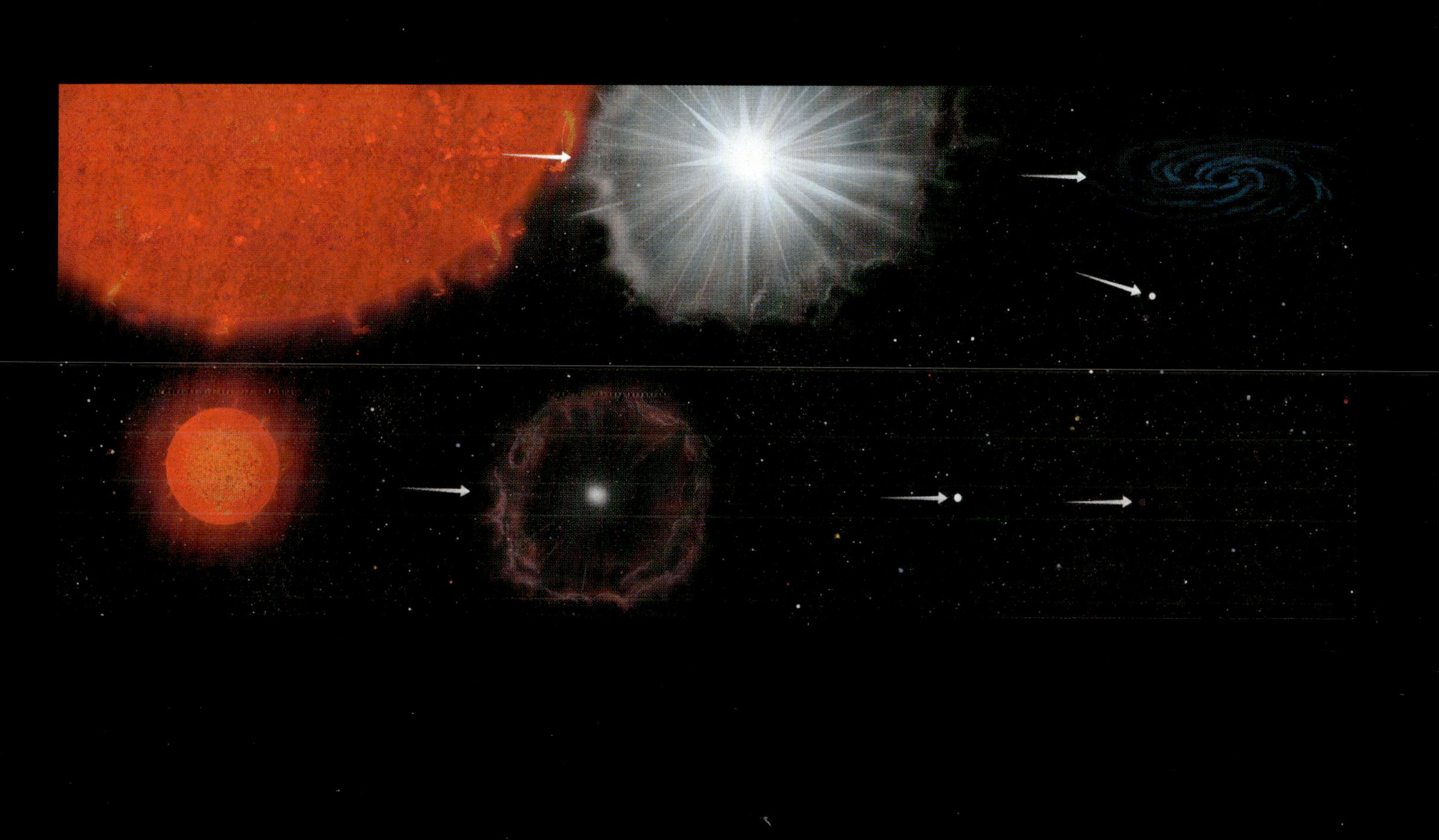

SUSANNE BRÄUNIG - HARALD VORBRUGG

Germany

Title of Work
Puppies from around the world

Original Publisher and Date of Publication
Franckh.Kosmos Verlag, August 1995
ISBN 3-440-06918-4

Technique
Watercolour

Legend
. Where do pups come from?
. Altricial and precocial birds

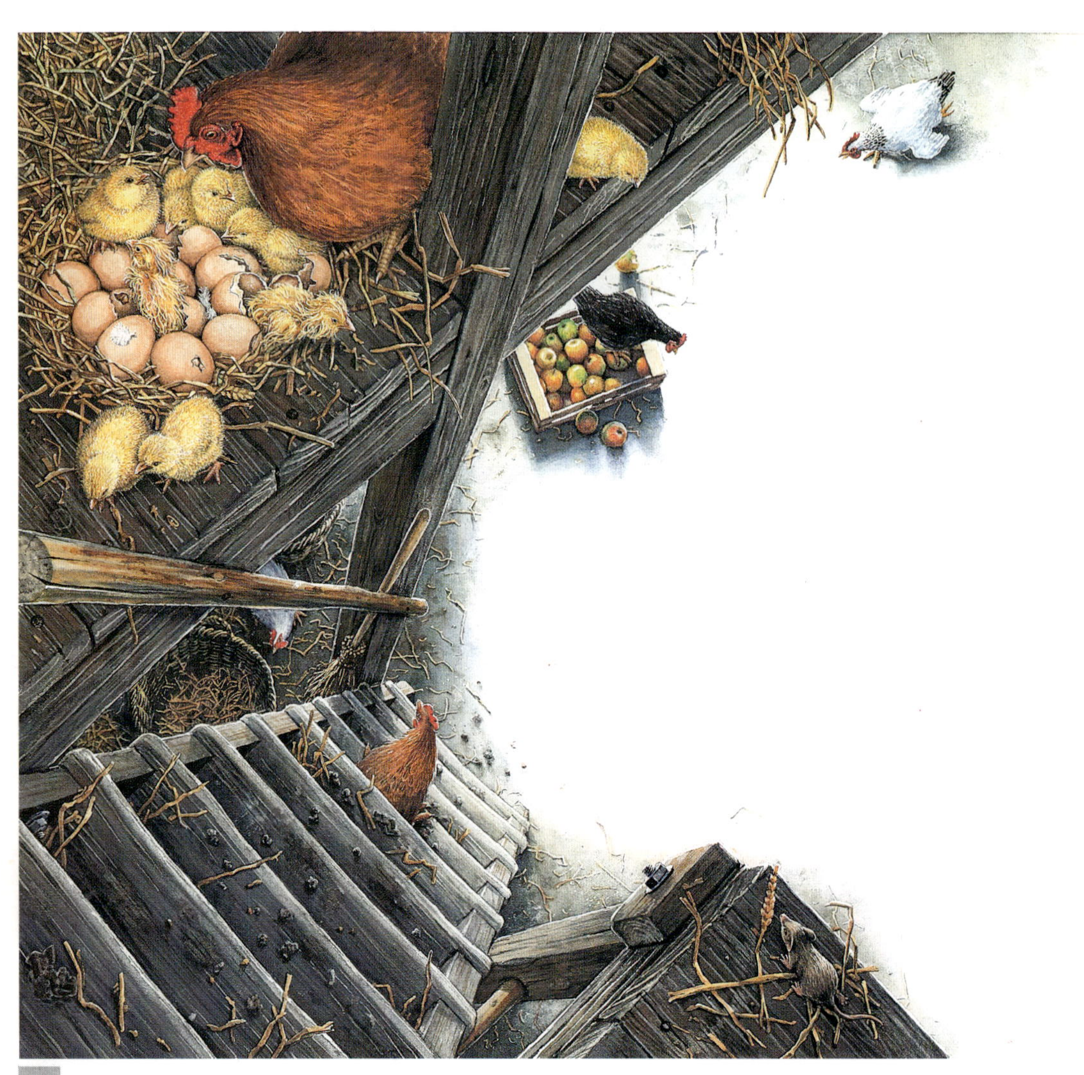

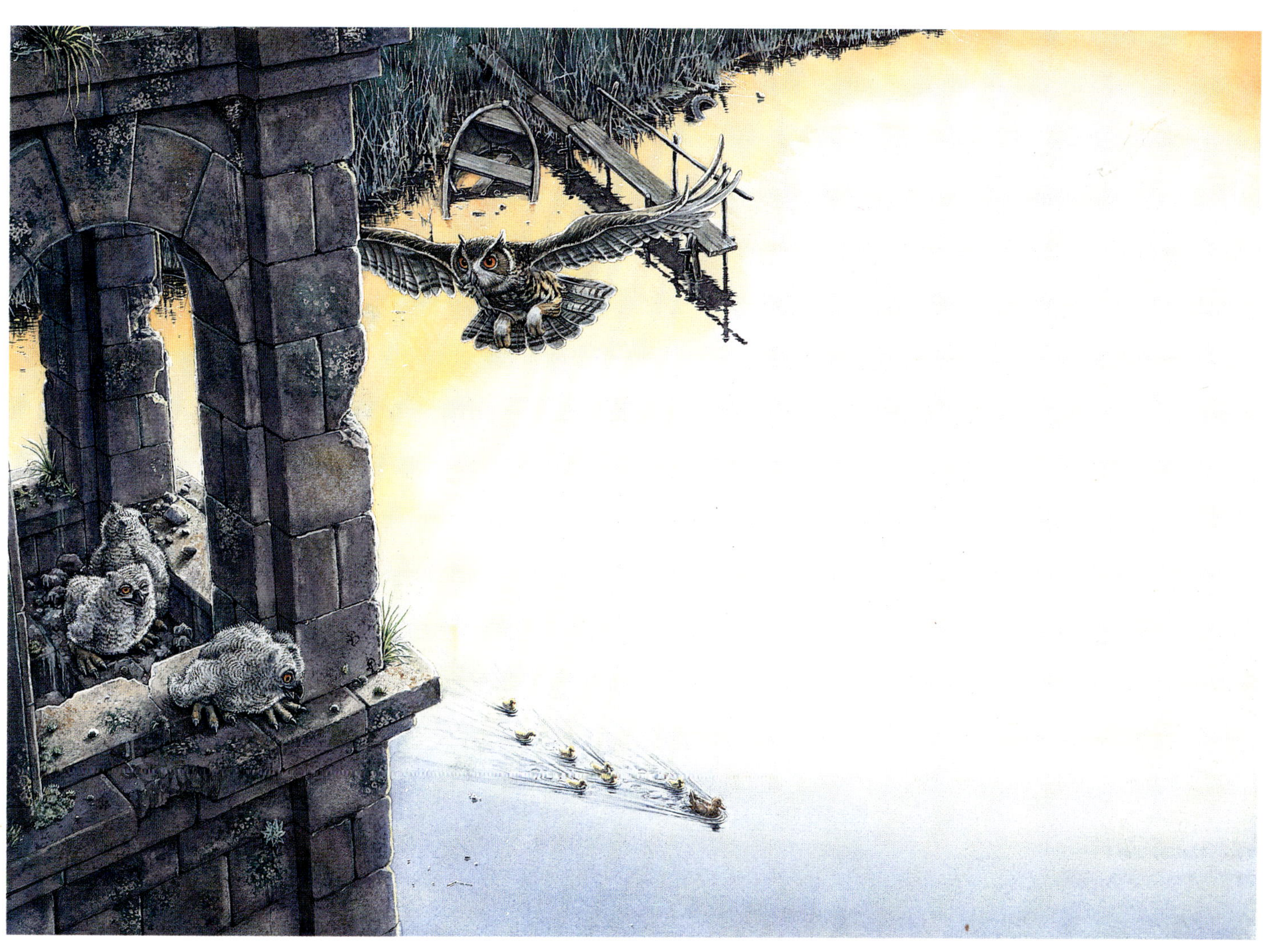

Laura Bruni

Italy

Title of Work
Wood dwellers

Technique
Watercolour, acrylic

Legend
. *Hare*
. *Dormouse*

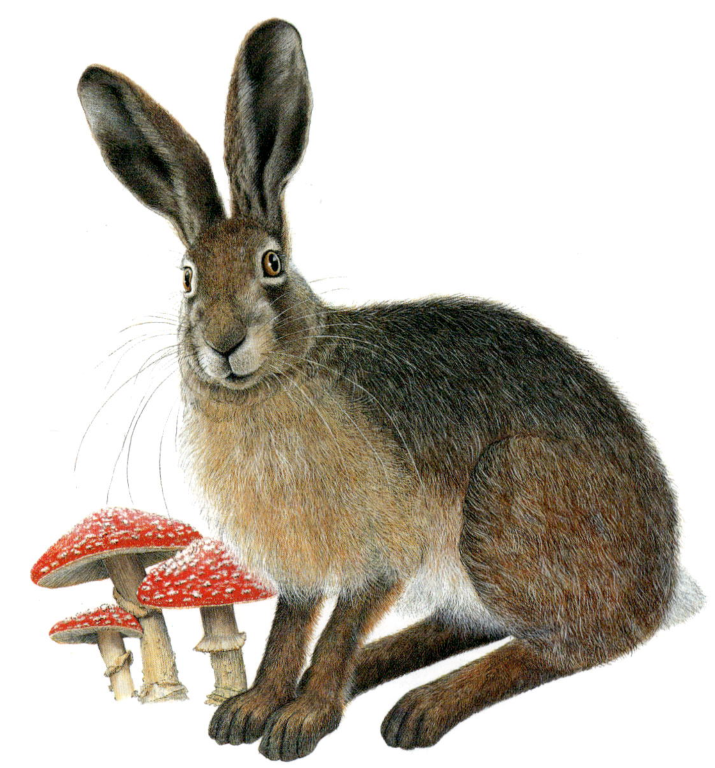

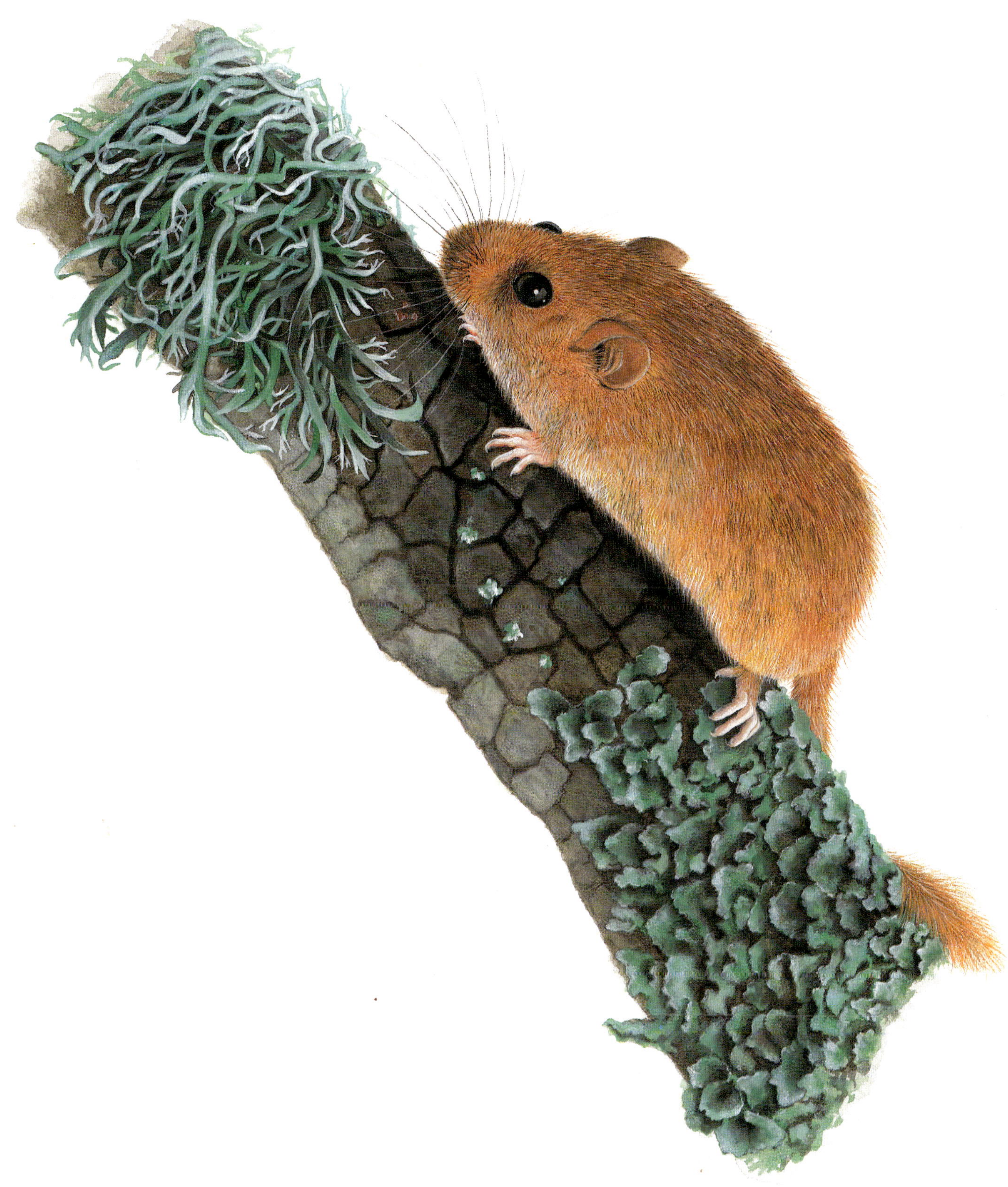

Giovanni Caselli

Malta

Title of Work
The descent of man

Original Publisher and Date of Publication
Istituto Geografico De Agostini, 1994
ISBN 88-415-1850-2

Technique
Watercolour, china ink

Legend
. *Homo erectus*
. *The giant ape*

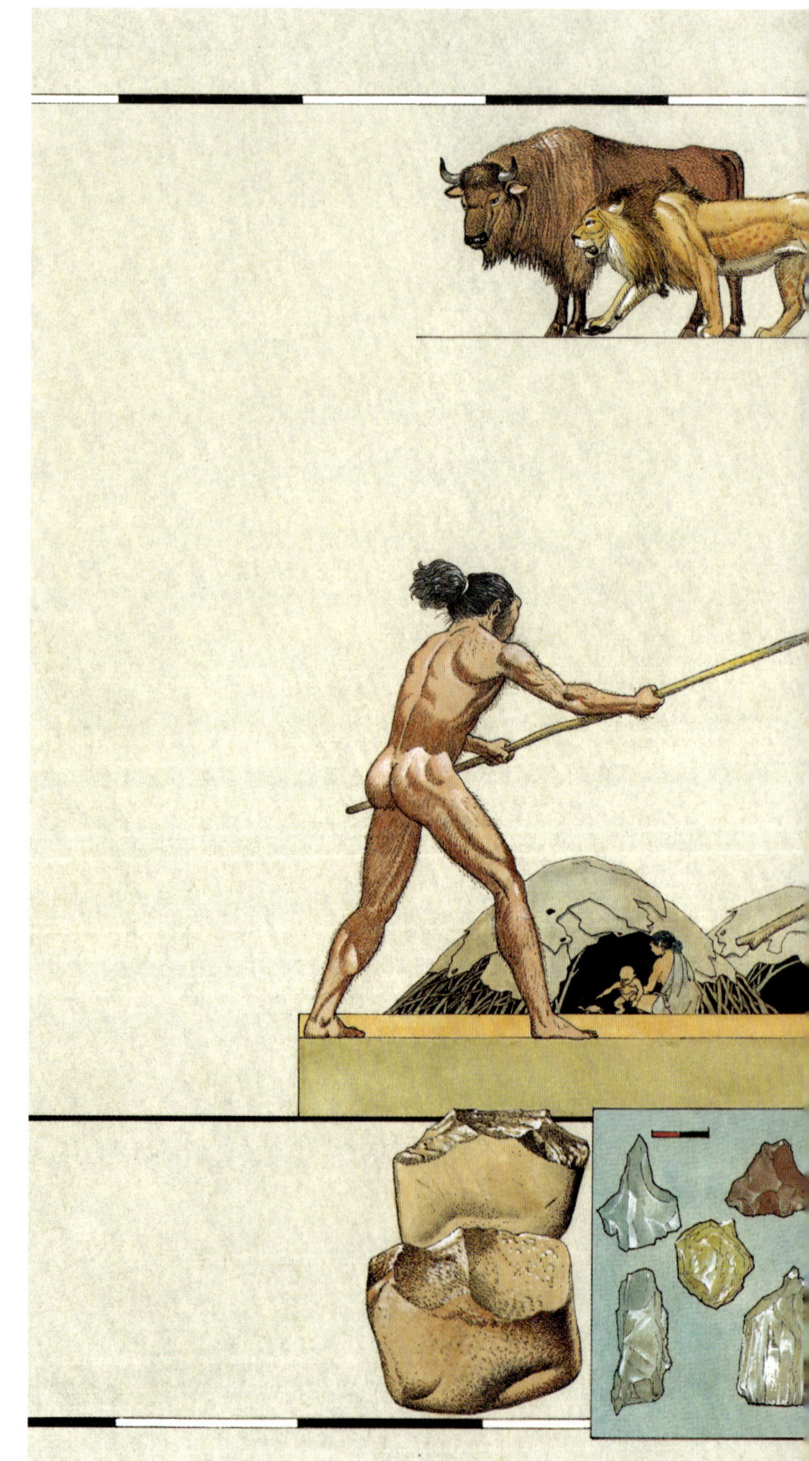

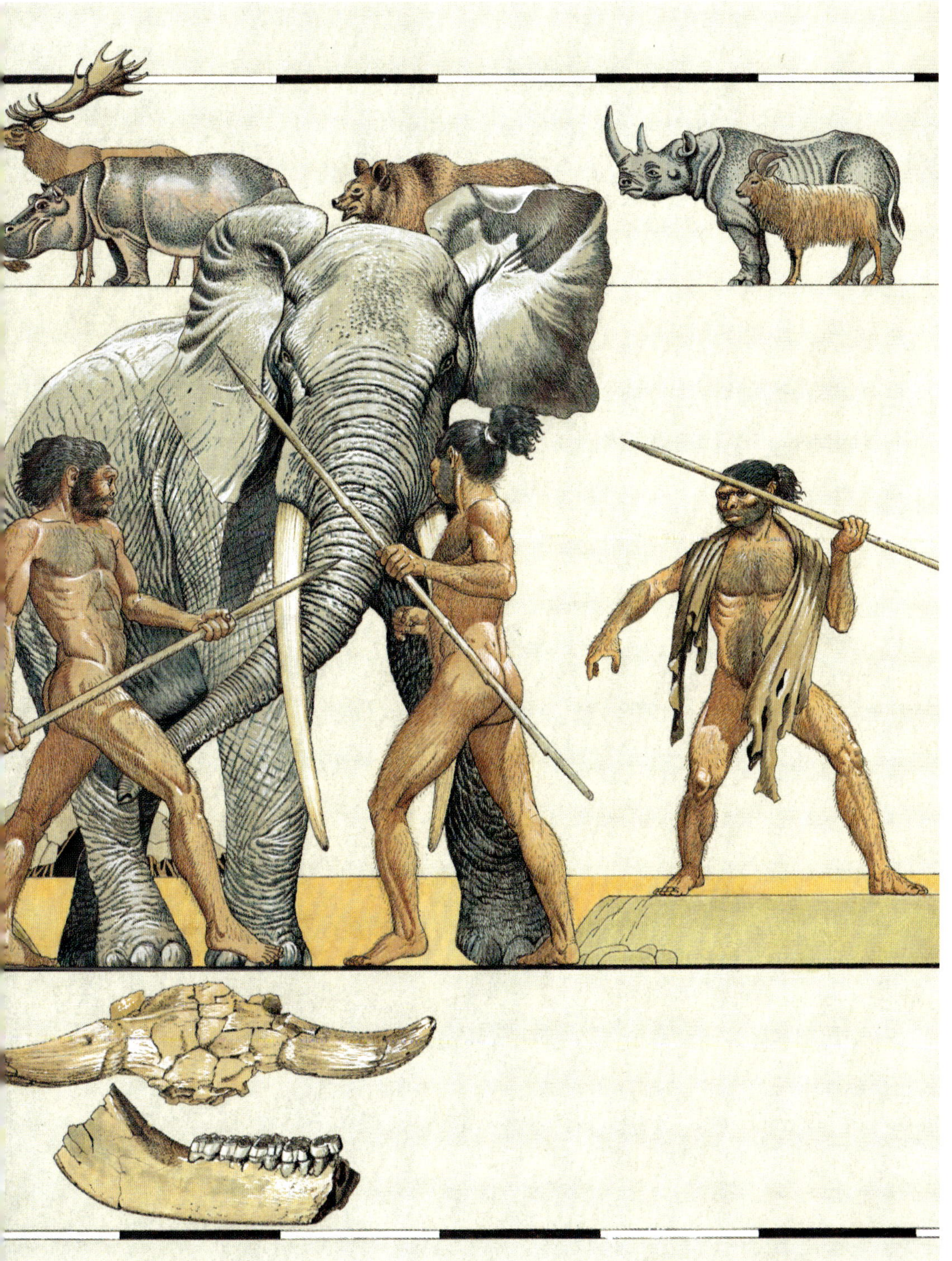

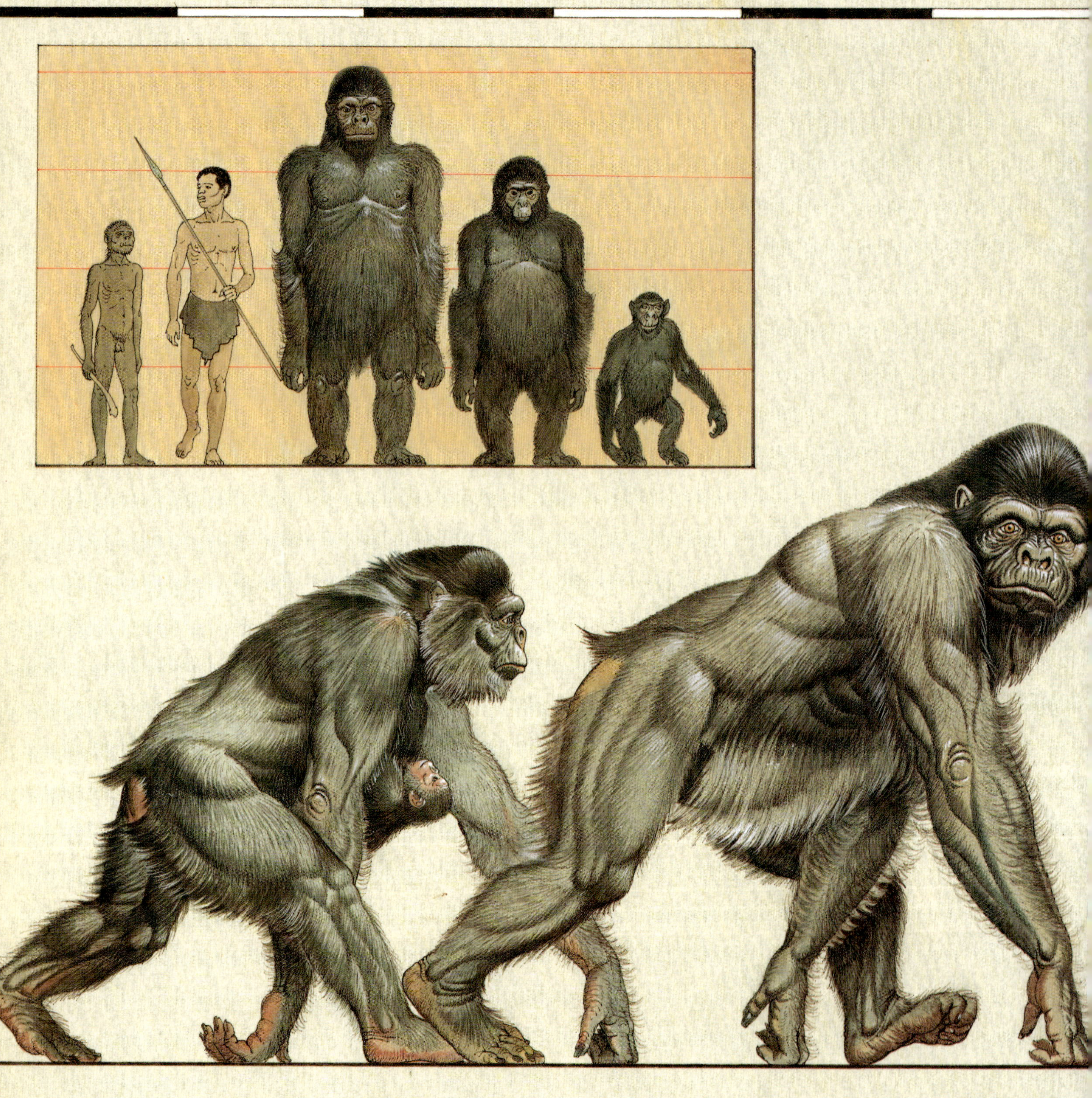

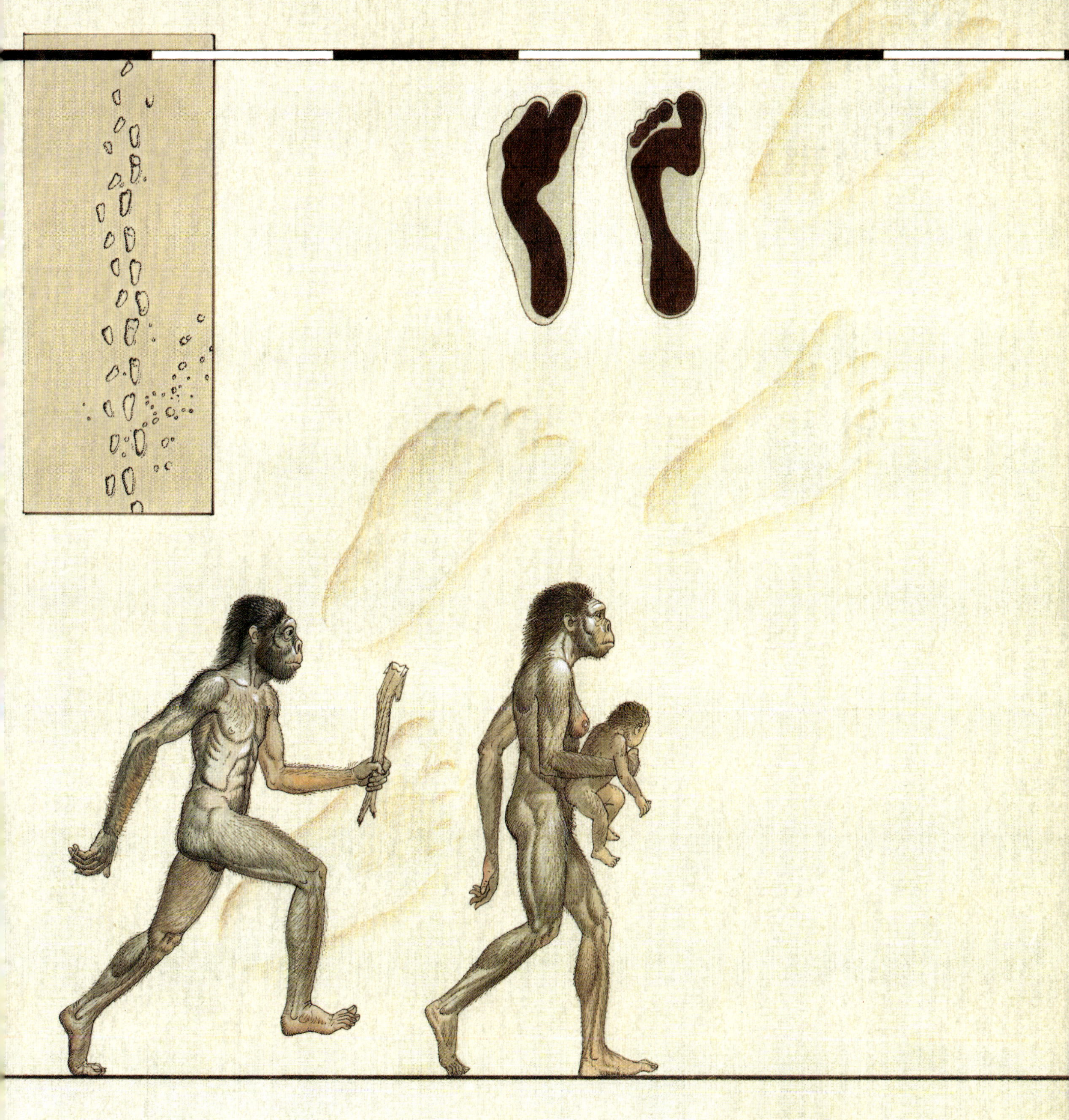

Matteo Chesi

Italy

Title of Work
Peoples, races and animals

Technique
Acrylic

Legend
. Australian aborigine
. Inuit children

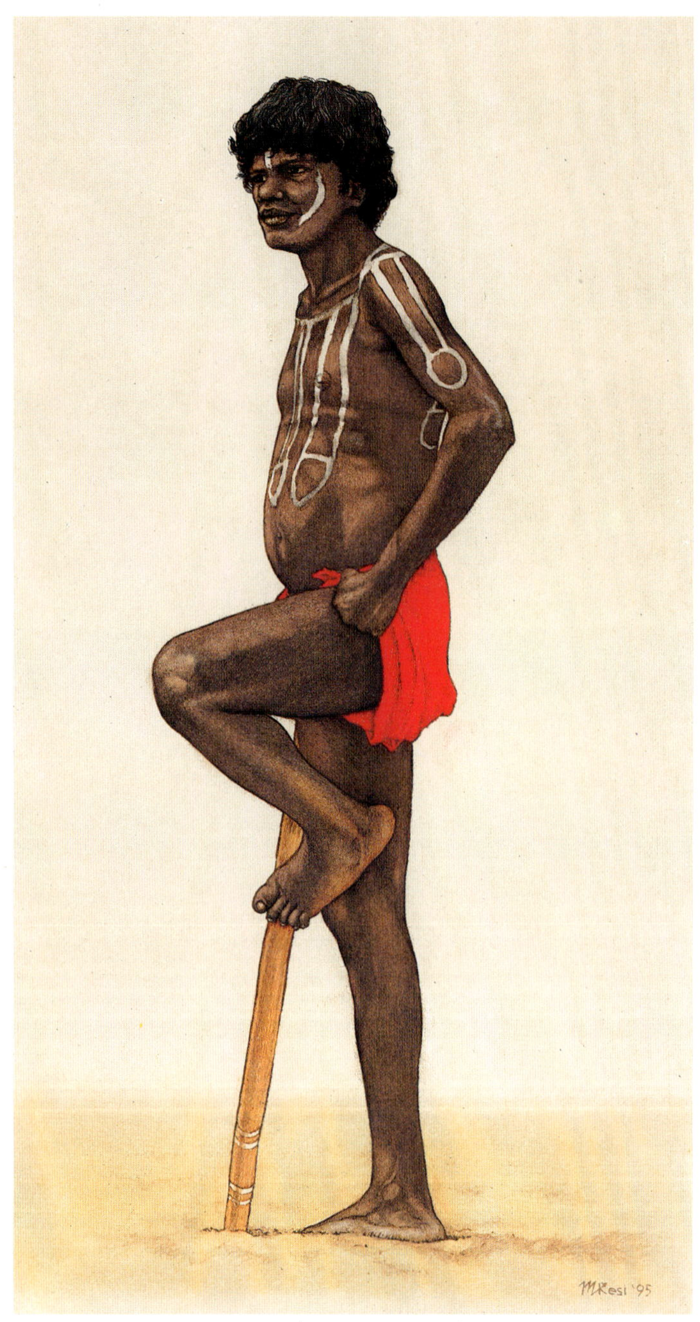

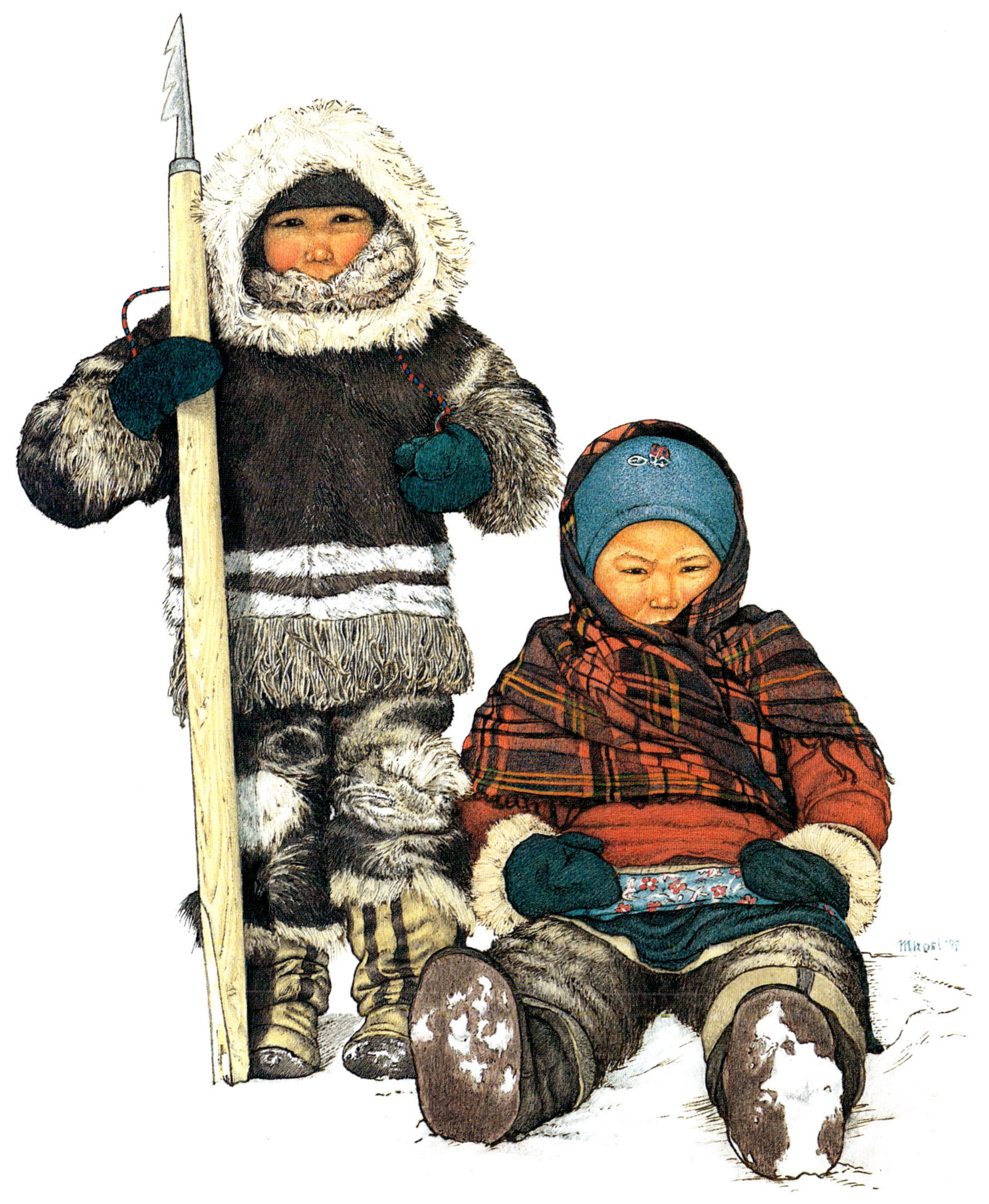

M. Gabriella Colombo

Italy

Title of Work
A Journey through Kenya

Technique
Coloured pencil

Legend
. Mukululu mission
. Archer's Post mission

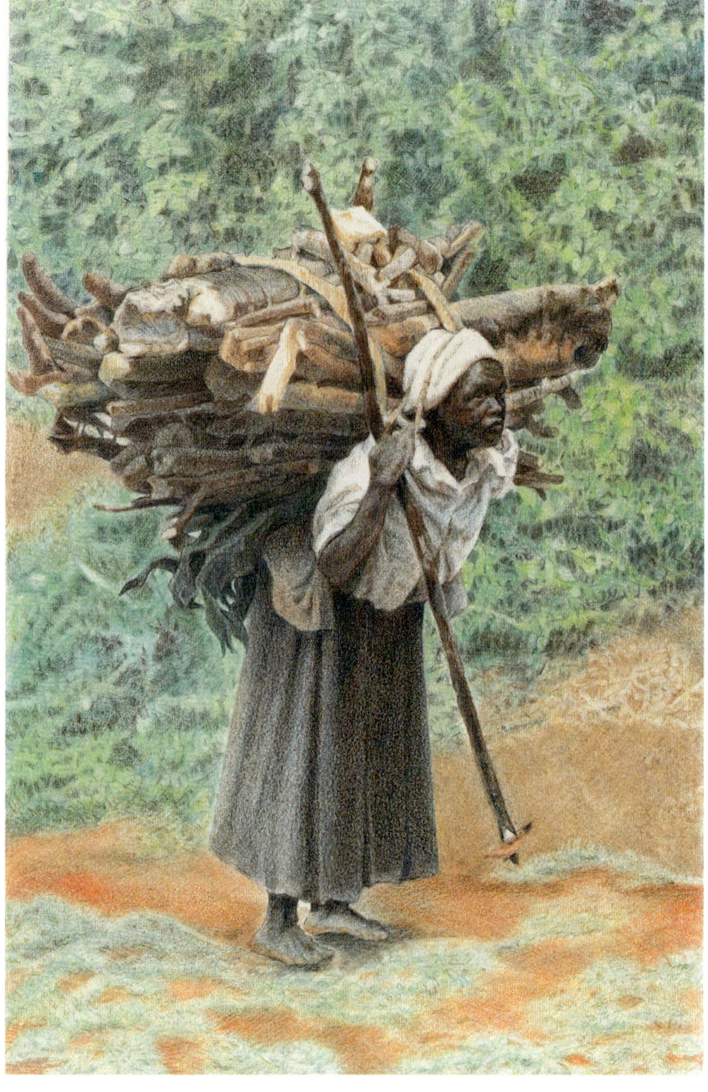

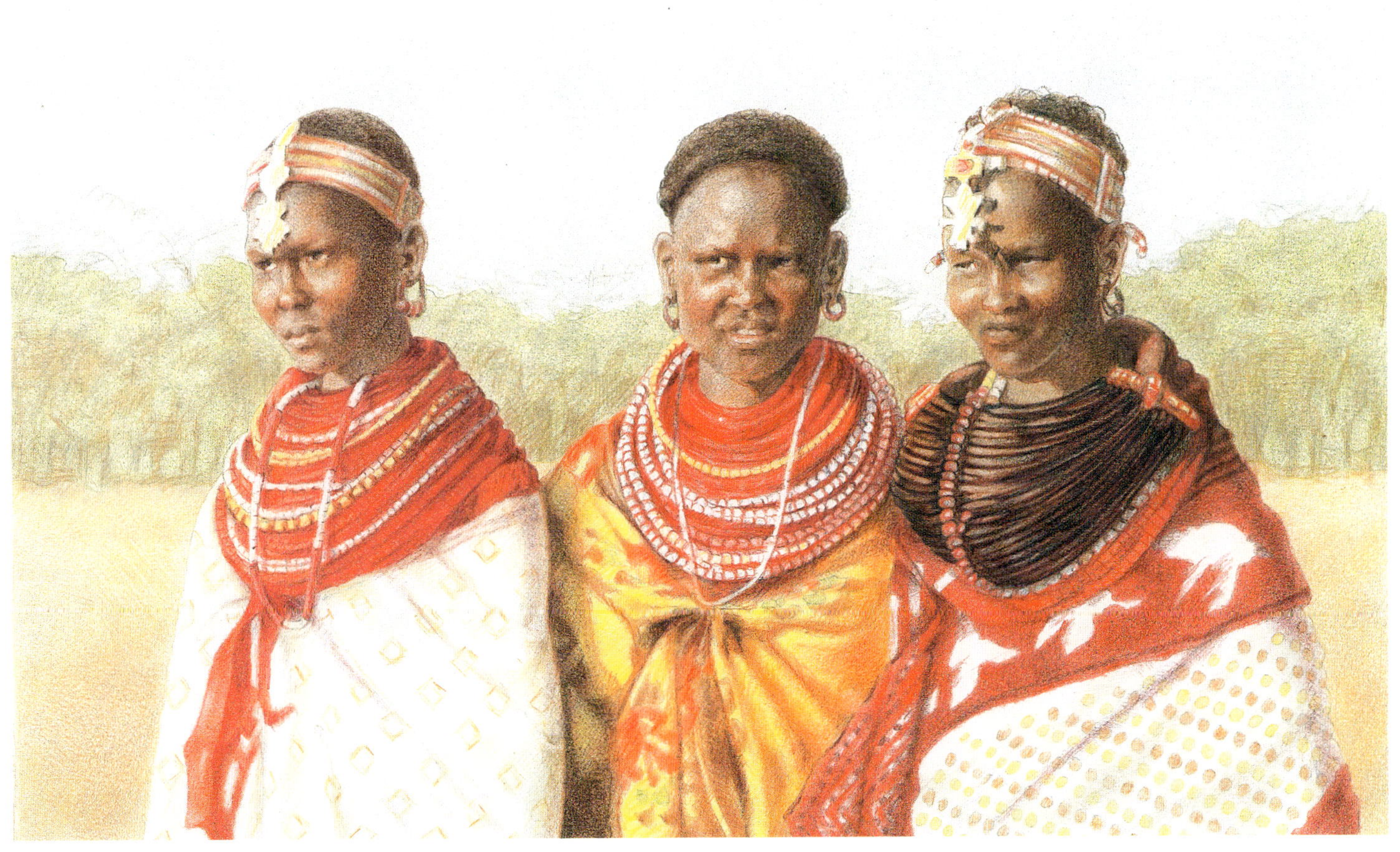

Isabelle Courmont

France

Title of Work
Ulysses, Hero of the Odyssey

Original Publisher and Date of Publication
Editions Alif, August 1995
ISBN 2-218-03101-9

Technique
Watercolour and gouache

Legend
. Poseidon's planet

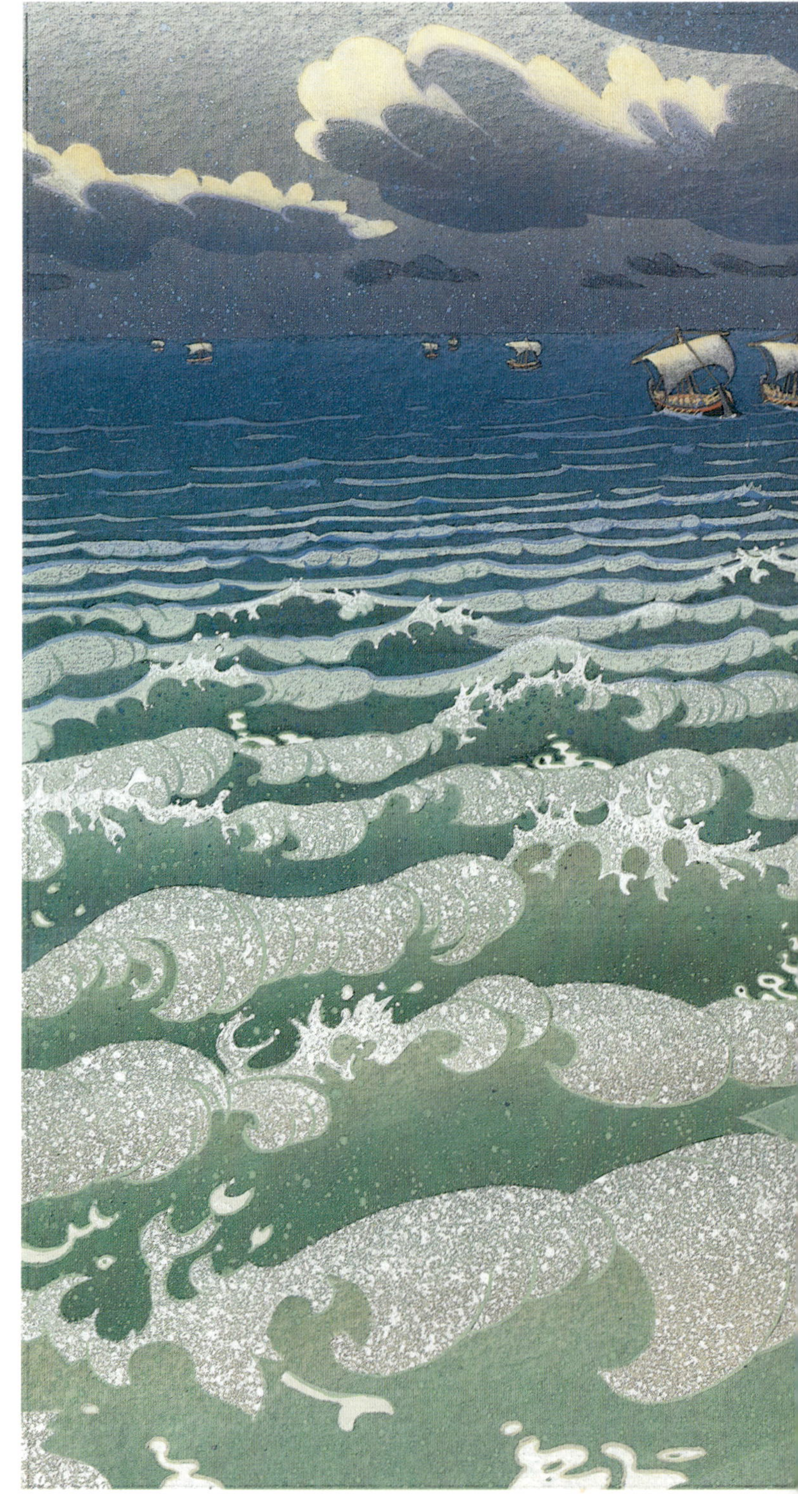

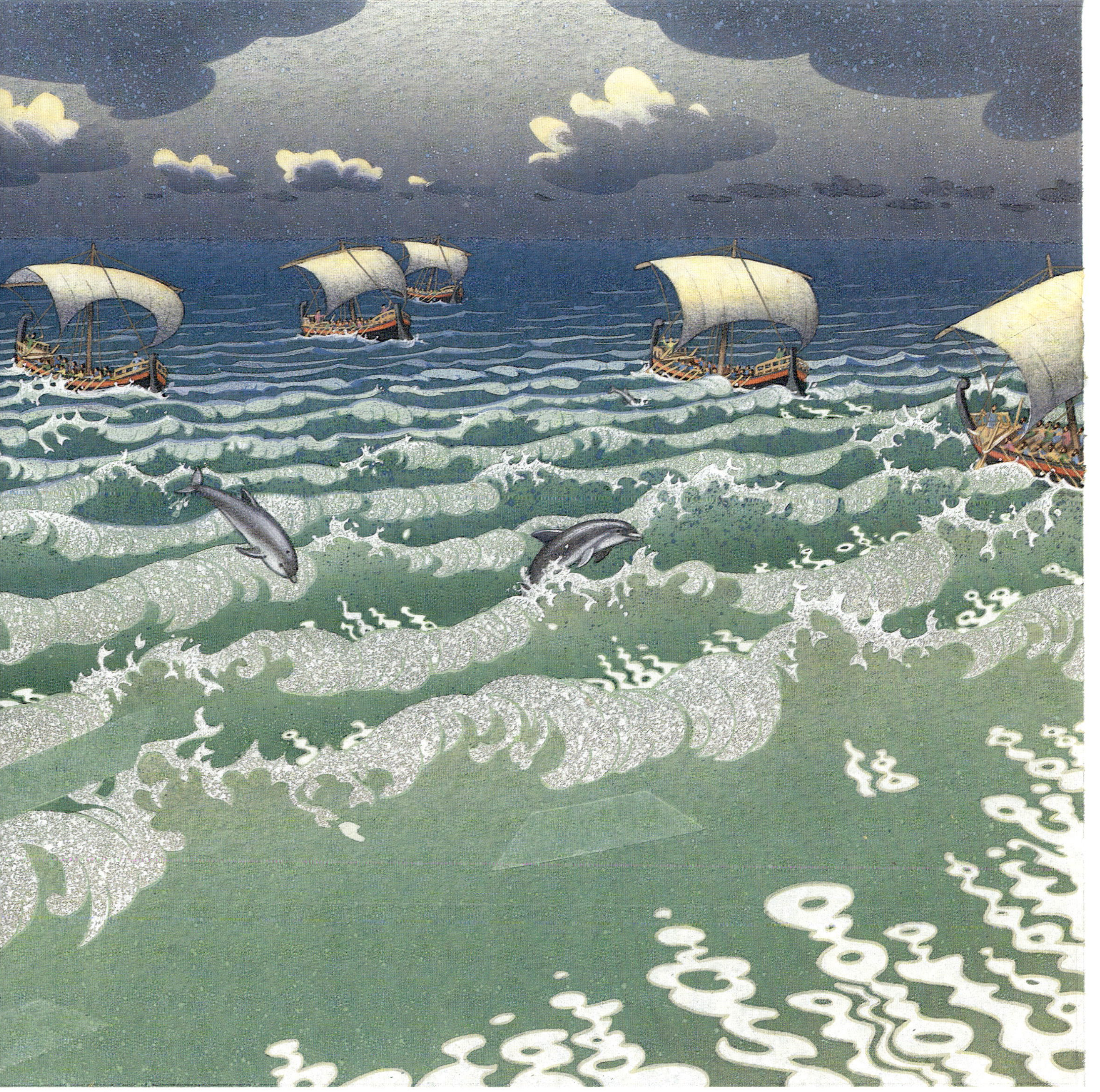

Brian Delf

Great Britain

Title of Work
In the Beginning

Original Publisher and Date of Publication
Dorling Kindersley, 1995
ISBN 0-7513-53183

Technique
Pen and ink

Legend
. Costumes
. Trains

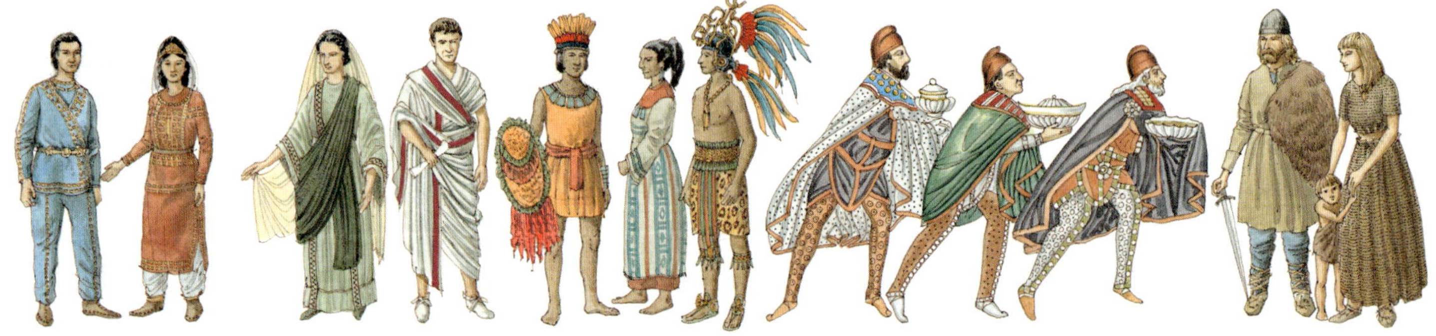

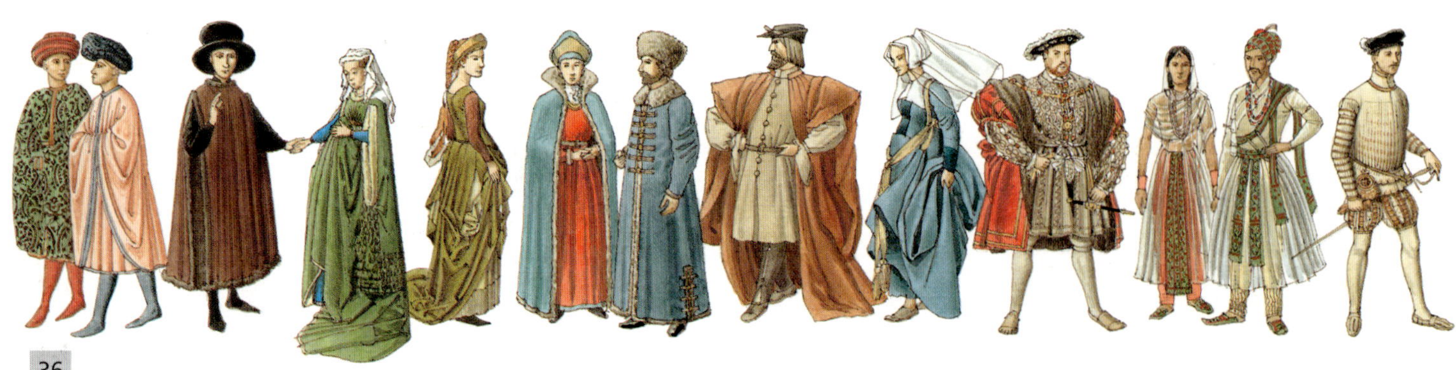

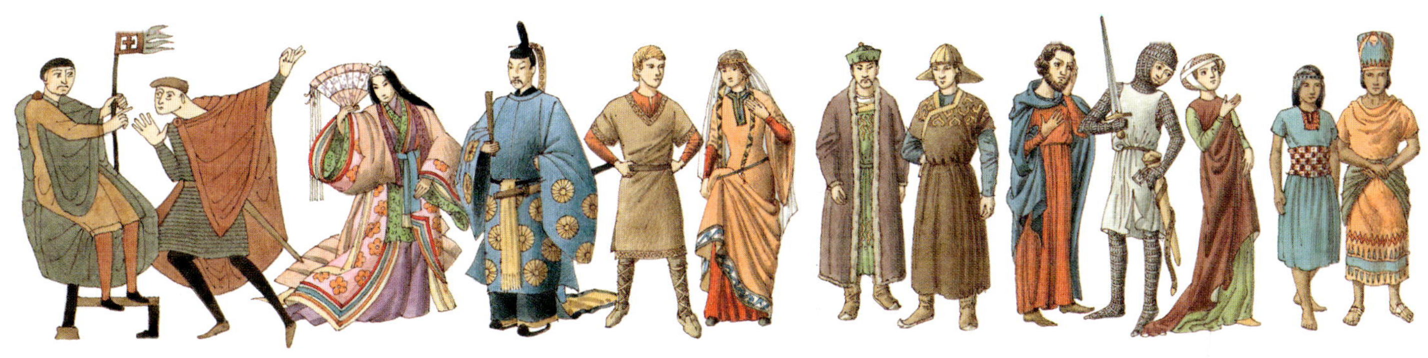

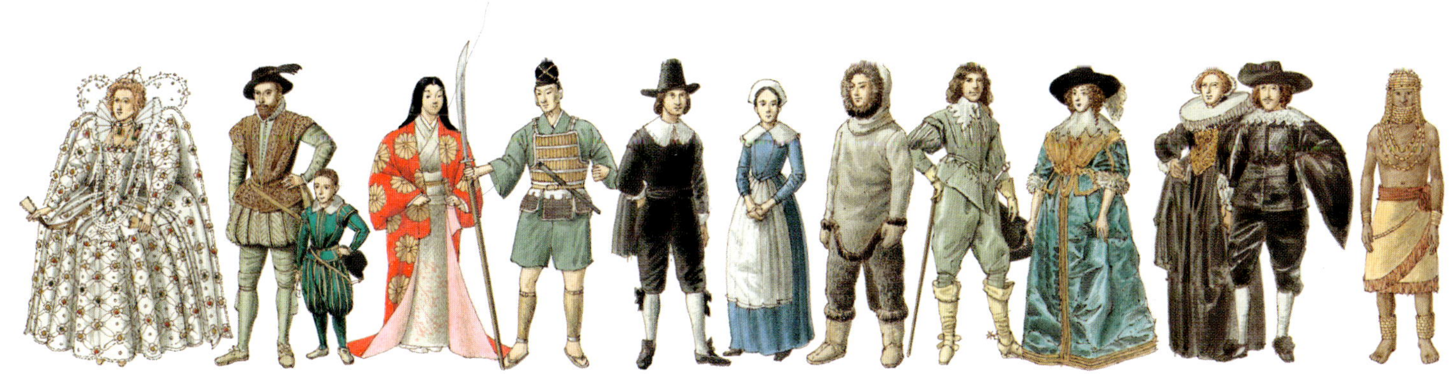

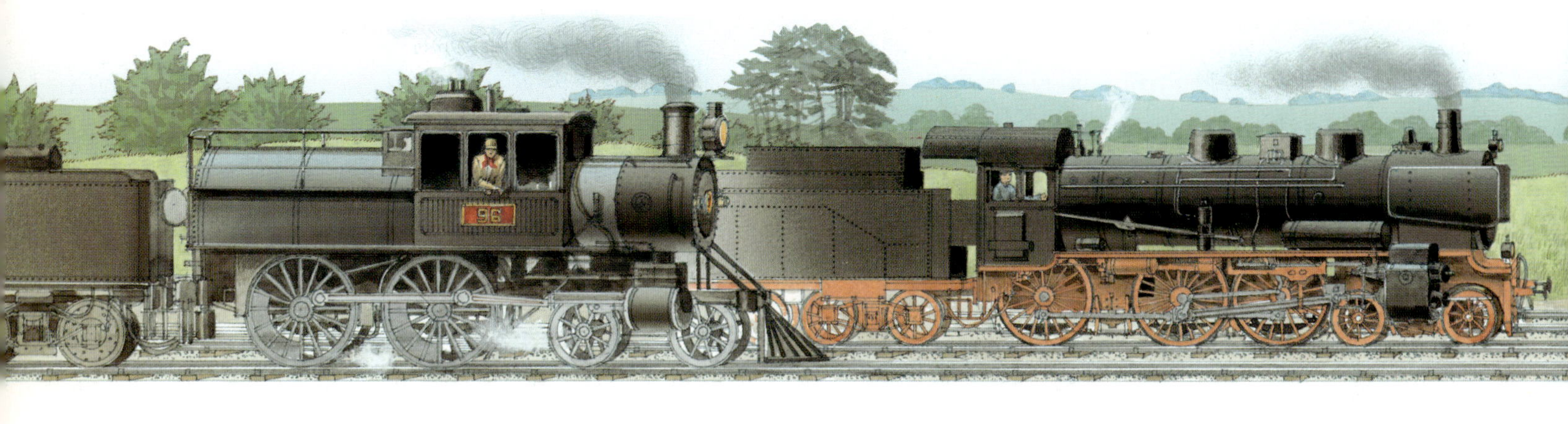
96

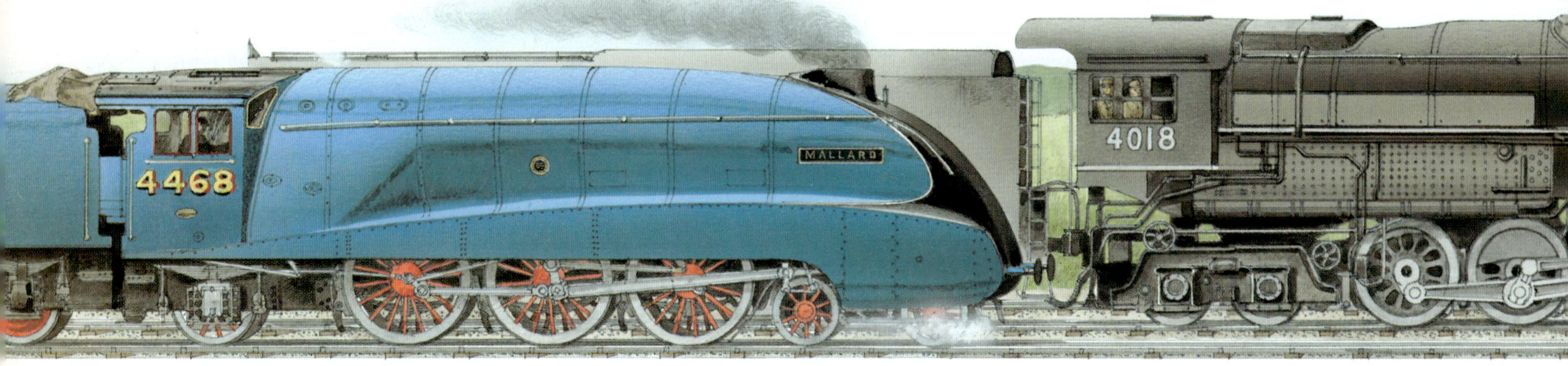
4468
MALLARD
4018

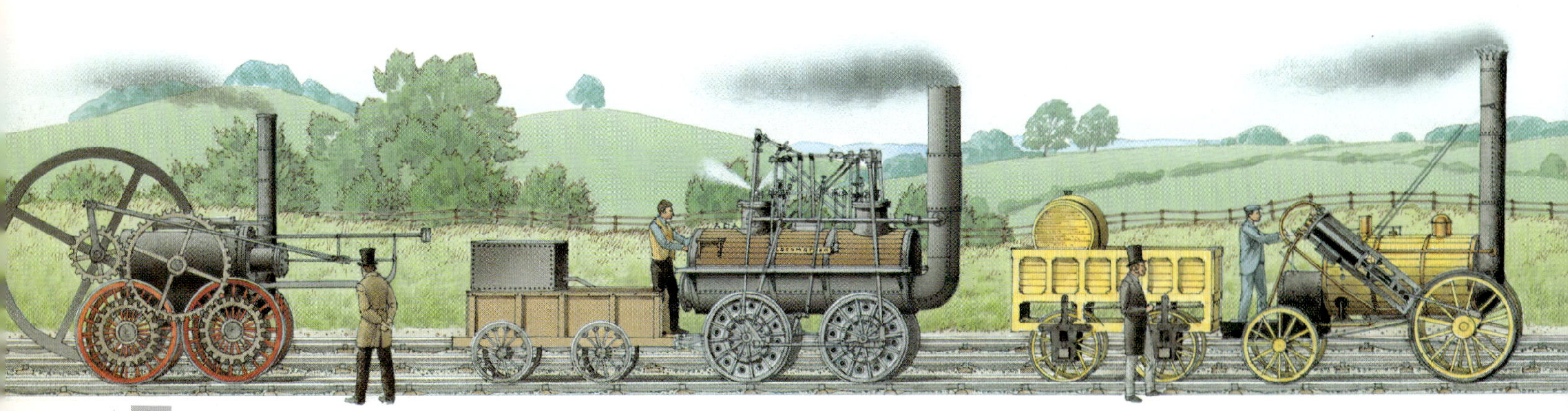

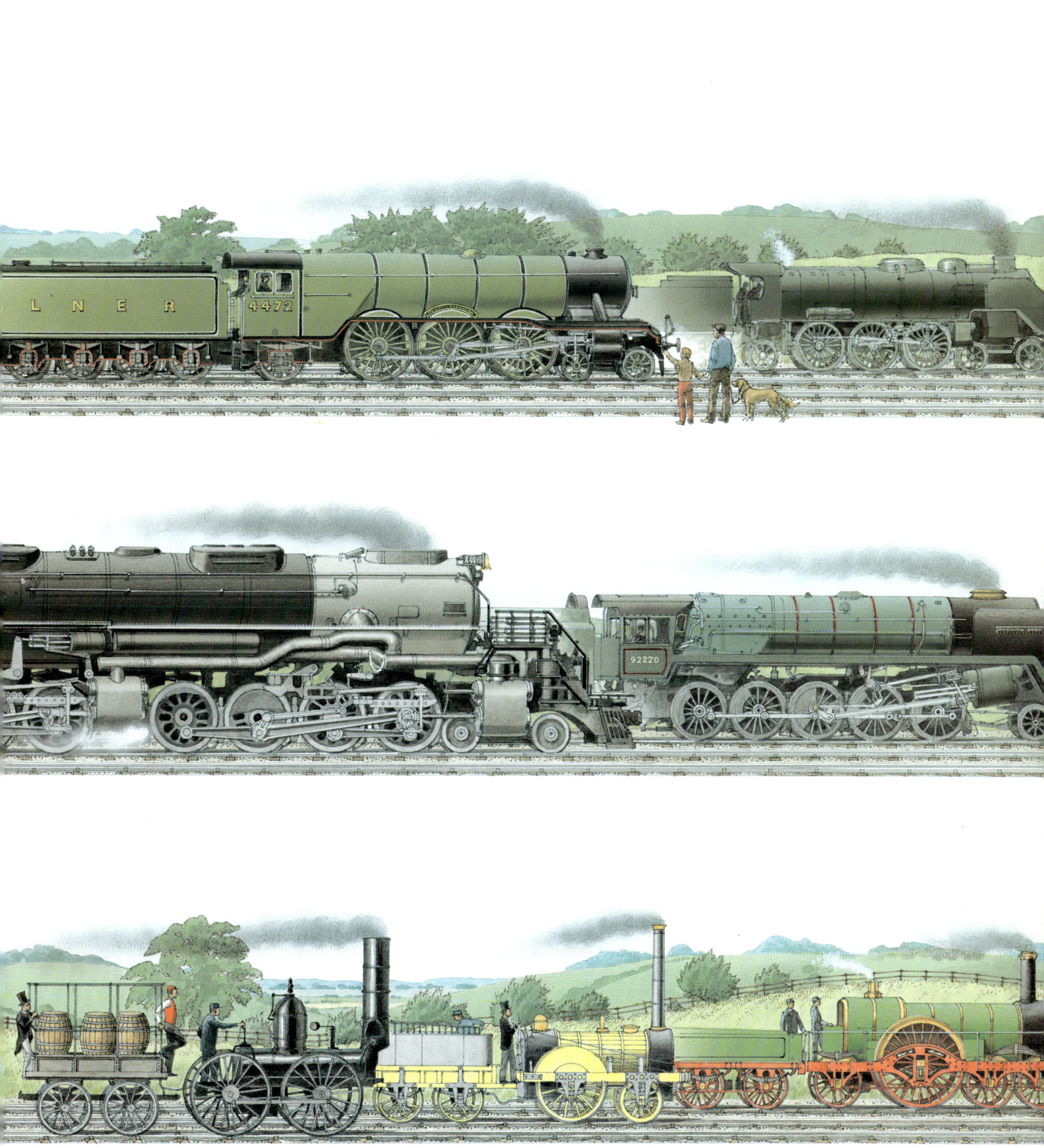
L N E R
4472
92220

Myriam Deru

Belgium

Title of Work
Early in the morning

Original Publisher and Date of Publication
Editions Fernand Nathan, 1995
ISBN 2-09-210156-0

Technique
Watercolour, pencil, pastel

Legend
. The sleeping garden

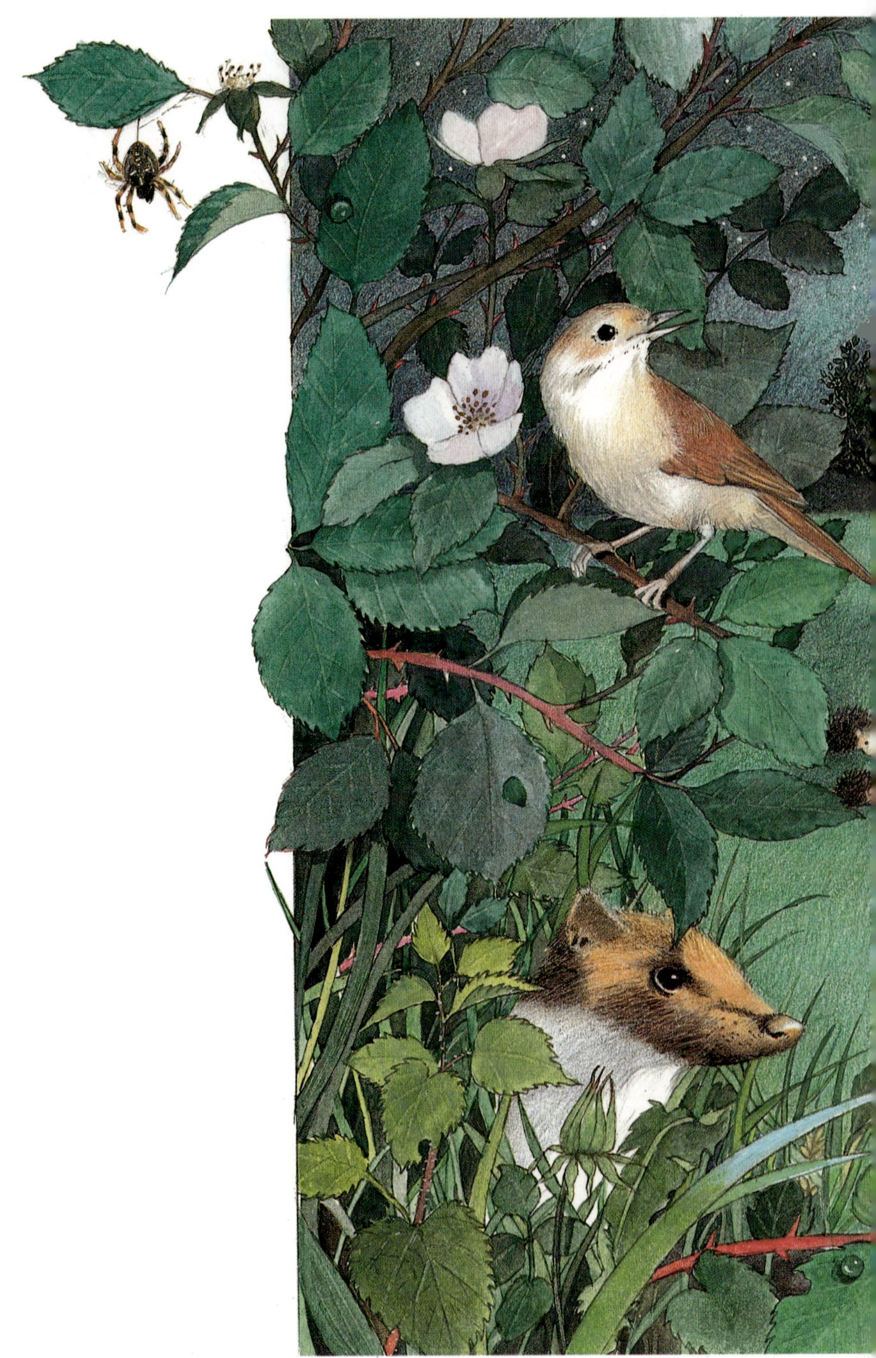

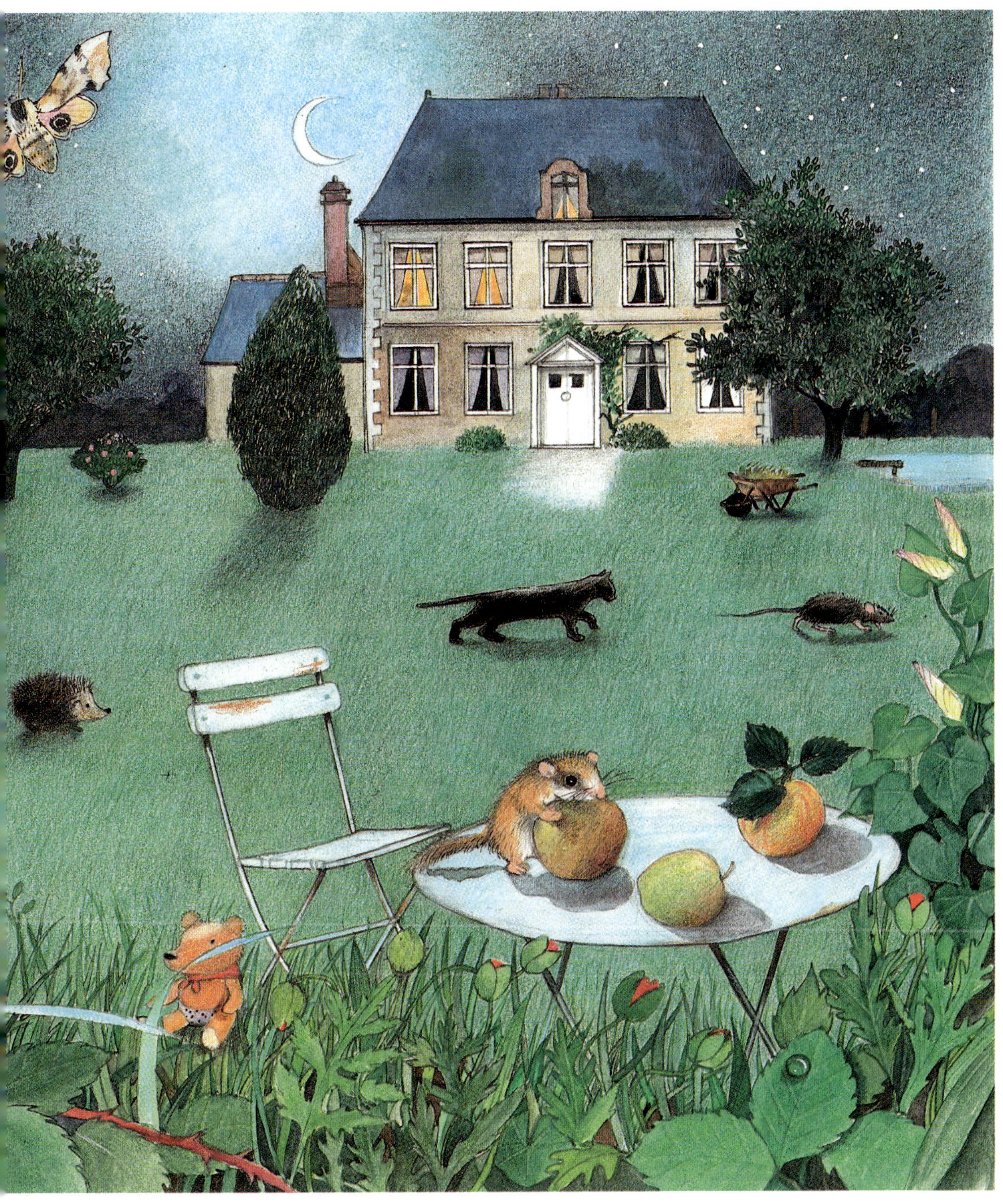

François Desbordes

France

Title of Work
Carnets de la Nature:
Winter birds

Original Publisher and Date of Publication
Editions Gallimard,
October 1995
ISBN 2070592065

Technique
Watercolour

Legend
. Robin red.breast

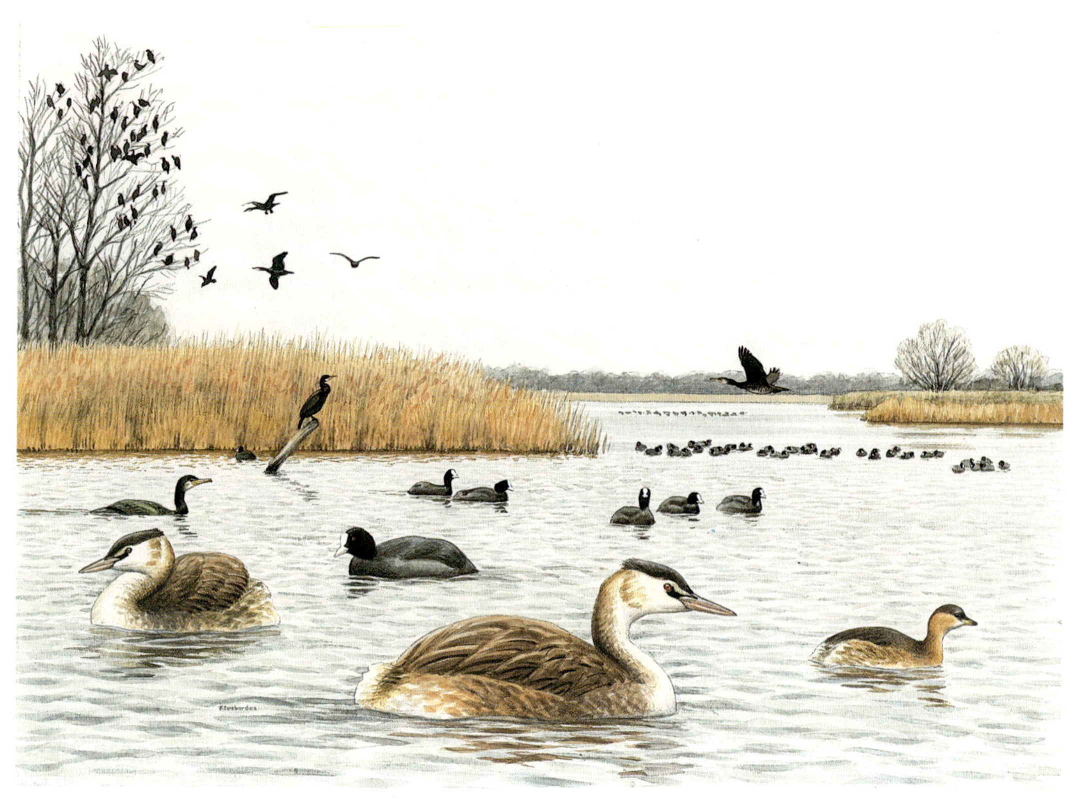

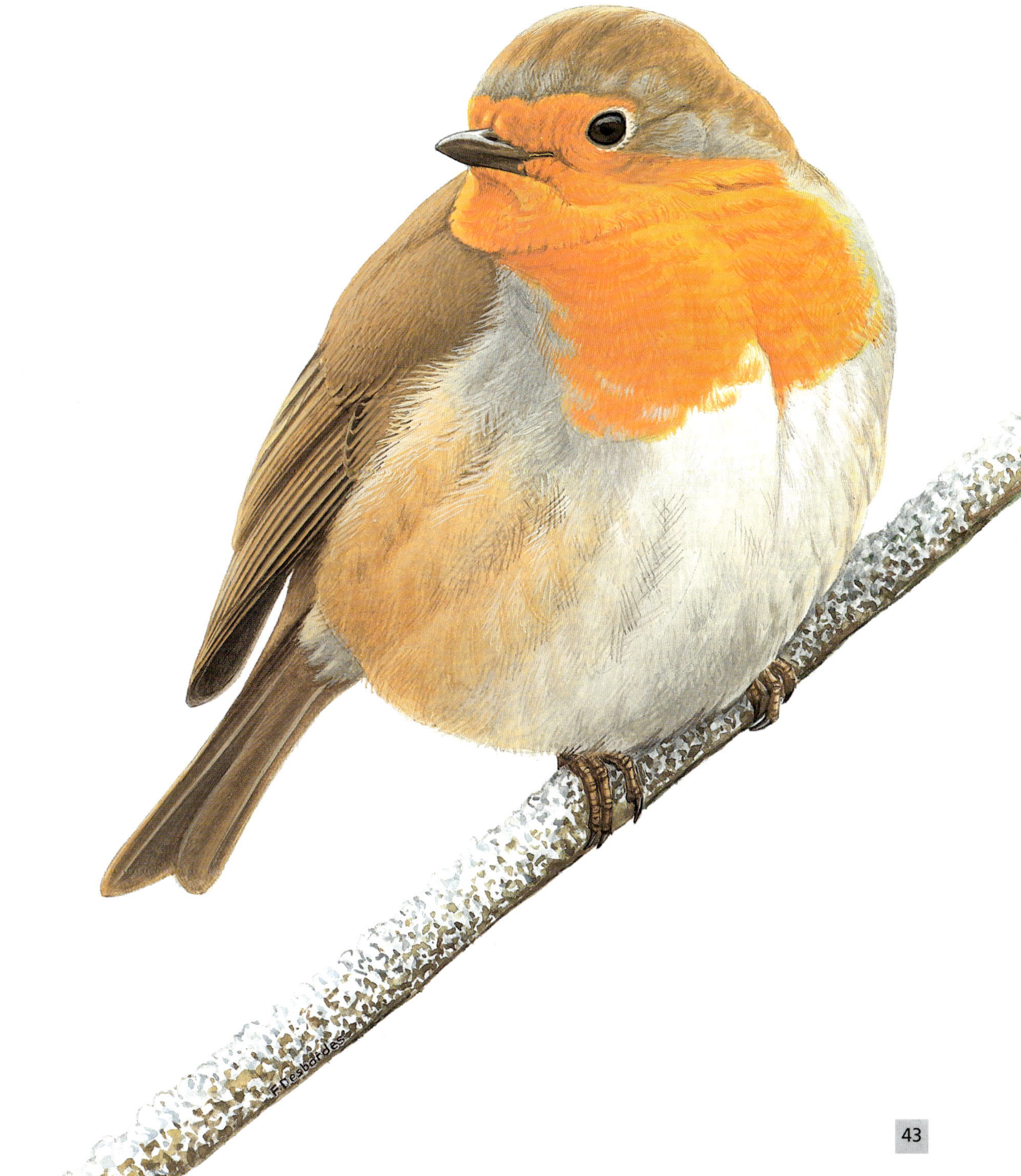
F.Desbordes

Stephane Dessaint

France

Title of Work
Motorcycles (3D computer images)

Technique
Infography (3 dimensional)

Legend
. Original drawing for Laetitia, Esmeralda, Amelie, Eloise

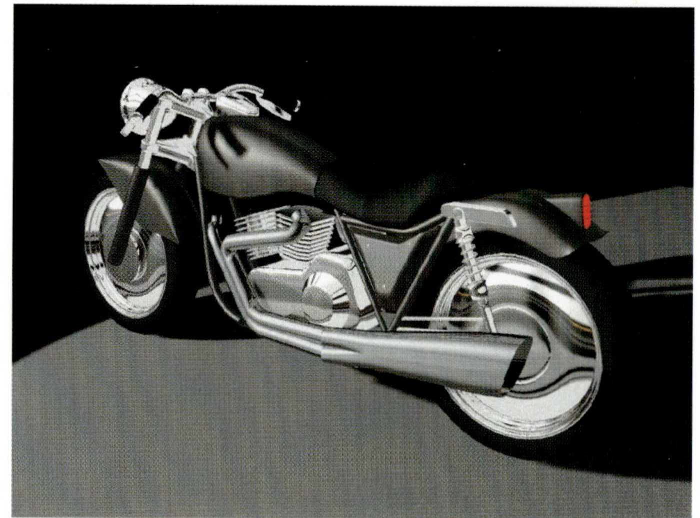

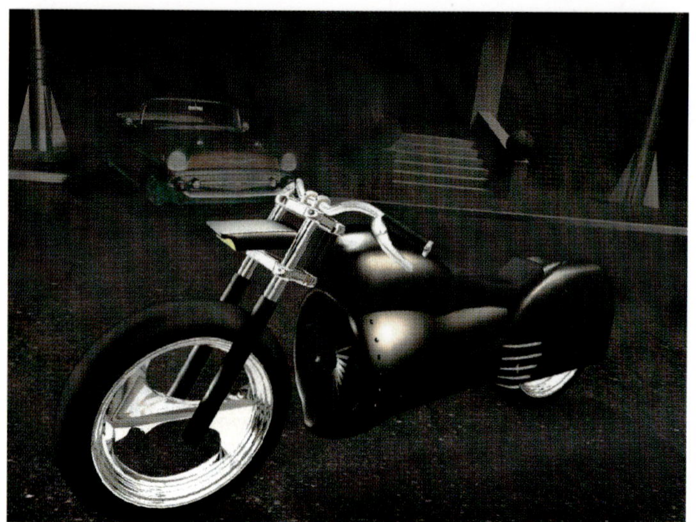

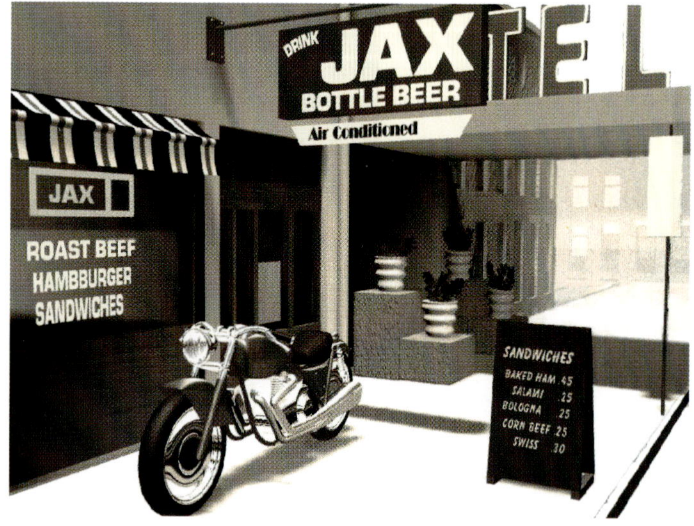

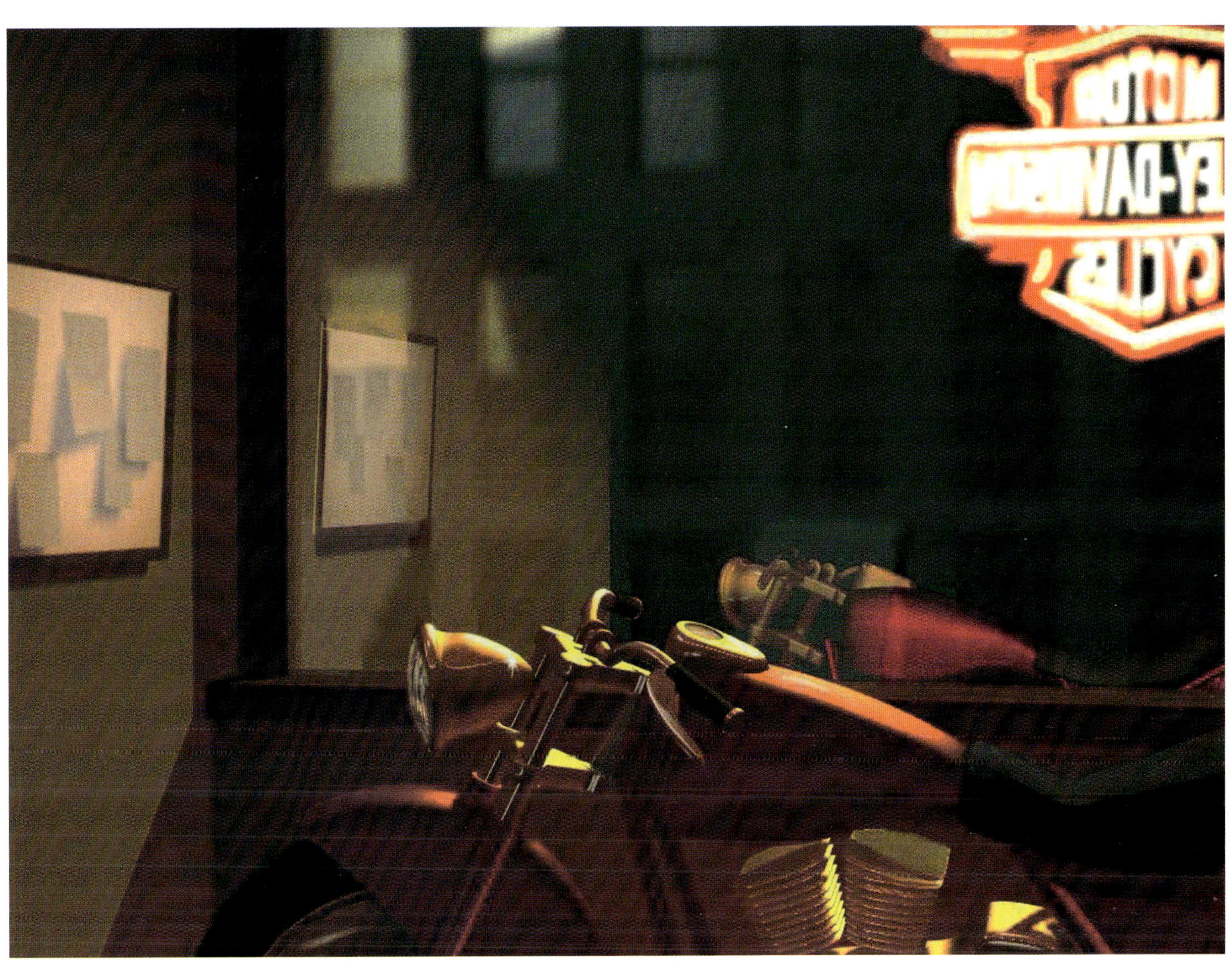

Marina Durante

Italy

Title of Work
Comparative Tables

Technique
Mixed

Legend
. Comparative tables of several species of the Rallidae and the Dendrobatidae families

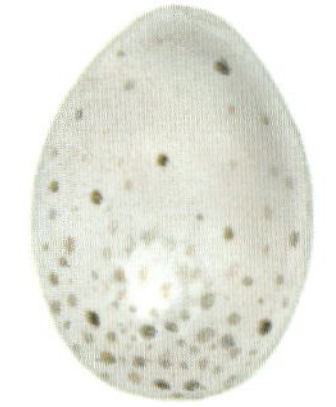

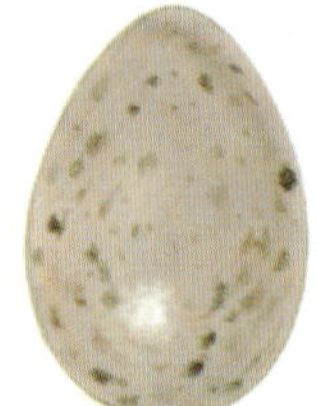

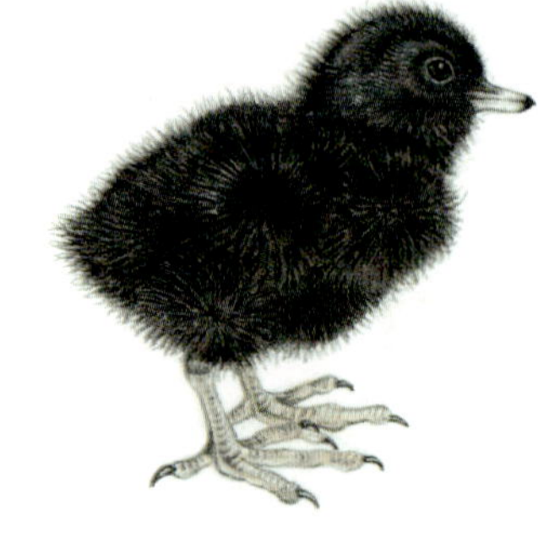

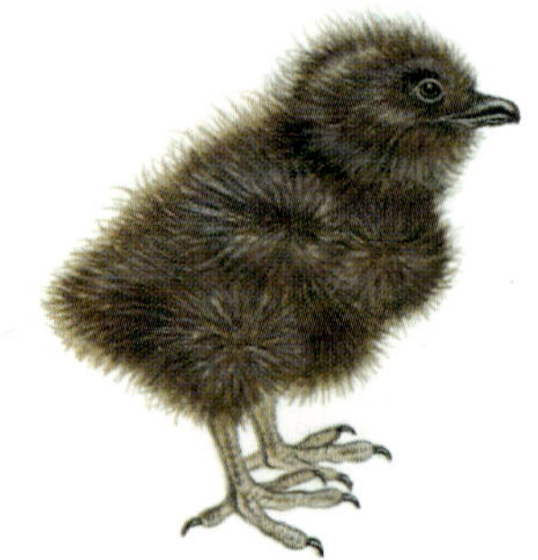

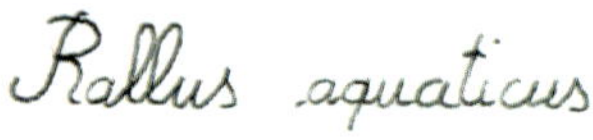

Crex crex

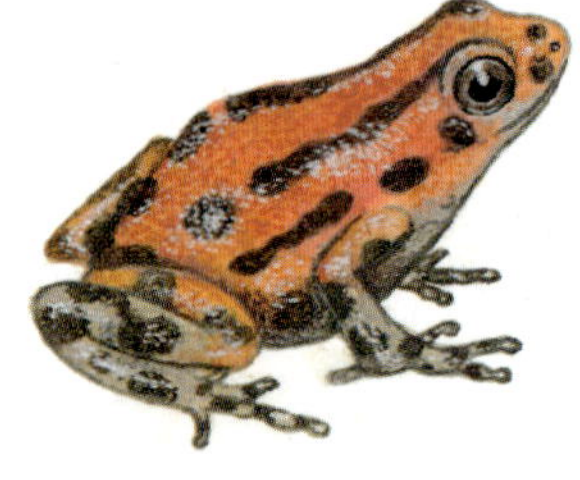

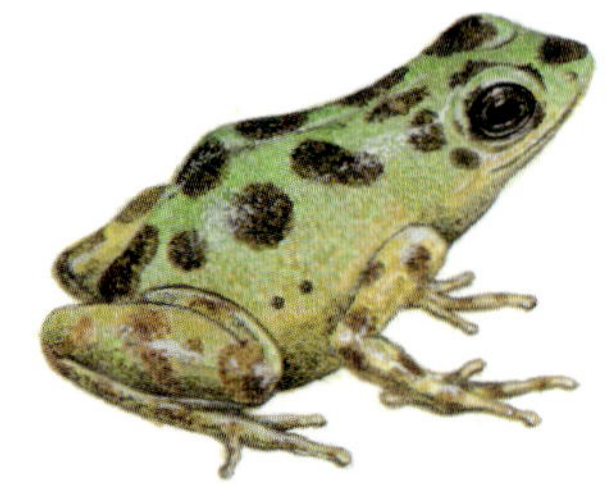

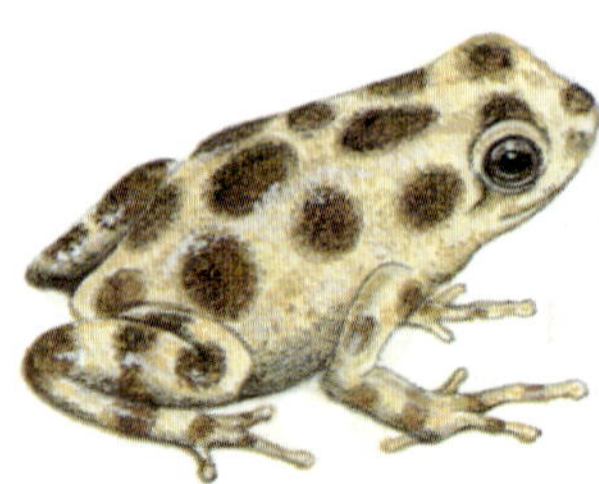

D. pumilio

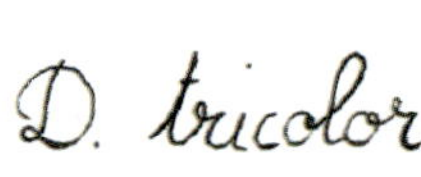

D. pumilio

D. pumilio

Dendrobates sp.

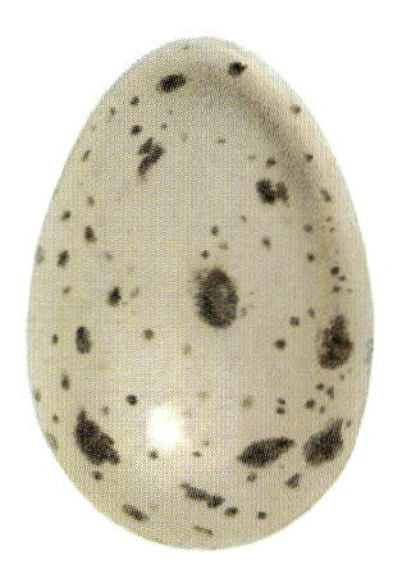
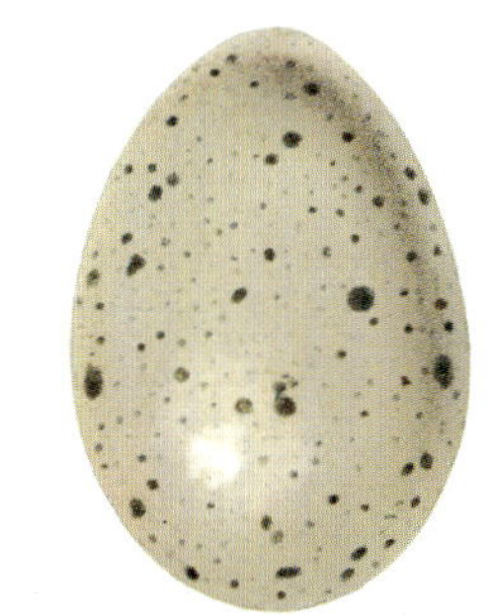
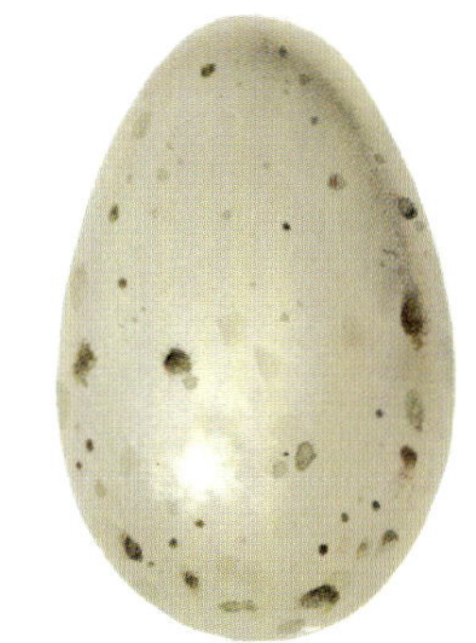

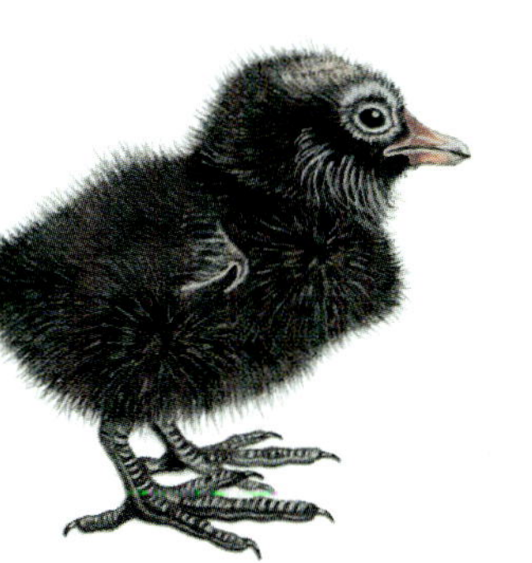
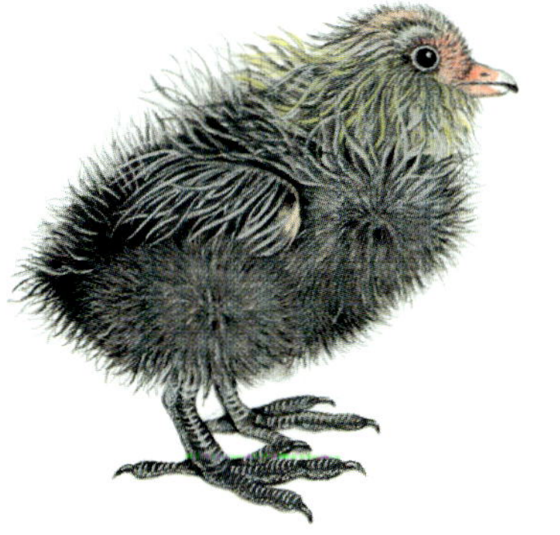
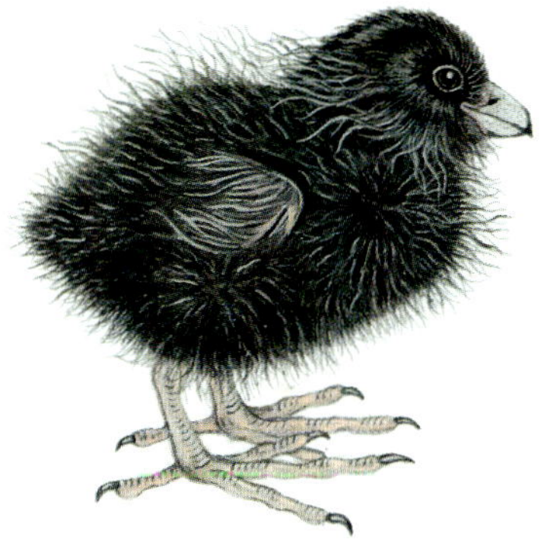

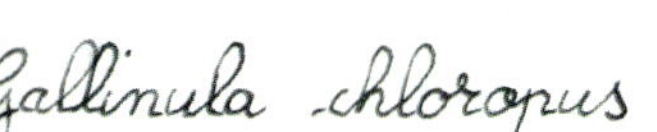

Gallinula chloropus *Fulica atra* *Porphyrio porphyrio*

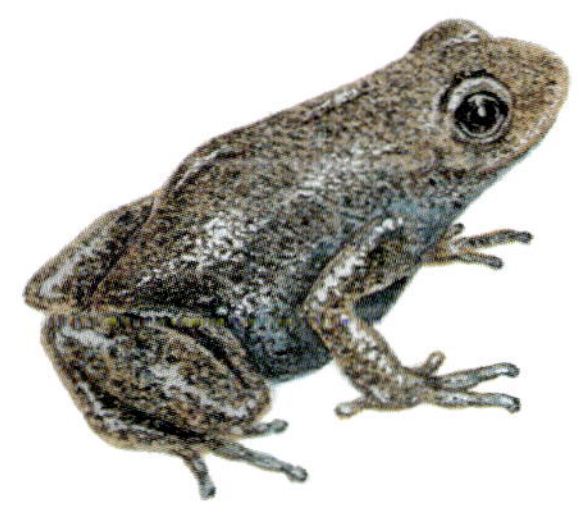
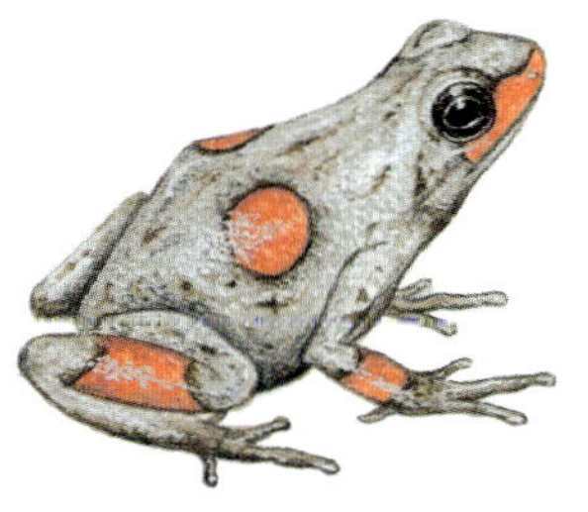
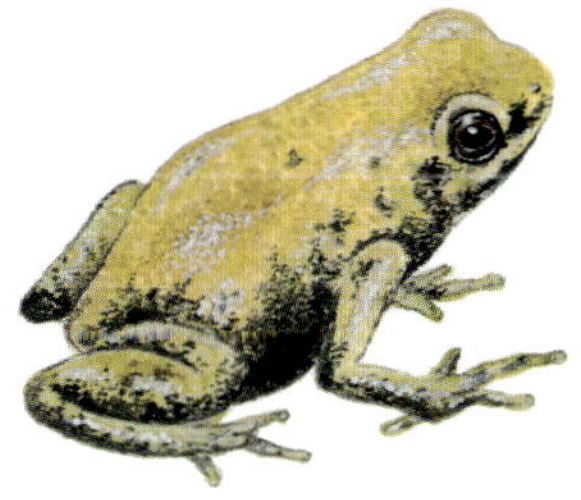
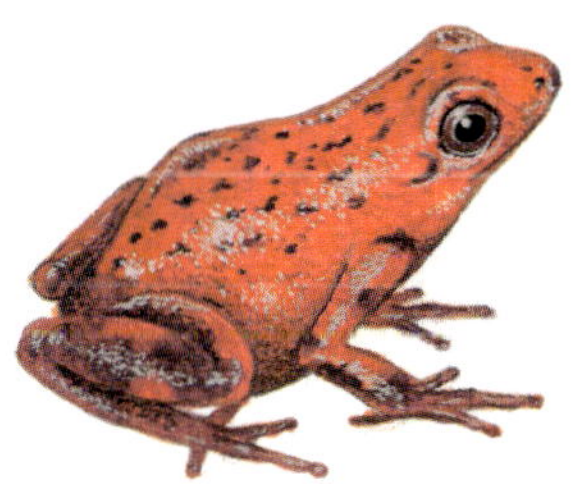

D. pumilio *D. histrionicus* *D. terribilis* *D. pumilio*

Christer Eriksson

Sweden

Title of Work
Discoveries - Reptiles

Original Publisher and Date of Publication
Weldon Owen Publishing, pending publication 1996

Technique
Acrylic, gouache, ink, coloured pencil

Legend
. *Finding a meal*
. *Pit viper*
. *In and out of water*

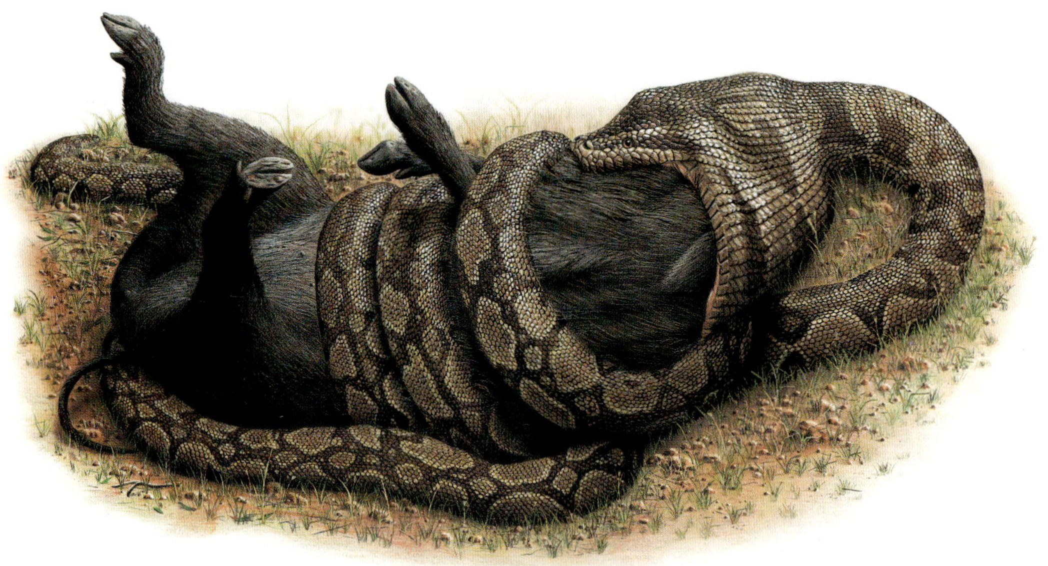

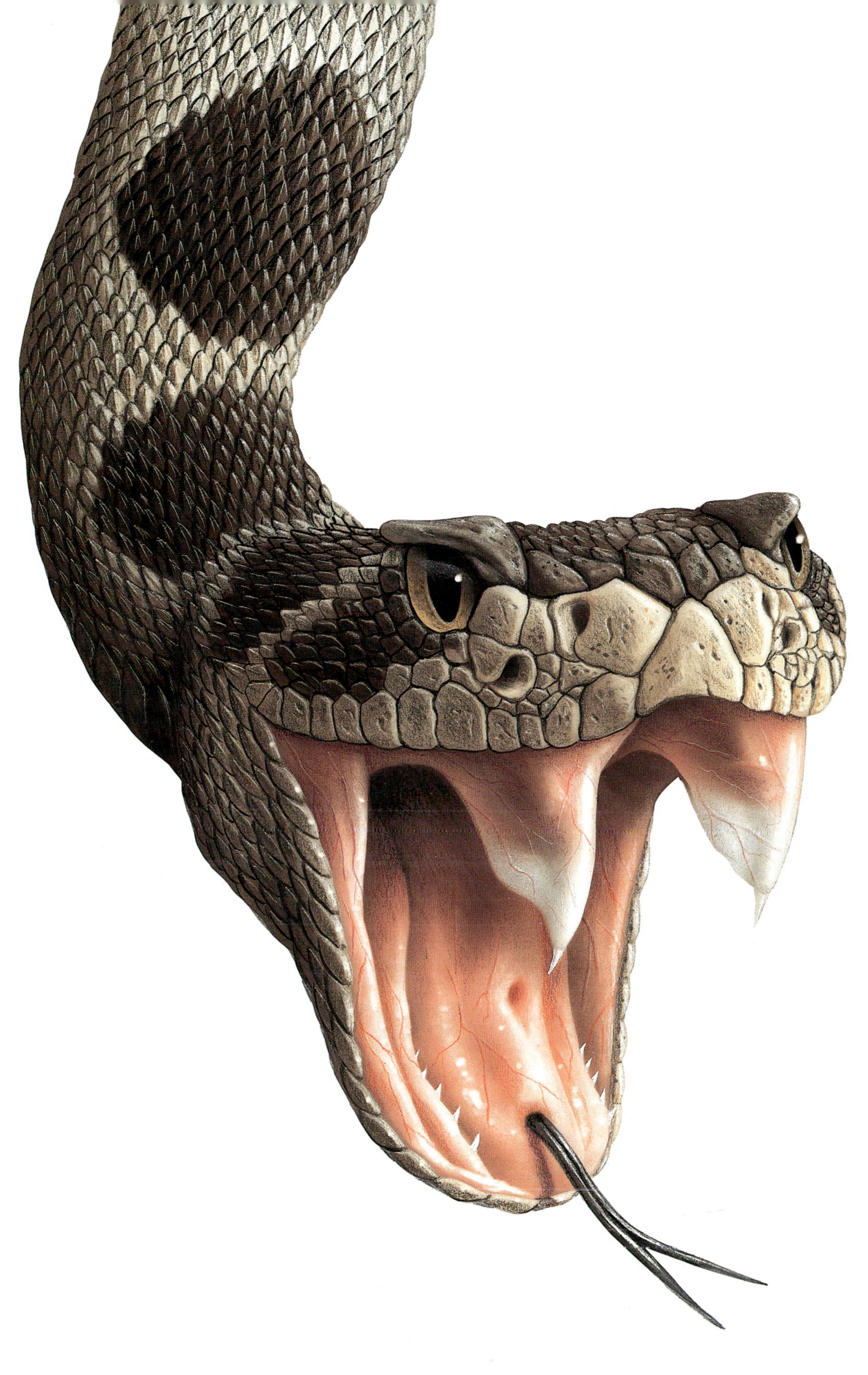

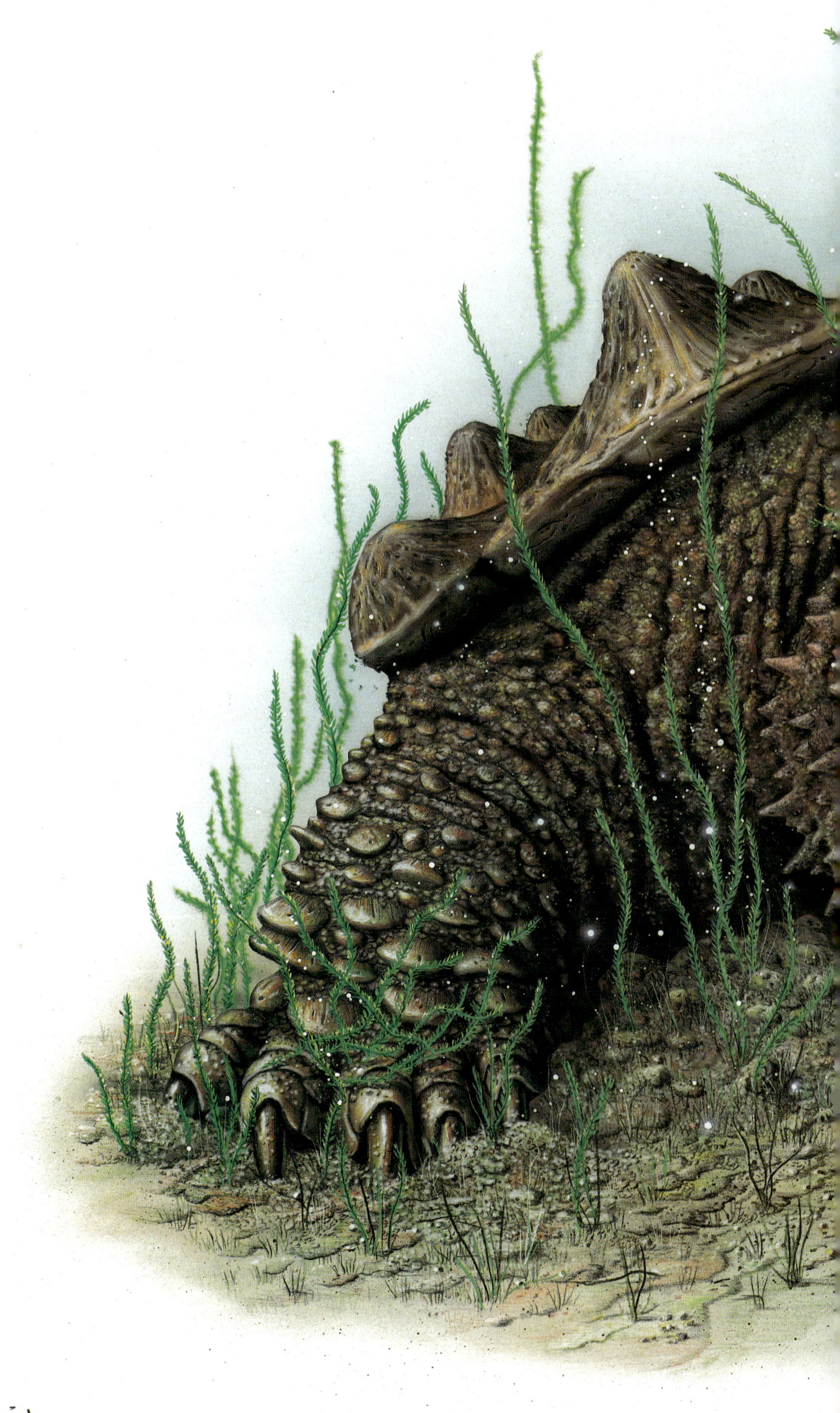

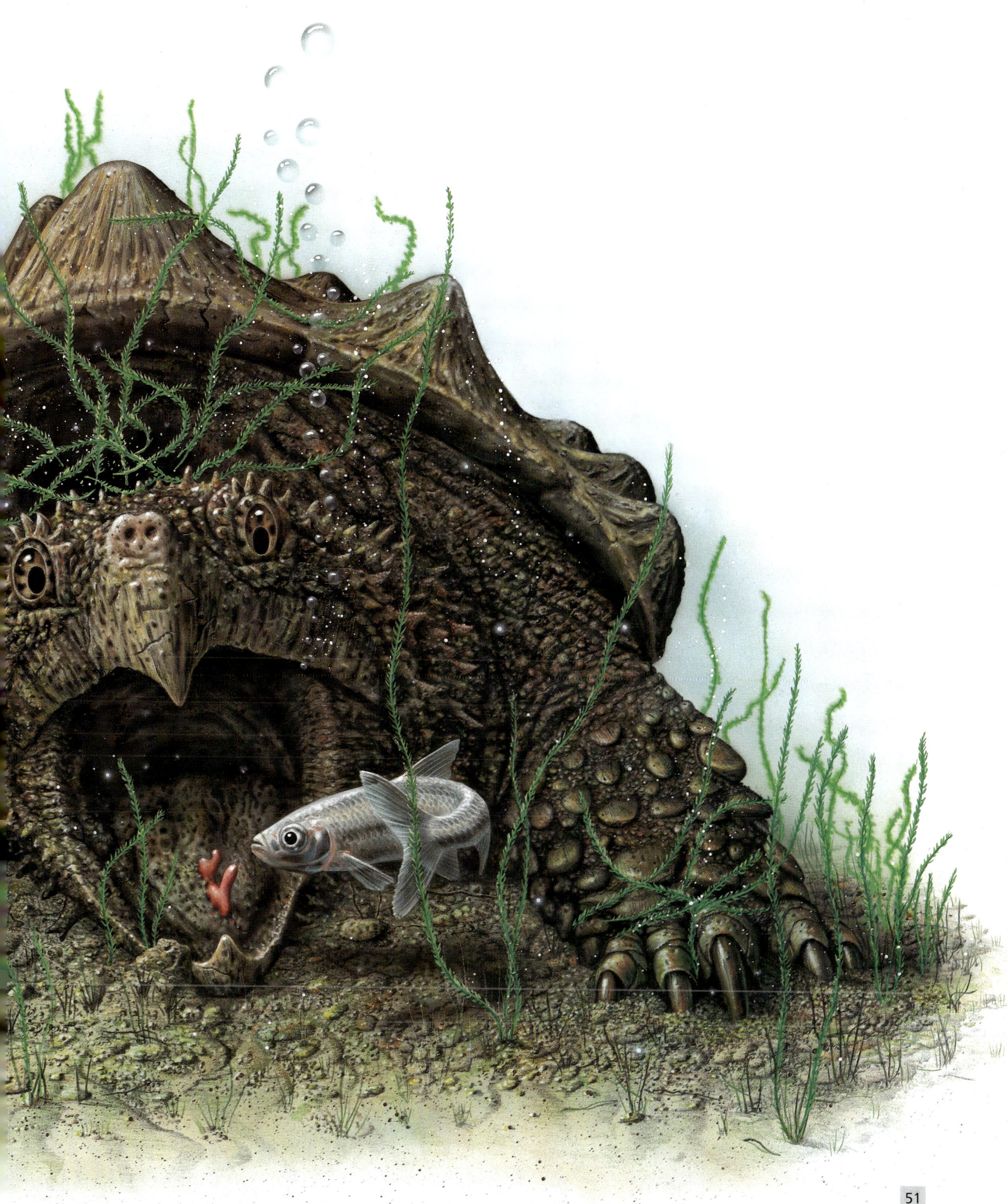

Carlo Ferrantini

Italy

Titles of Works
La macchina del tempo:
In the Jerusalem of David and Solomon
In the Florence of Lorenzo dei Medici

Original Publisher and Dates of Publication
Giunti Publishing Group, 1995
ISBN 88.09.20627.4 (In Jerusalem)
ISBN 88.09.20626.6 (In Florence)

Technique
Mixed

Legend
. Divine splendour
. The artist's atelier

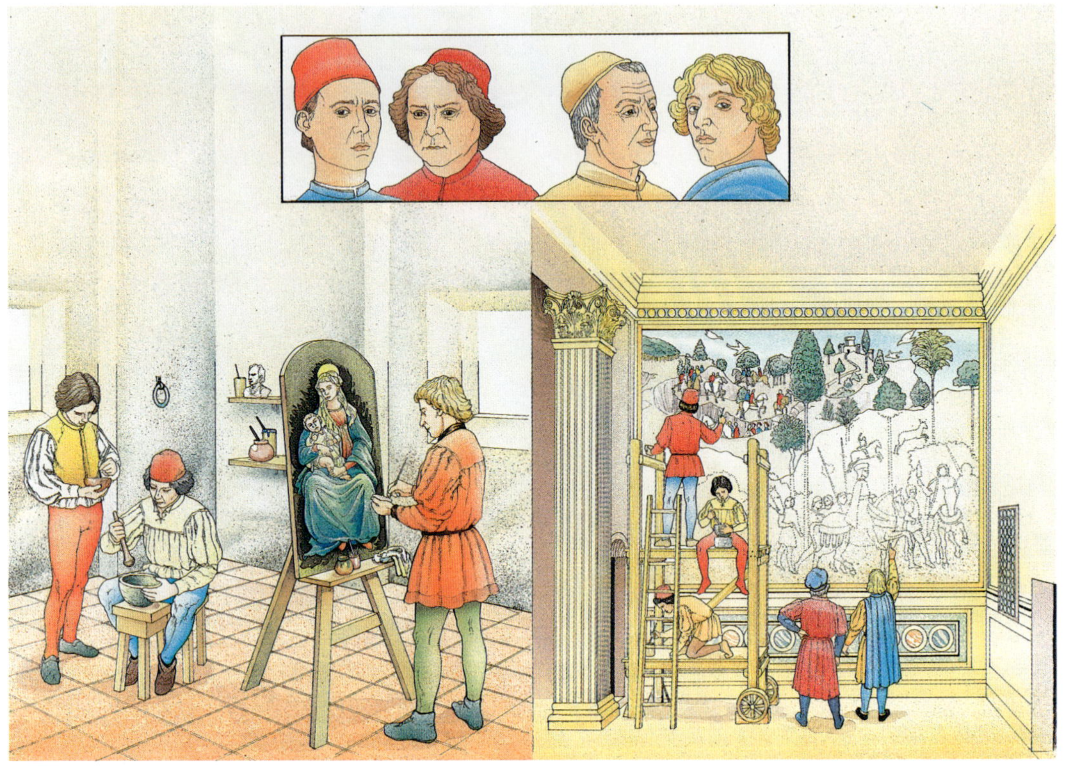

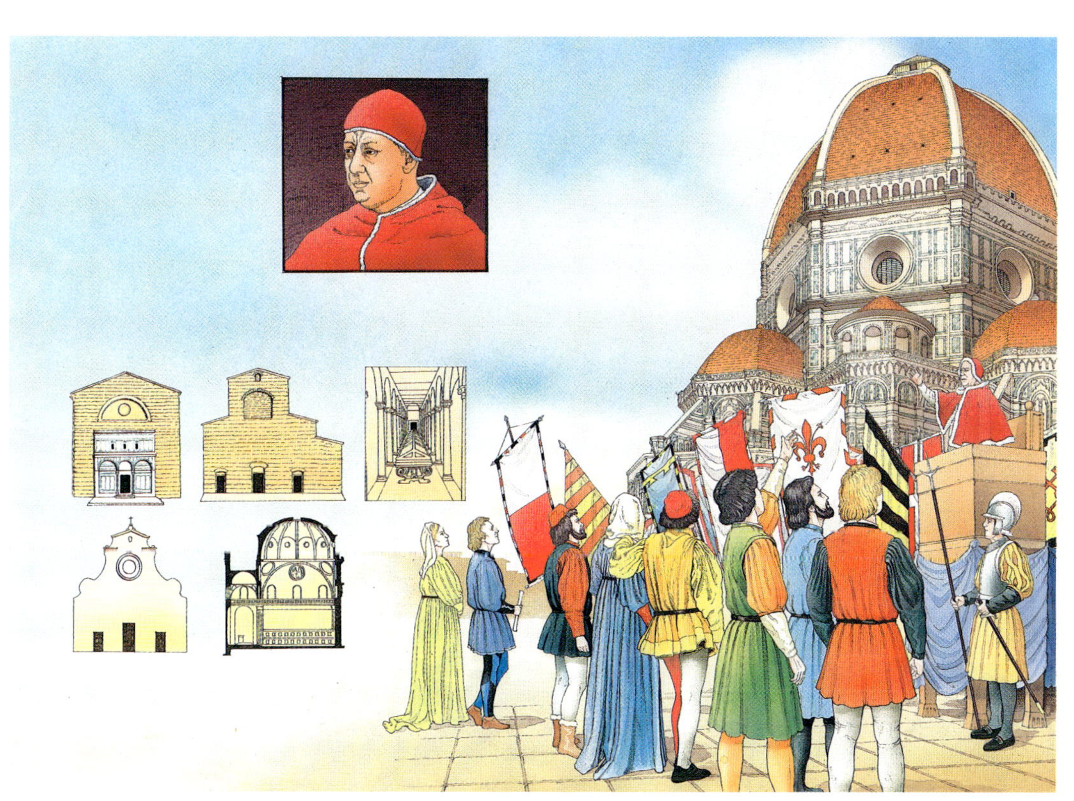

Elisabetta Ferrero

Italy

Title of Work
Animals in the home

Original Publisher and Date of Publication
Giunti Publishing Group,
October 1995
ISBN 88-09-20702-5

Technique
Ecoline, coloured pencil

Legend
. *All together*
. *Dogs*

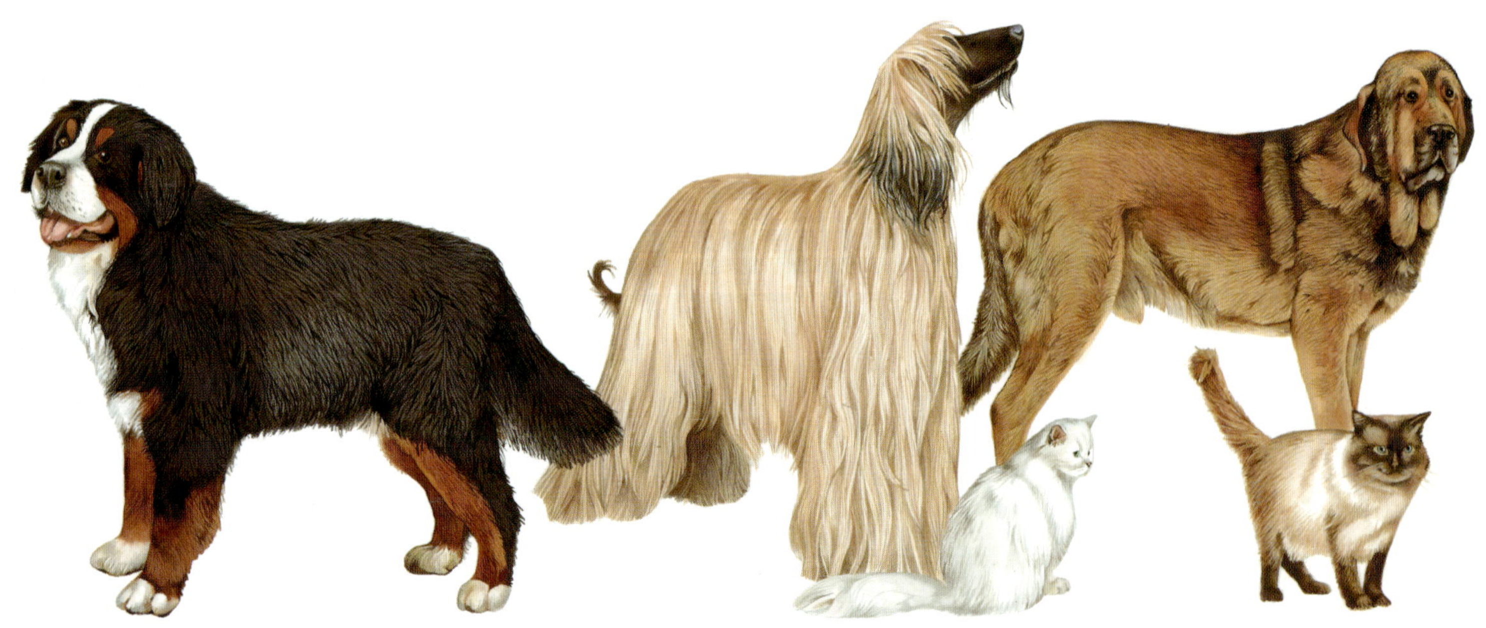

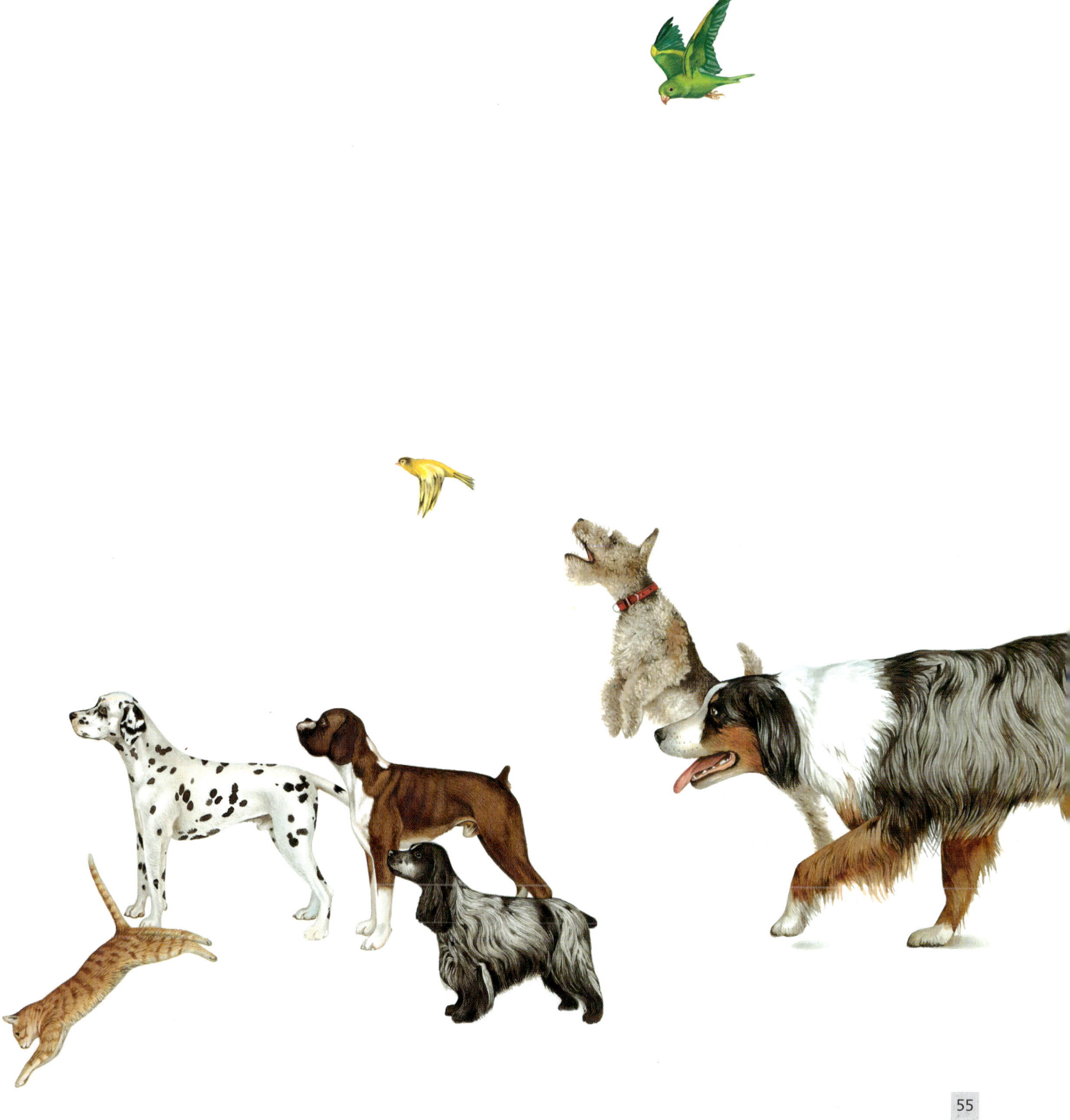

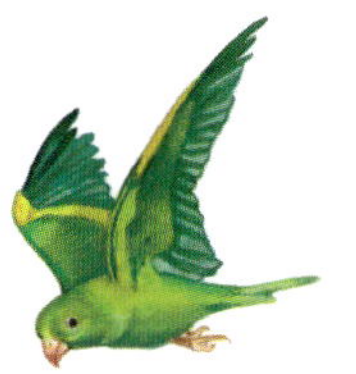

Giona Fiocchi

Italy

Title of Work
The tarot

Technique
Etching

Legend
. The Tower between the She-Pope and the Devil
. Earth, air, water, fire

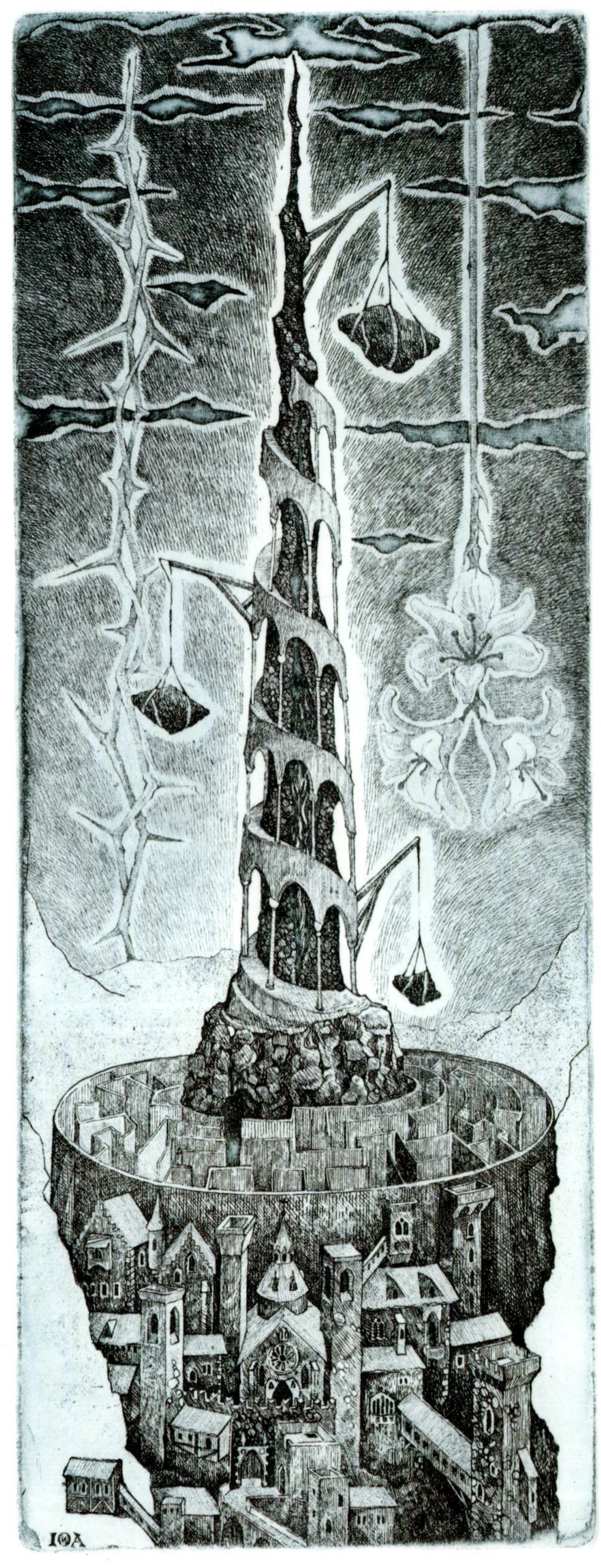

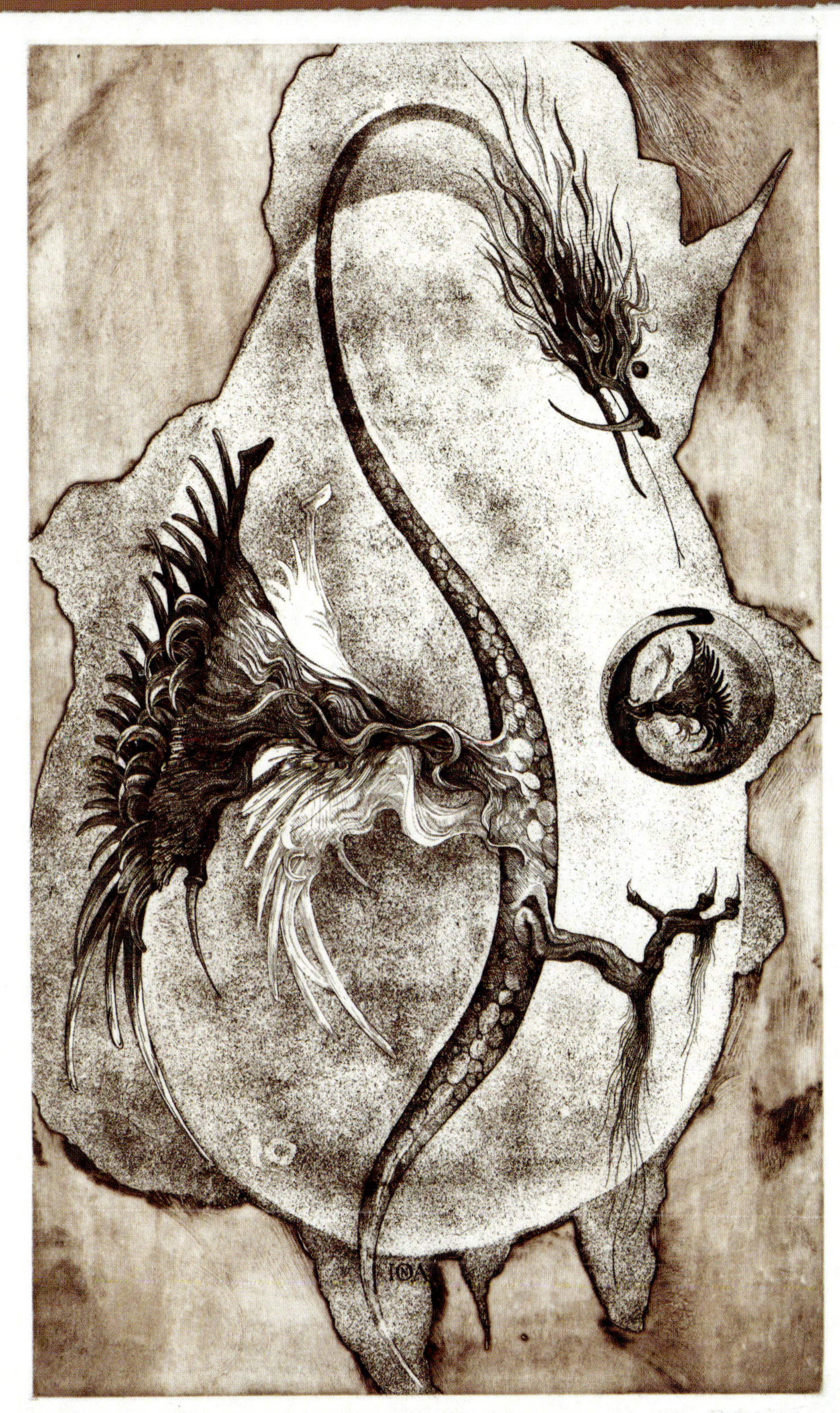

Concetta Flore Harris

Italy

Title of Work
Animals around us

Original Publisher and Date of Publication
Happy Books, 1994
ISBN 88-415-1756-5

Technique
Watercolur, gouache

Legend
. *Birds*

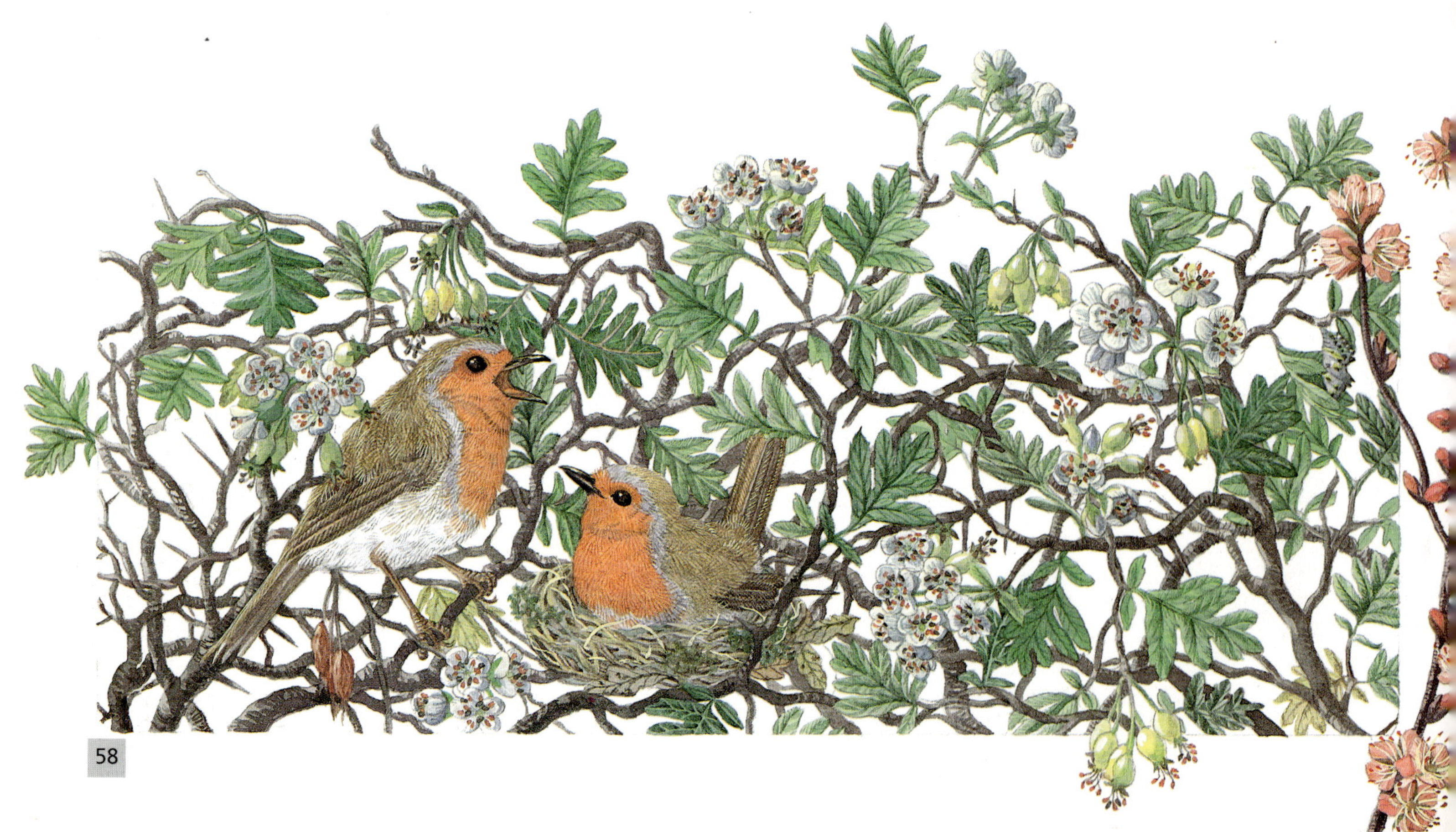

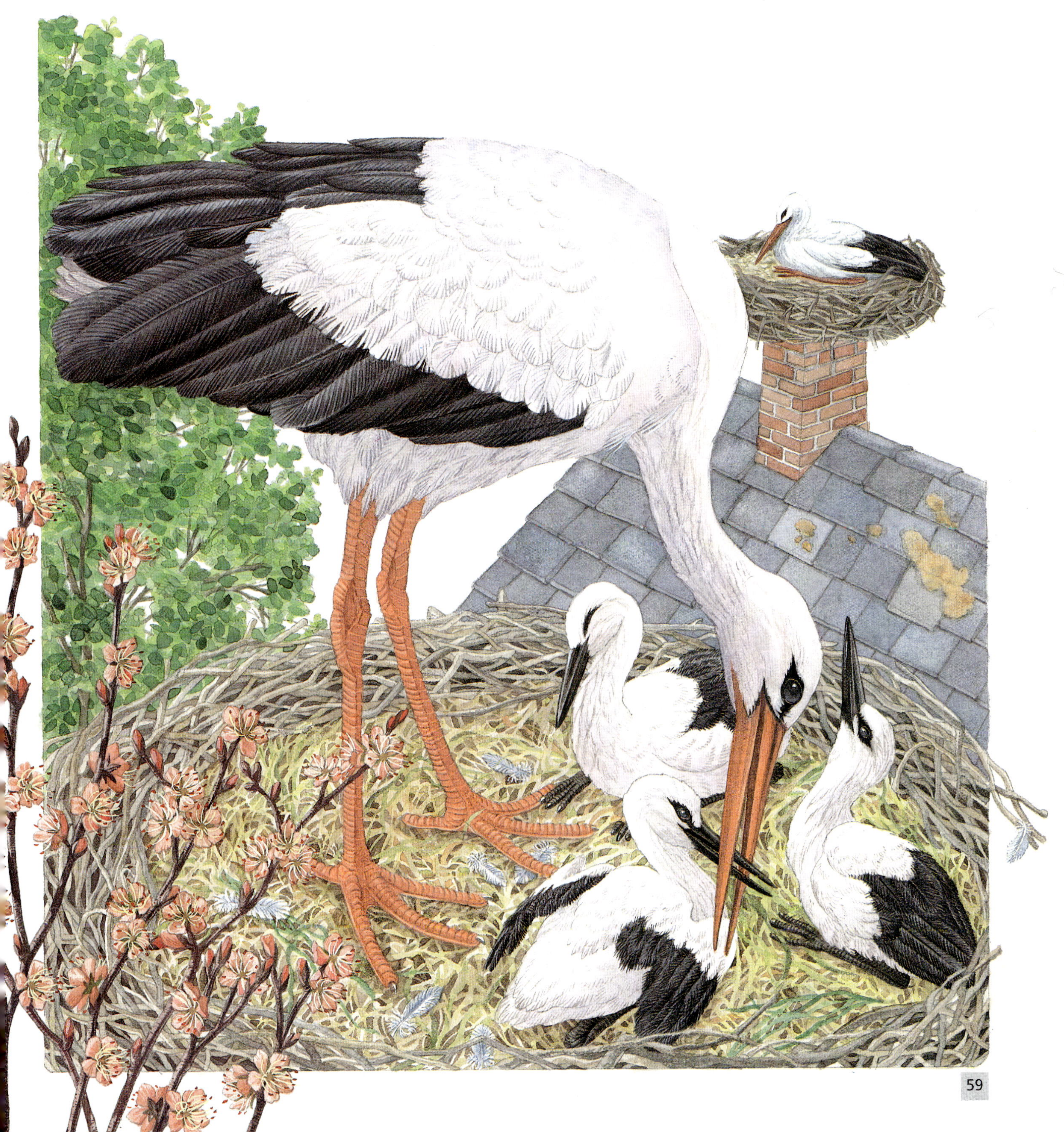

Henri Galeron

France

Title of Work
The bullfight

Original Publisher and Date of Publication
Editions du Mont-Blanc & Hachette Jeunesse, March 1995
ISBN 2-01-291434-9

Technique
Acrylic, watercolour and pencil

Legend
. *Raising the bulls*
. *Branding the young bulls*

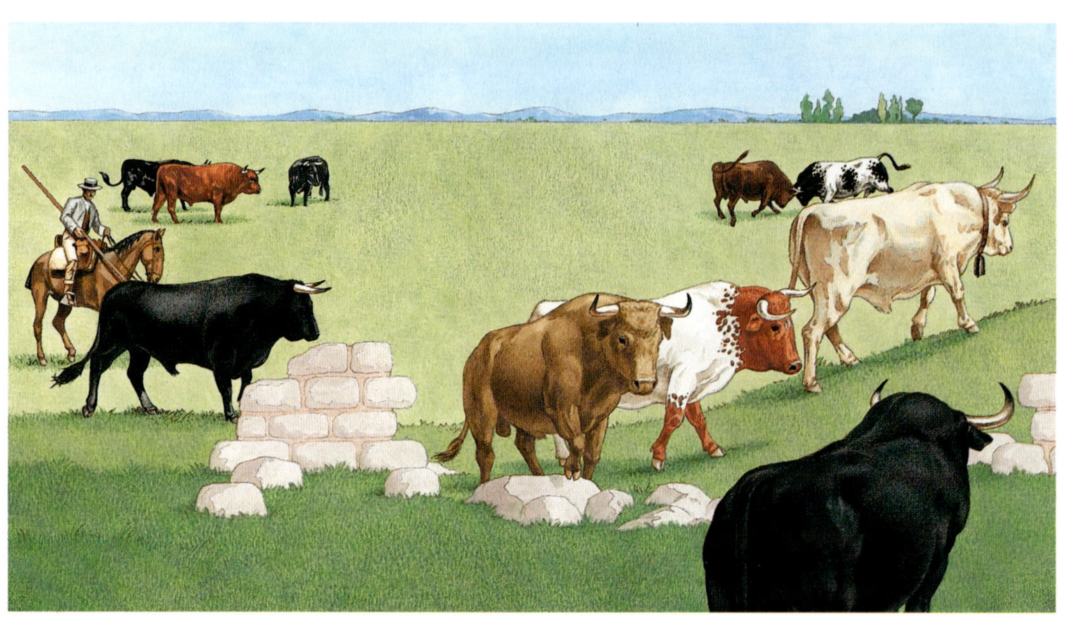

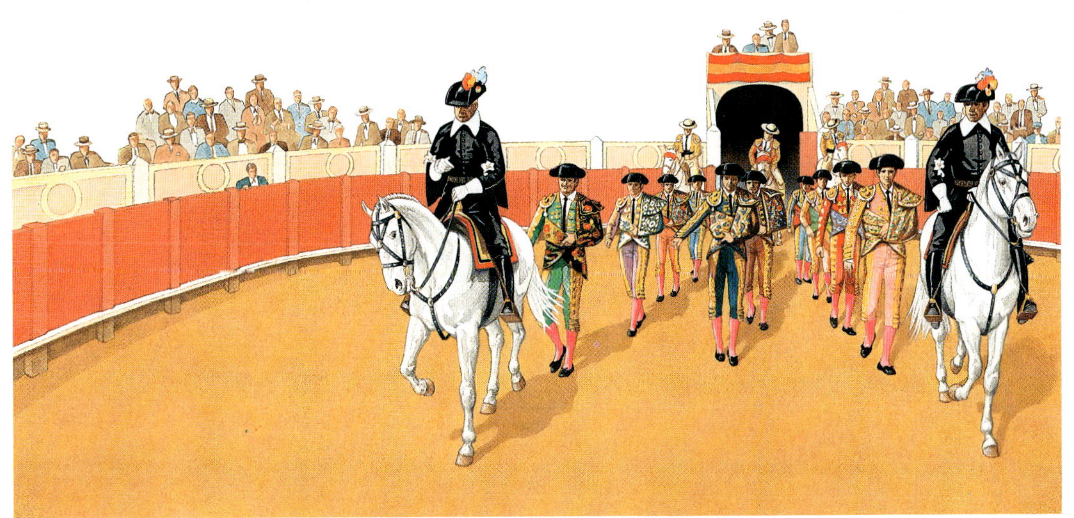

Jean-Marie Guillou

France

Titles of Works
Guides Gallimard:
Normandy
Paris

Original Publisher and Dates of Publication
Editions Gallimard,
September 1995
ISBN 2-7424-0267-5
(Normandy)
May 1995
ISBN 2-7424-0168-7
(Paris)

Technique
Gouache, watercolour, acrylic

Legend
. Geometrical motifs on small castles in Normandy
. Church of St. Louis des Invalides, Paris

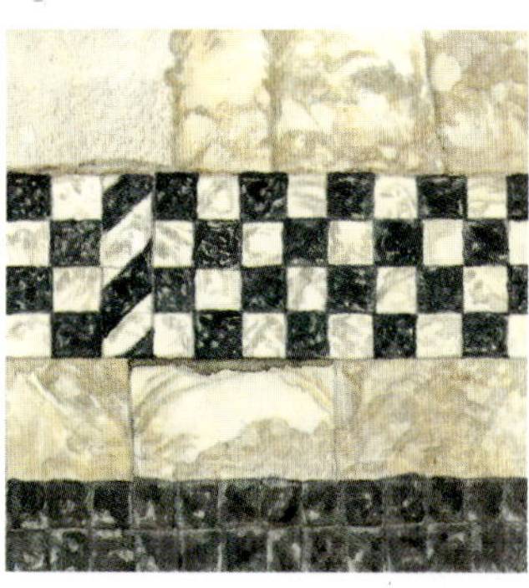
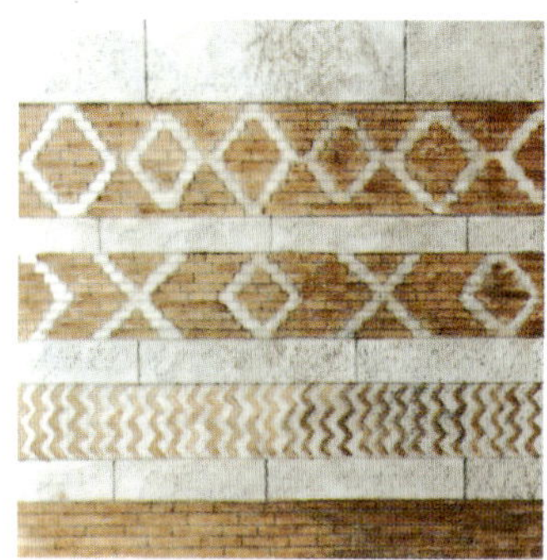
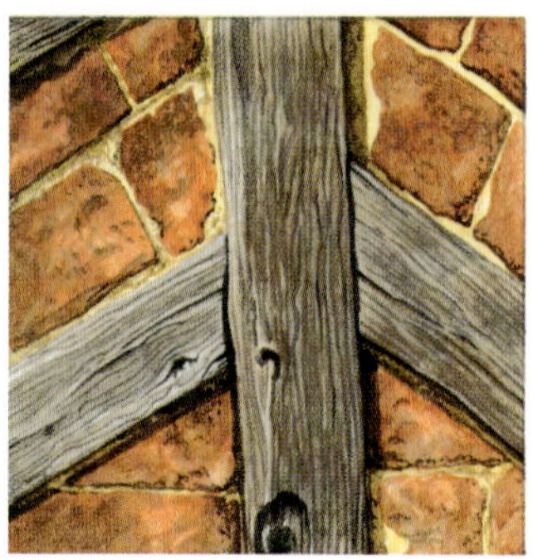
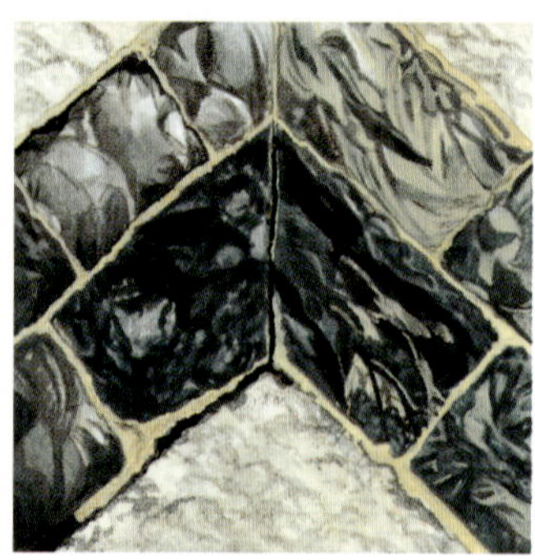
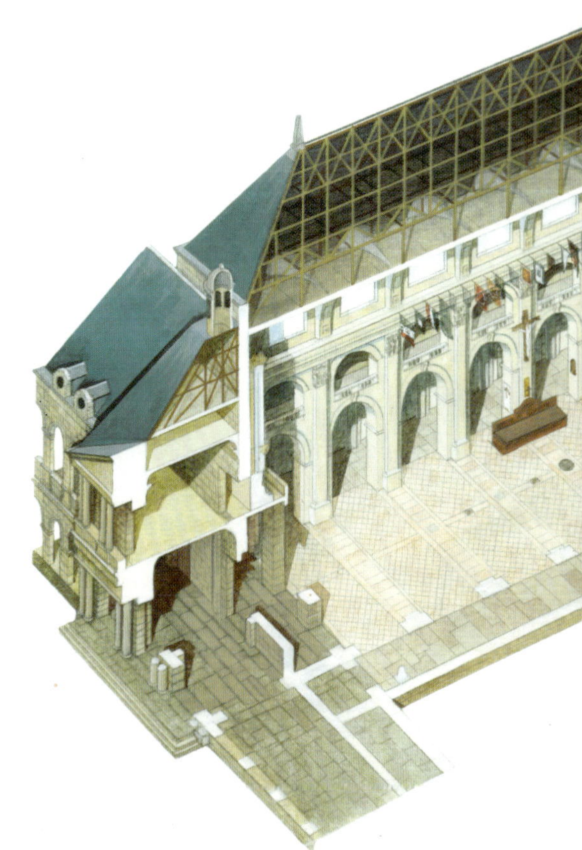

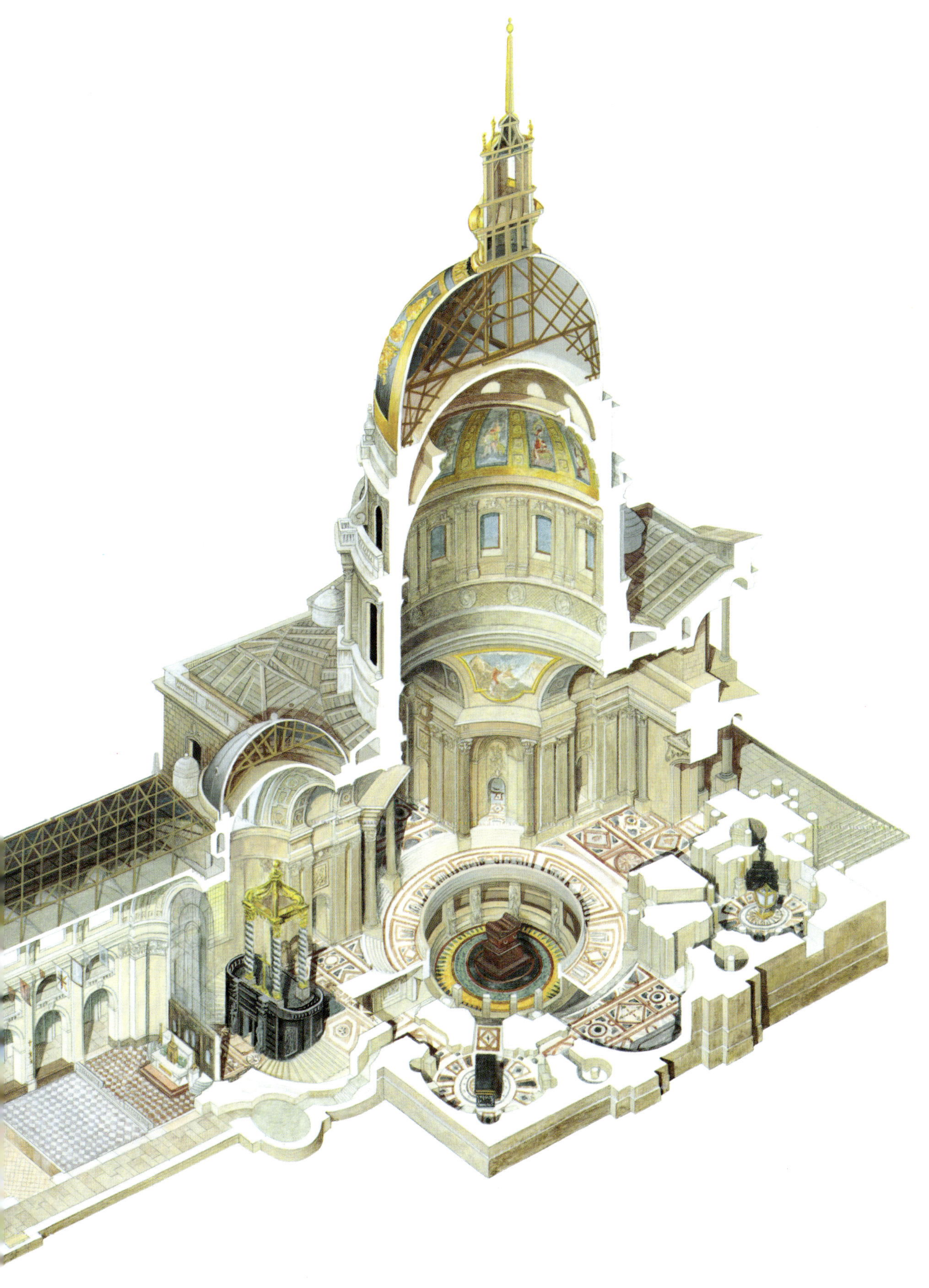

Matthias Haab

Switzerland

Titles of Works
Extinct and recent species of zebra
Nesting birds in danger in Switzerland
Impressions from the zoo

Technique
Watercolour

Legend
. Burchell zebra
. Black grouse, wood grouse, and members of the goosander family
. Siamese crocodile

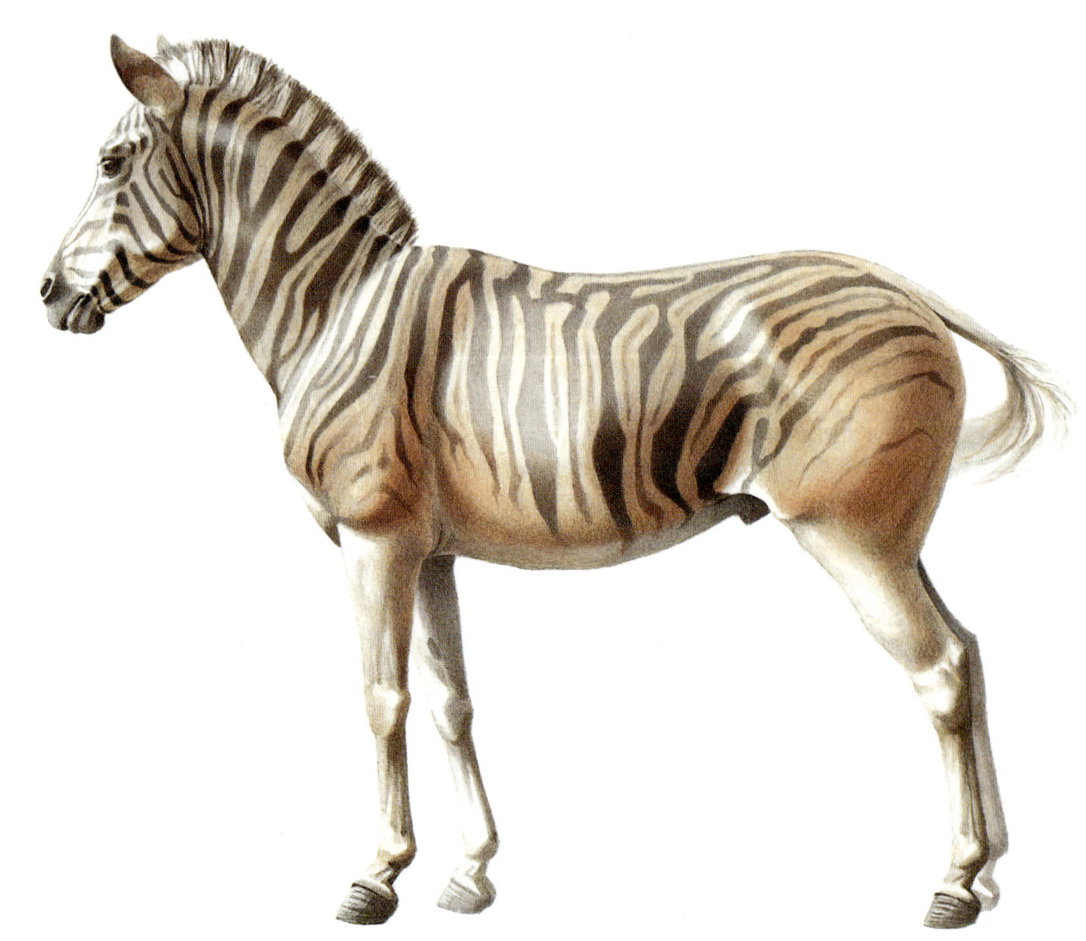

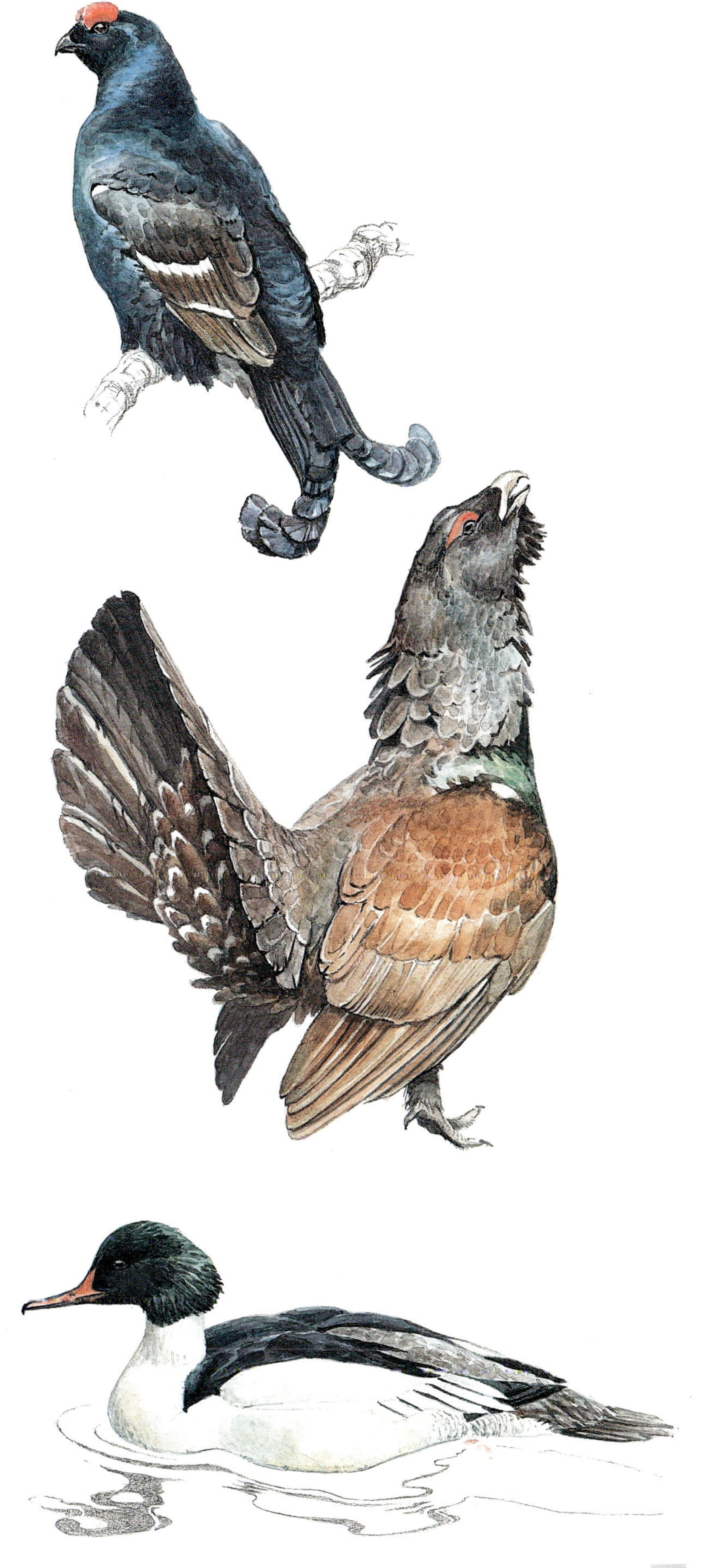

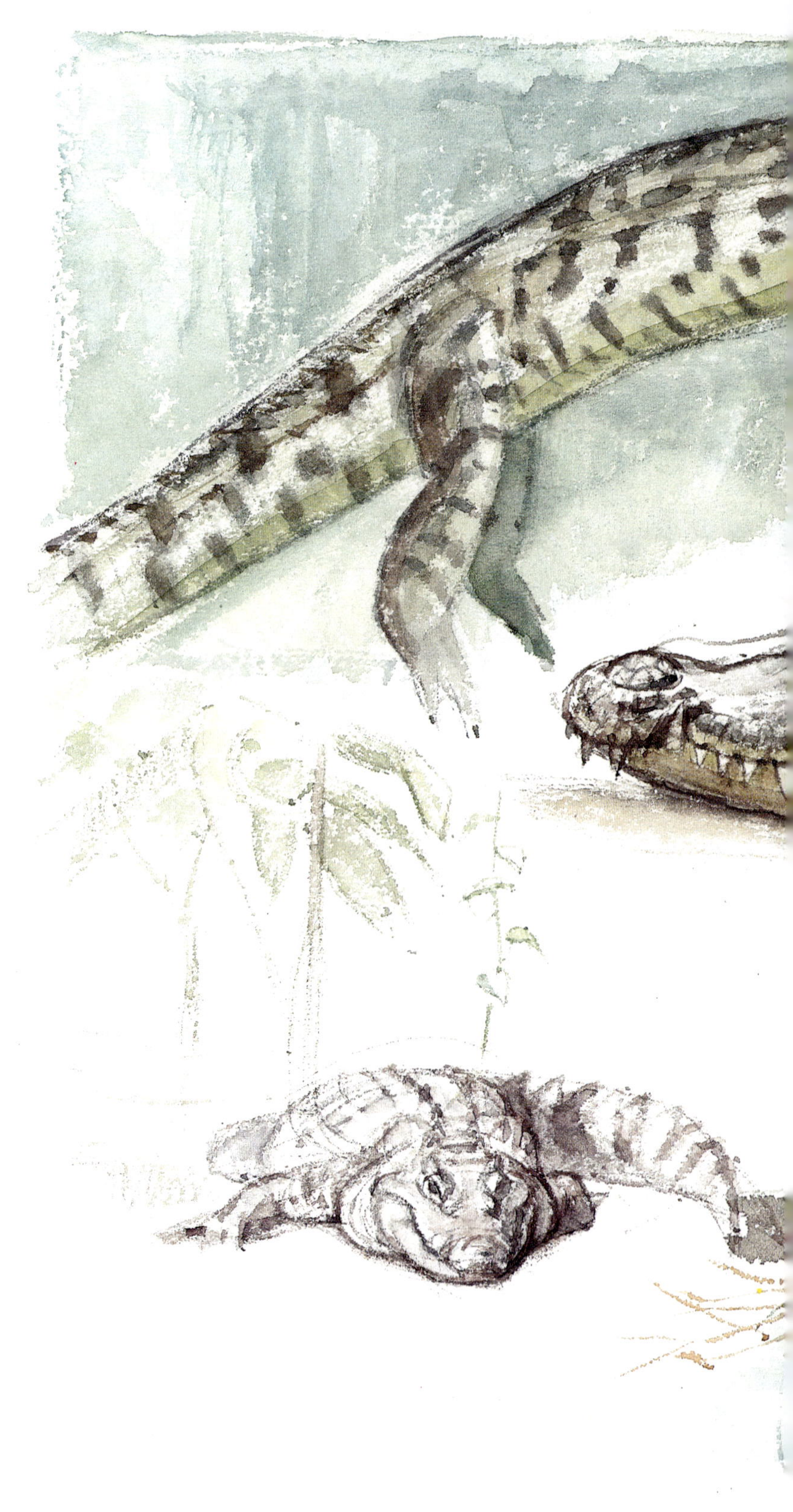

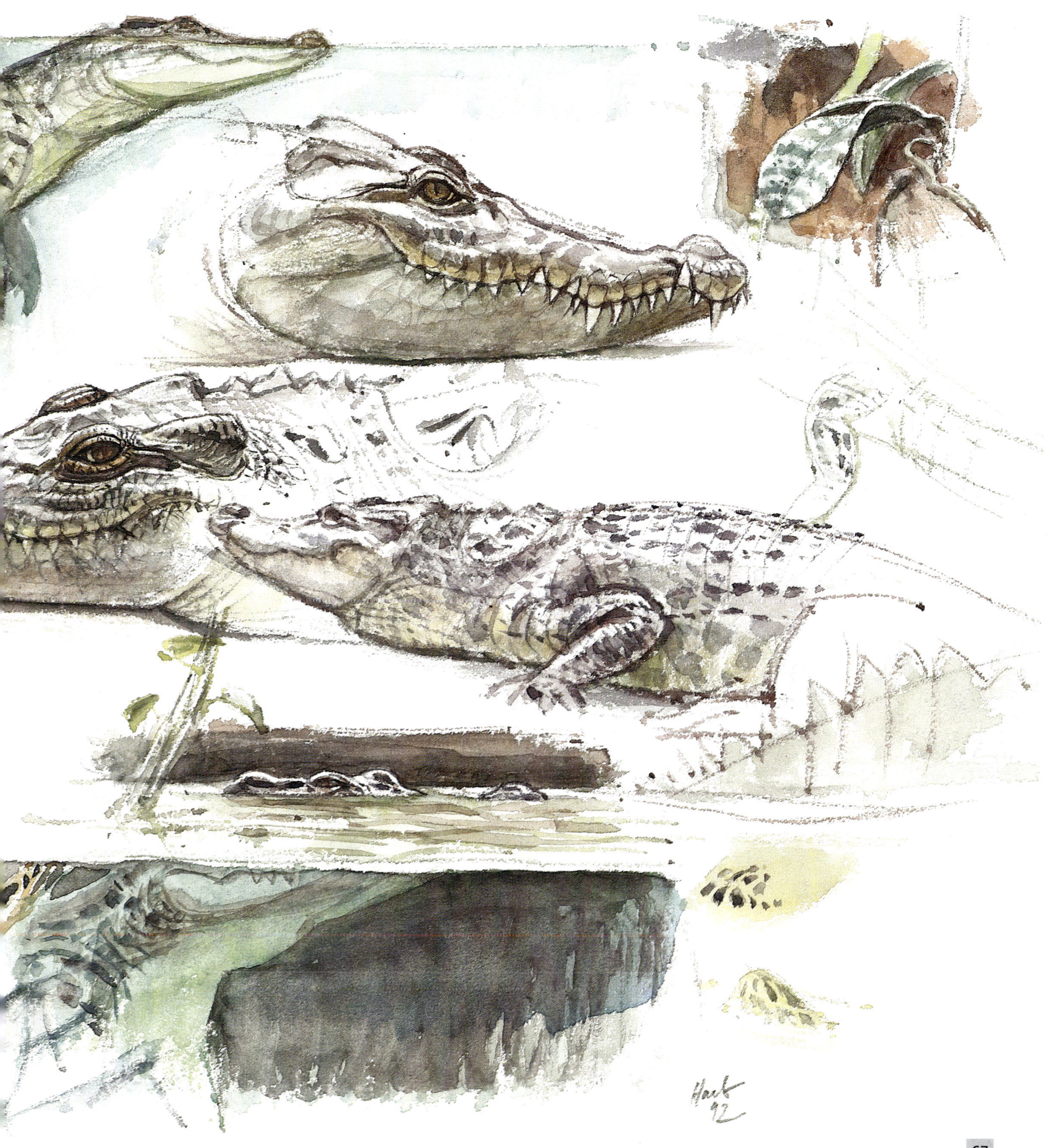
Hart
92

Andrea Hebrock

Germany

Title of Work
From a bumble bee's life

Technique
Watercolour and coloured pencil

Legend
. The bumble bee's nest
. First flight

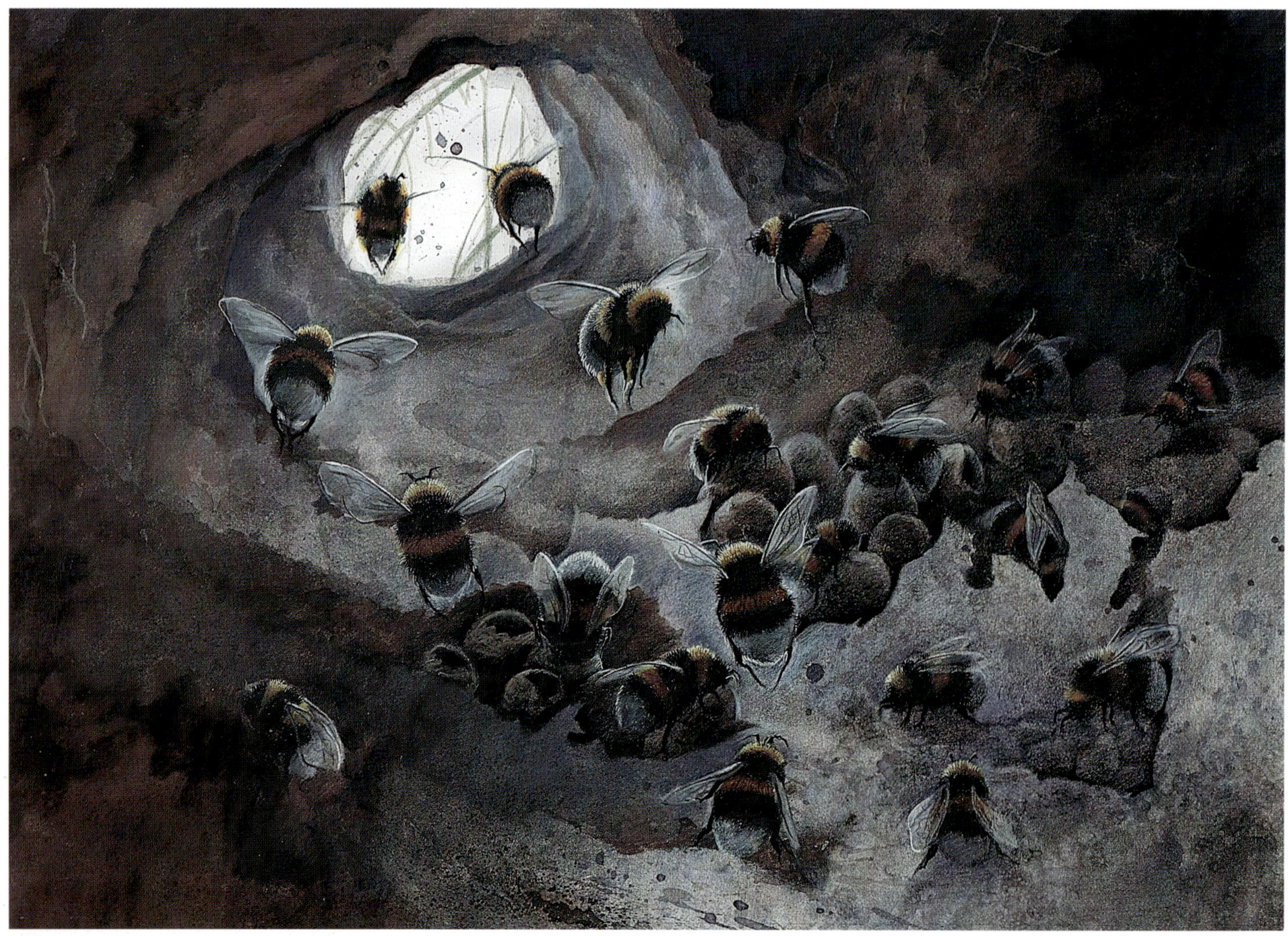

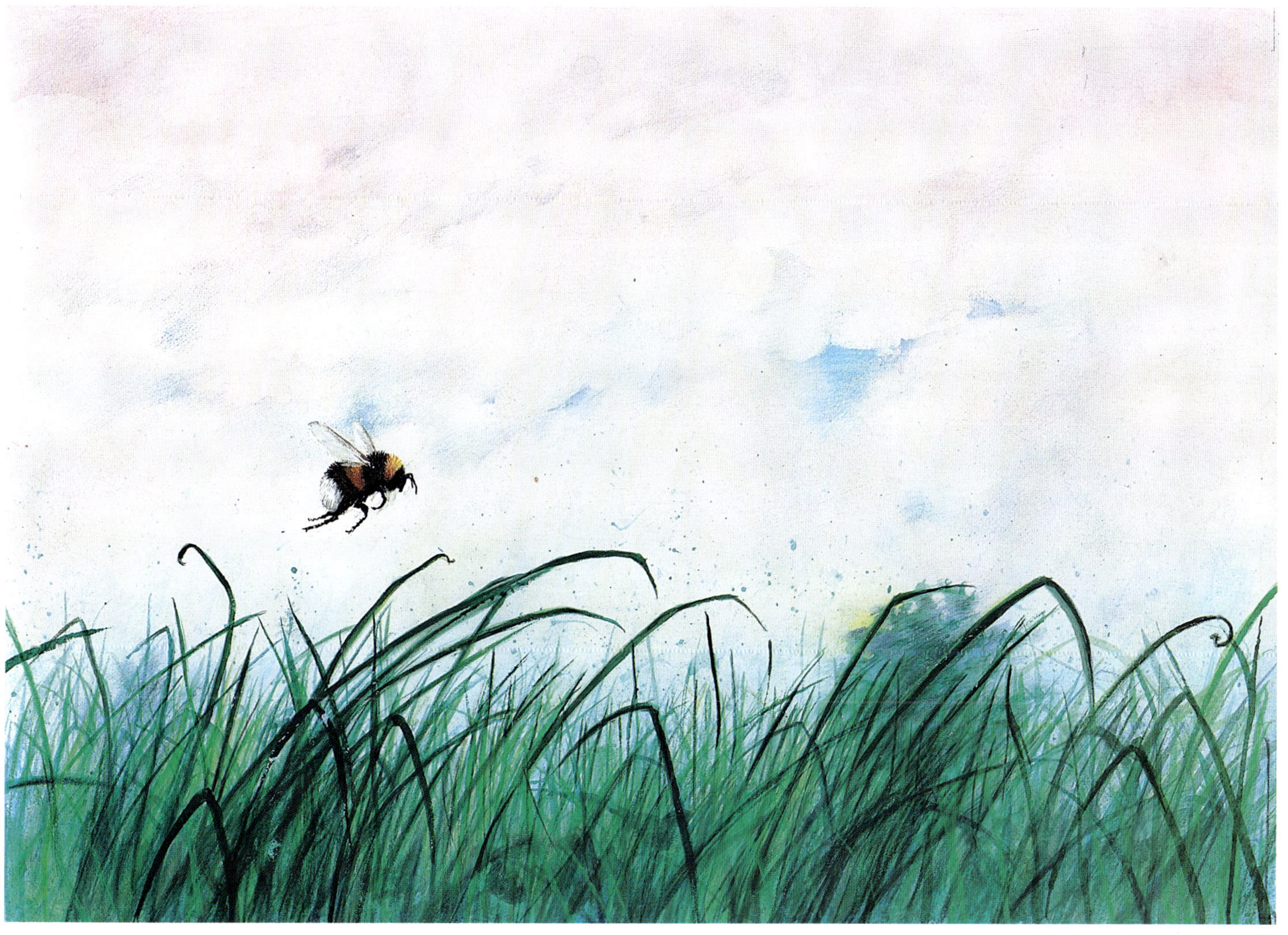

Istvan

Argentina

Title of Work
"Do two plus two always make four?"
(primary school maths book)

Original Publisher and Date of Publication
Ediciones del Eclipse,
November 1995
ISBN 987-9011-14-7

Technique
Collage

Legend
. *Chinese horoscope*
. *Western horoscope*
. *John the square*

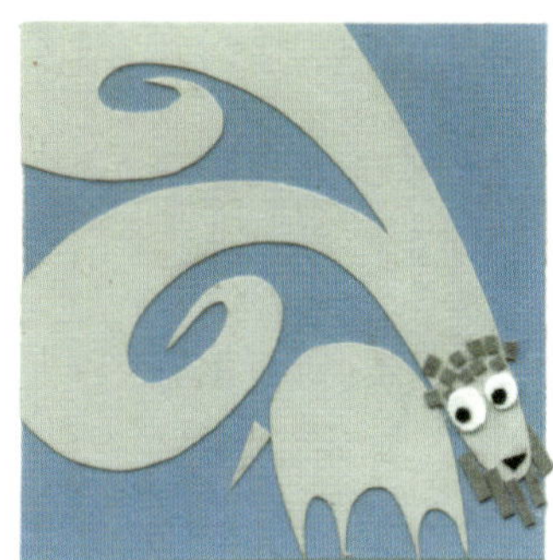

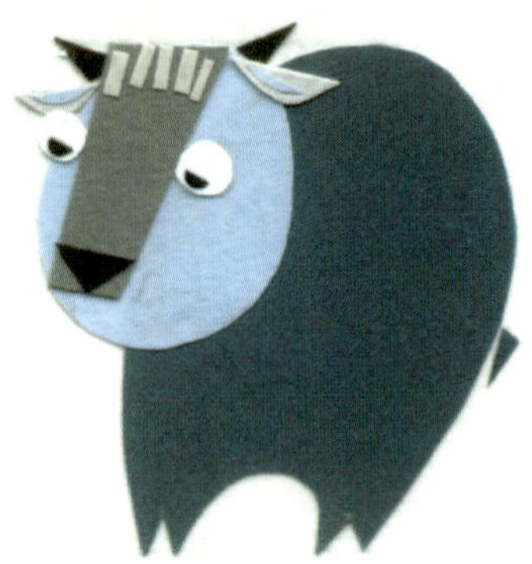

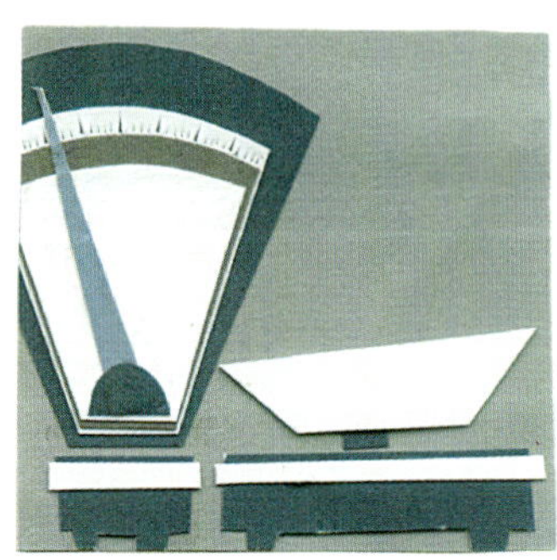

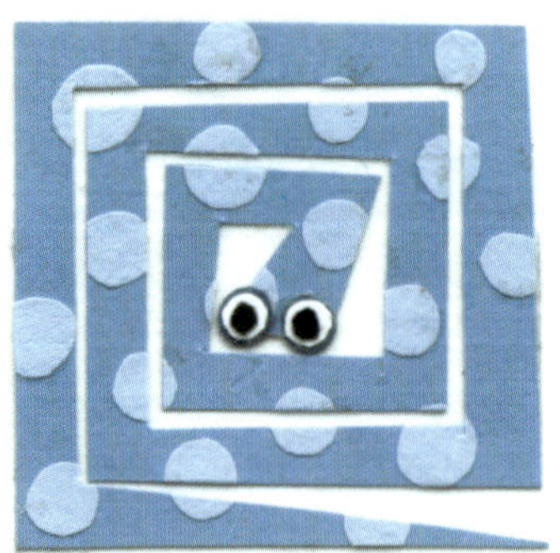

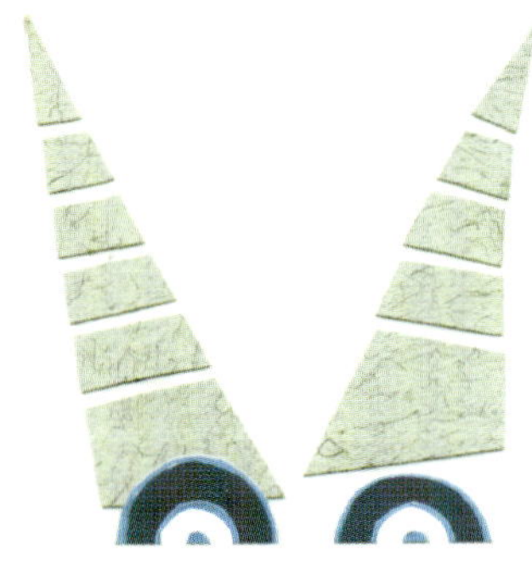

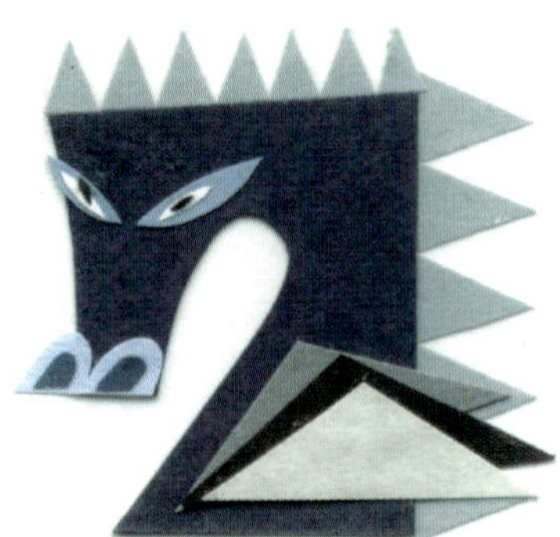

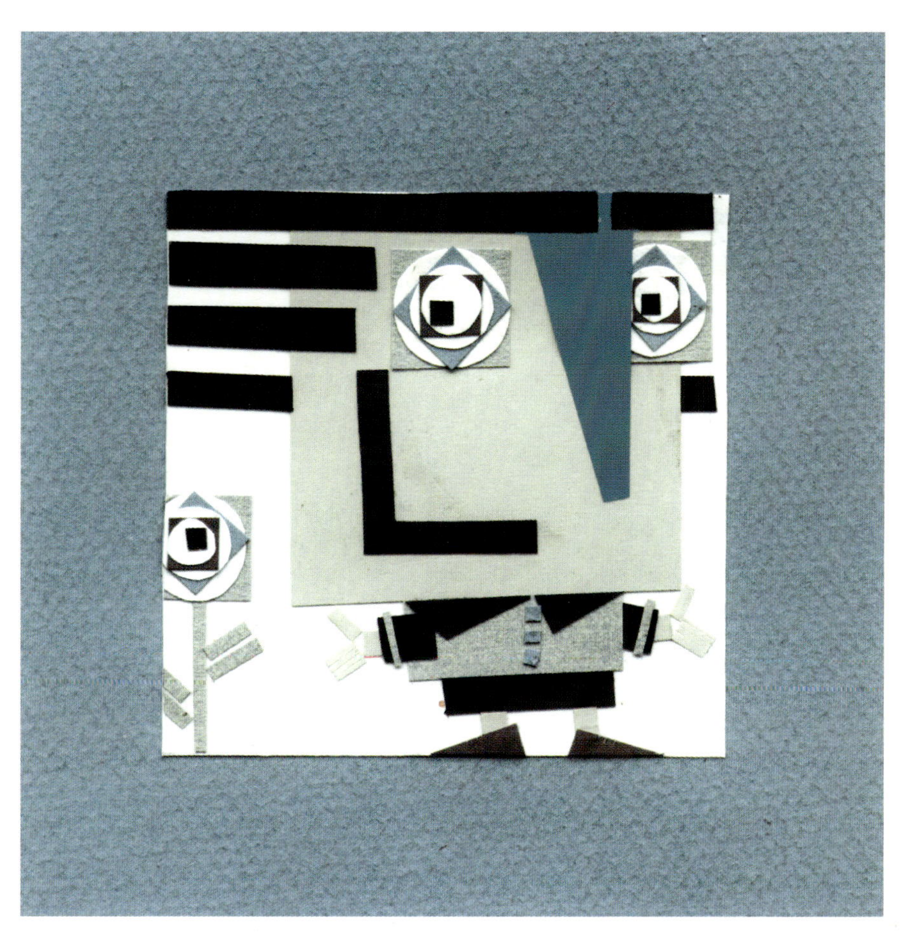

JEAN-MICHEL KACÉDAN

France

Titles of Work
Guides Gallimard:
Orne
Racines:
A history of pictures

Original Publisher and Dates of Publication
Editions Gallimard,
October 1995
ISBN 2-7424-0266-7
(Orne)
February 1995
ISBN 2-0705-8410-0
(A history of pictures)

Technique
Watercolour

Legend
. Casa Pilatos
. Anamorphosis: "The Ambassadors" by Holbein

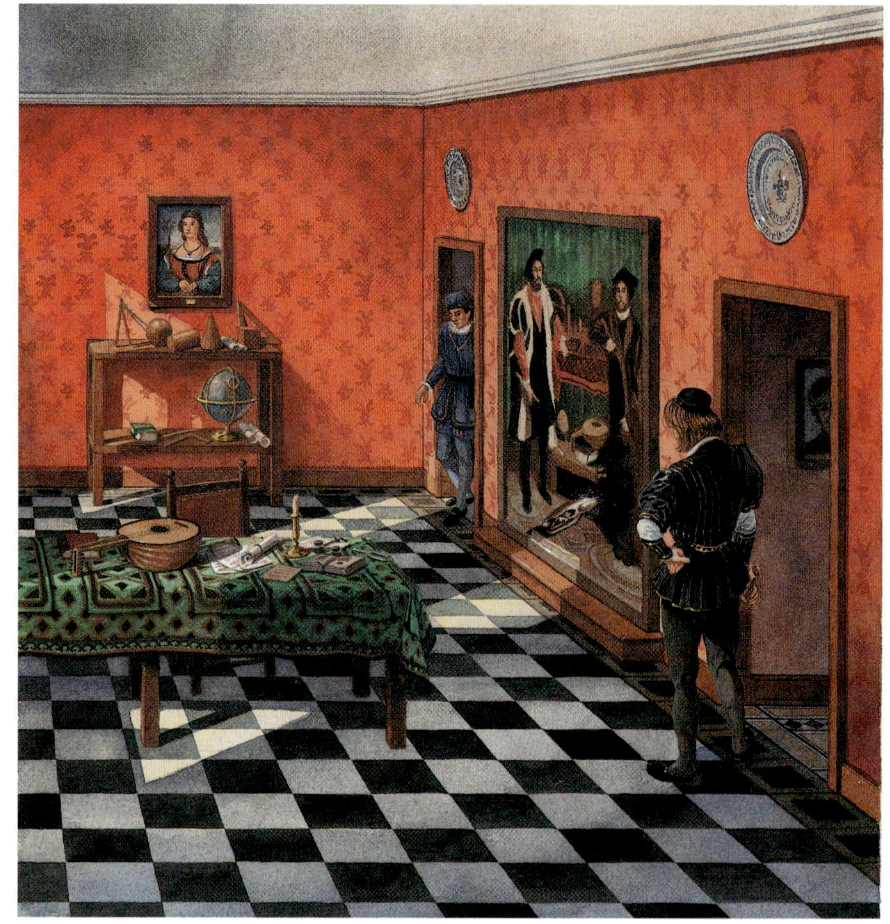

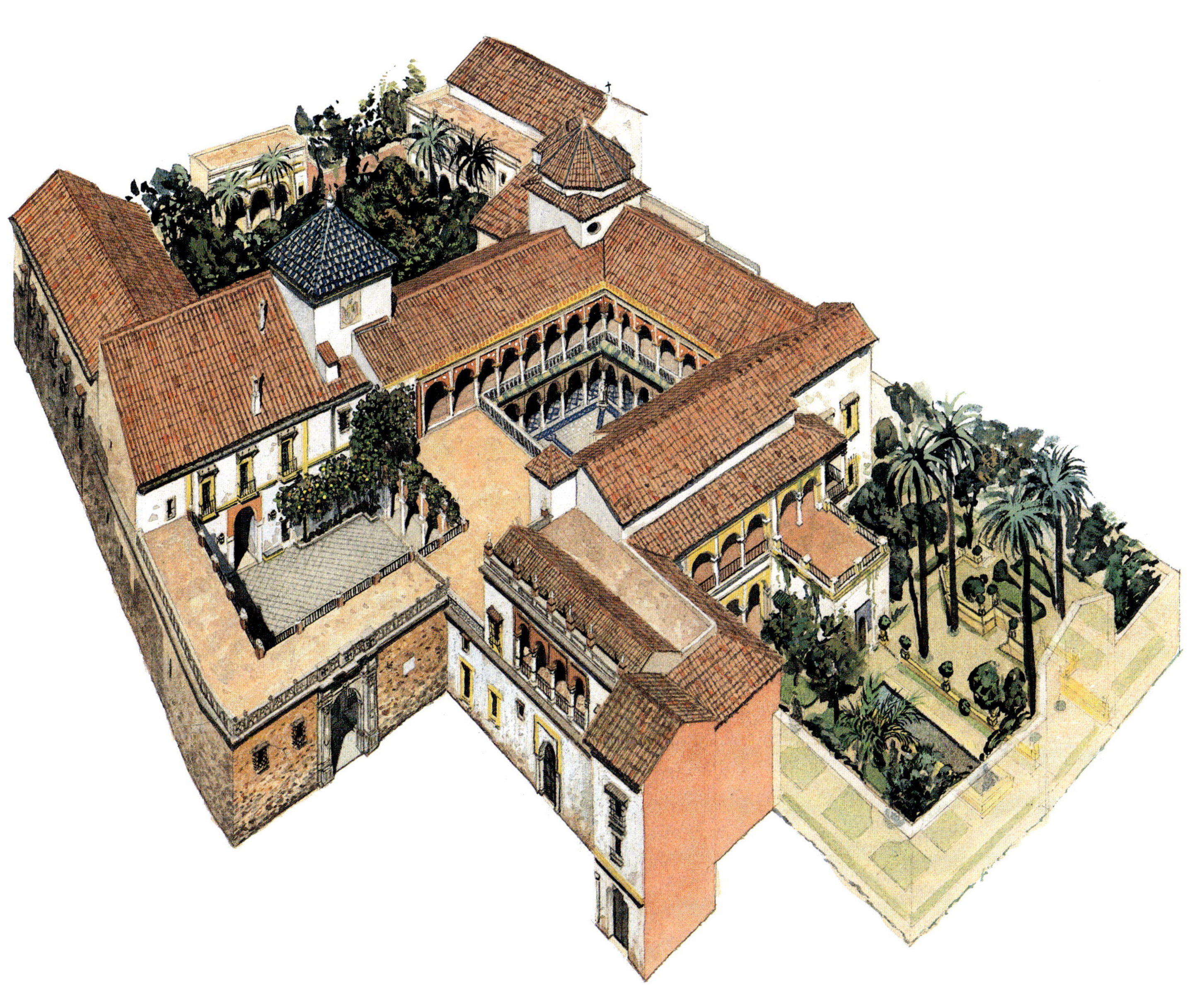

Marc Lagarde

France

Title of Work
Ma première encyclopédie: Peoples

Original Publisher and Date of Publication
Larousse S.A., 1994
ISBN 2-03-651812-5

Technique
Watercolour and gouache

Legend
. A monastery in Bhutan
. A Chinese city

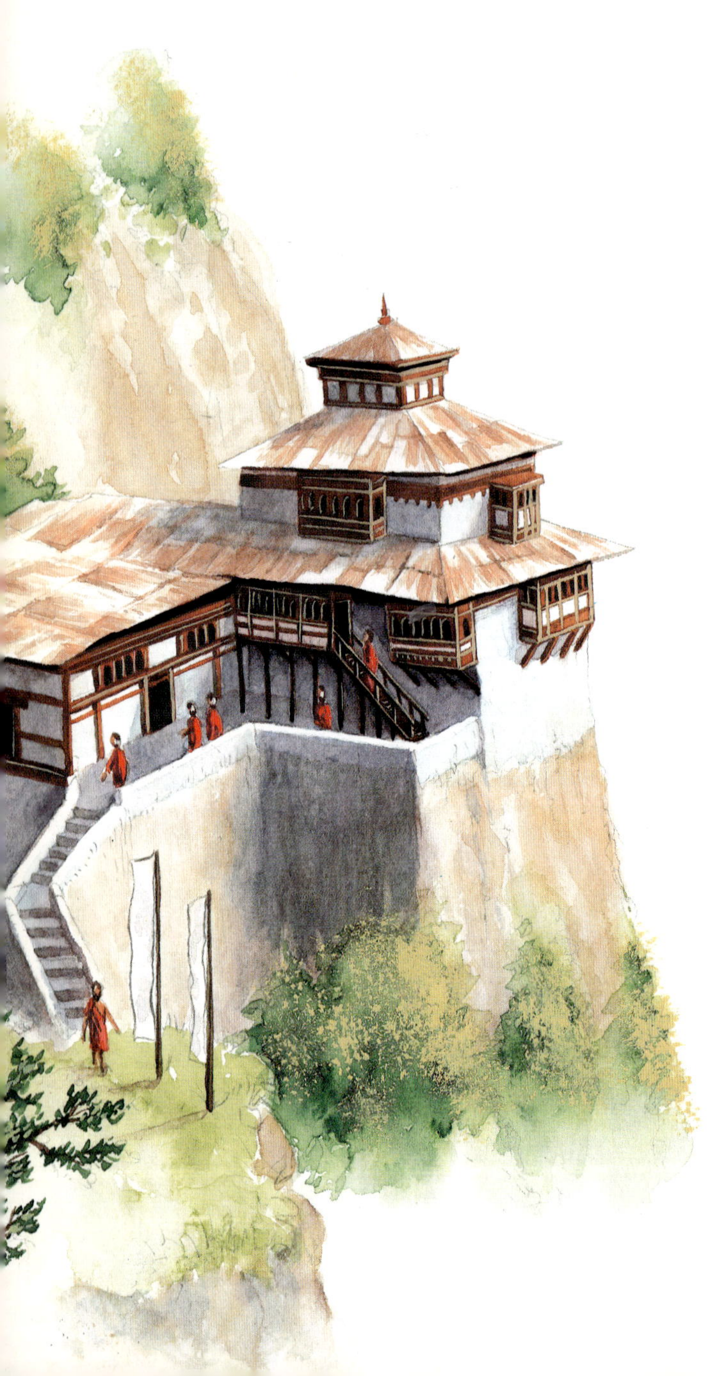

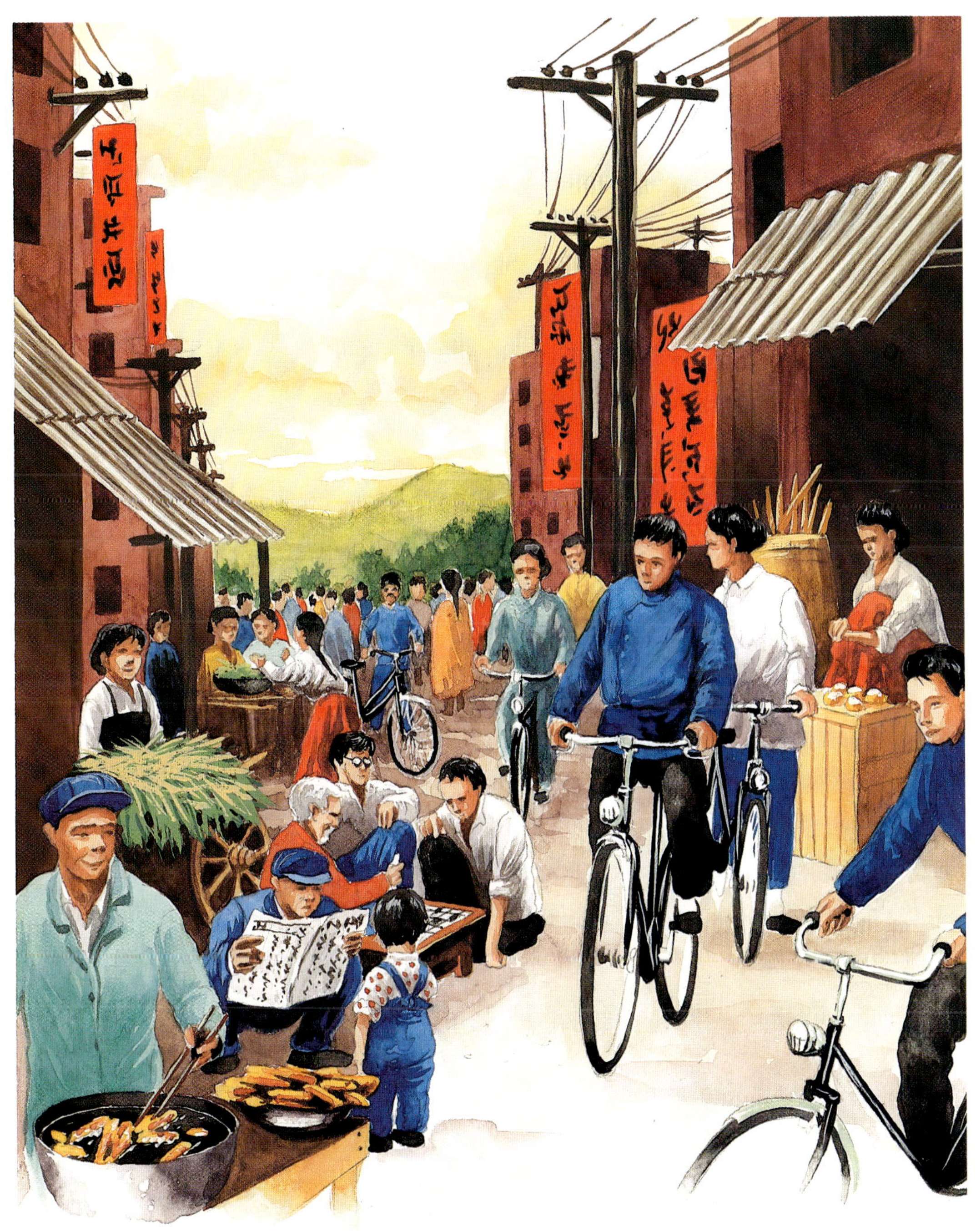

Doris Lecher

Switzerland

Title of Work
Illustrated primer

Original Publisher and Date of Publication
Verlag Herder AG,
January 1996
ISBN 3-451-23688-5

Technique
Watercolour

Legend
. L
. K

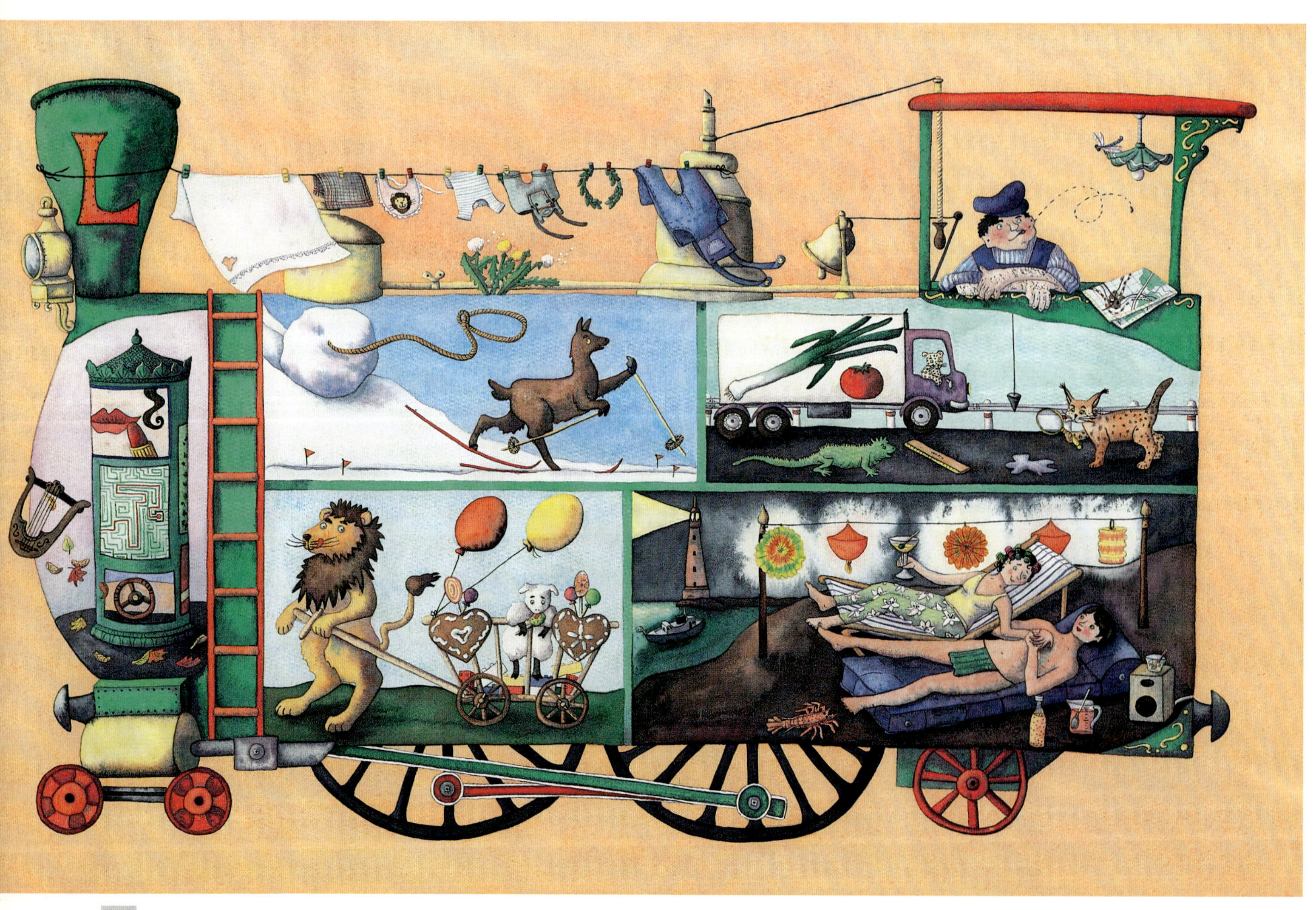

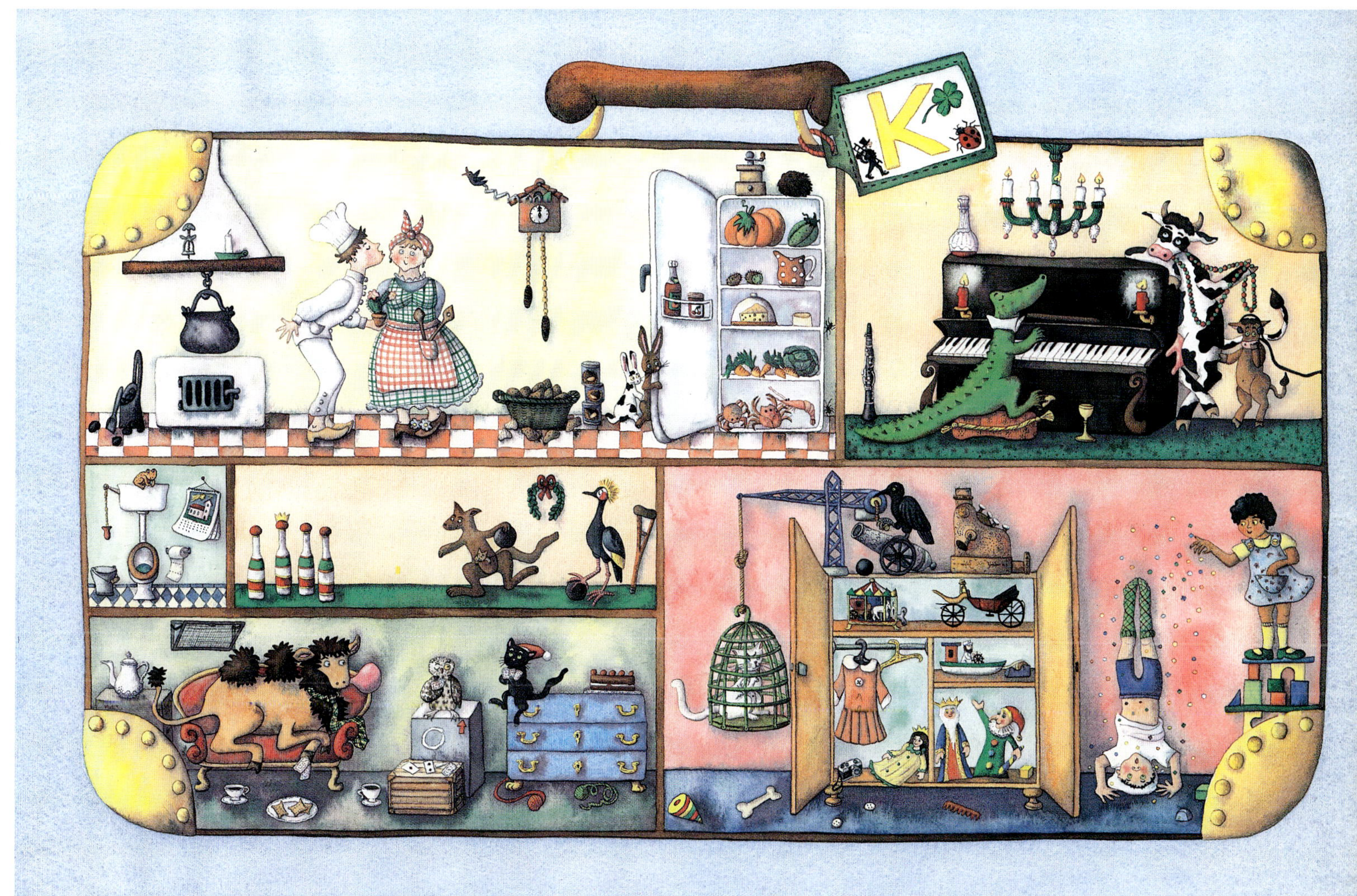
K

Sabrina Marconi

Italy

Title of Work
Ancient Rome

Technique
Tempera and gouache

Legend
. Kitchen and tableware

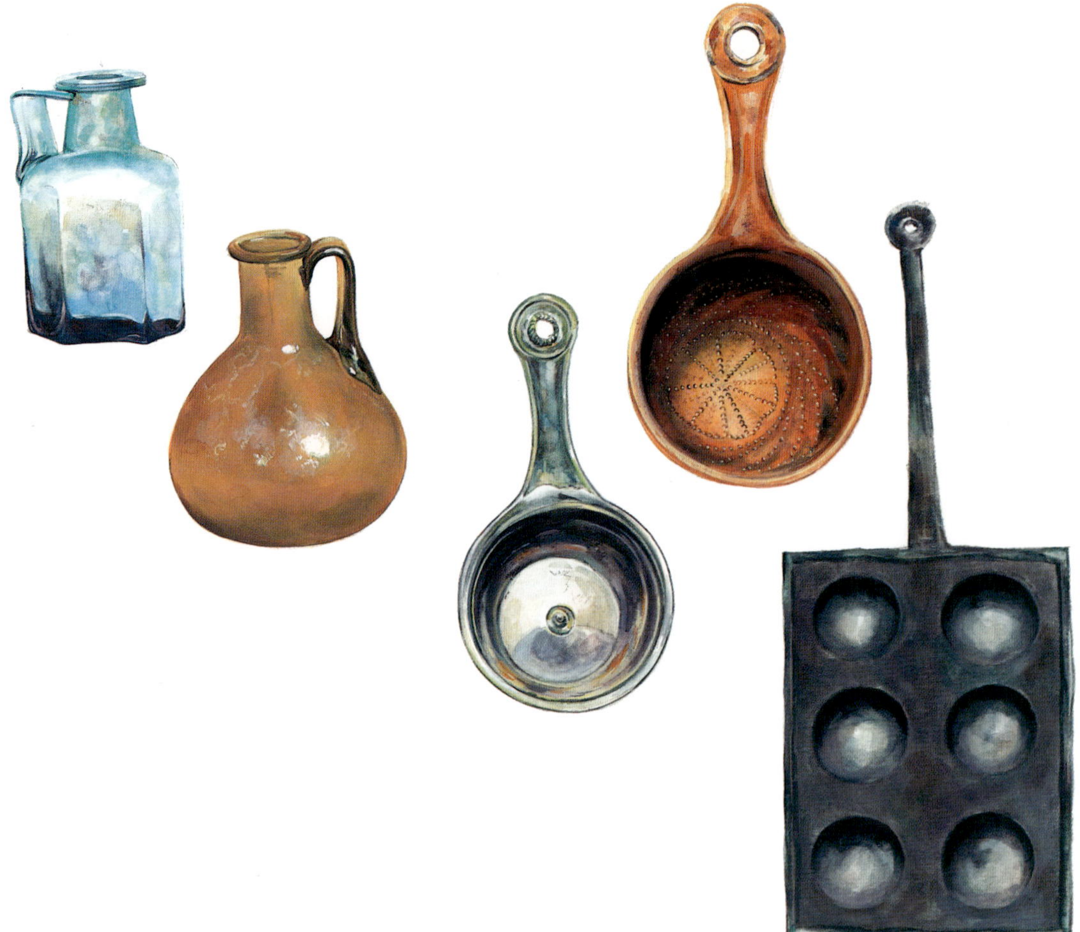

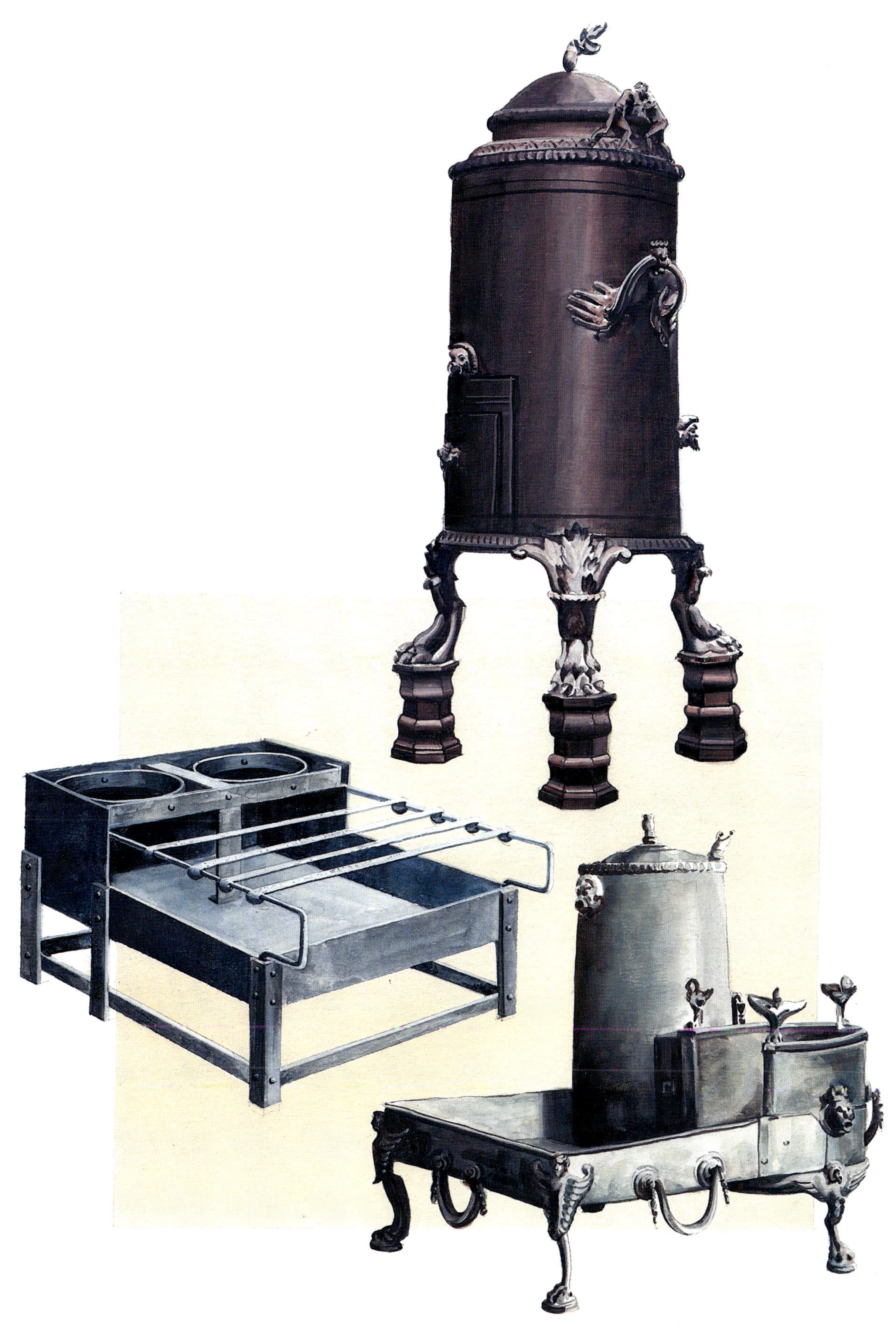

Gaia Marfurt - Maria Grazia Di Bernardo

Italy

Title of Work
Facial mimicry

Technique
Coloured pencil

Legend
. *Dynamics in expression*
(Marfurt)
. *Synergic action of the various mimicry muscles*
(Marfurt - Di Bernardo)

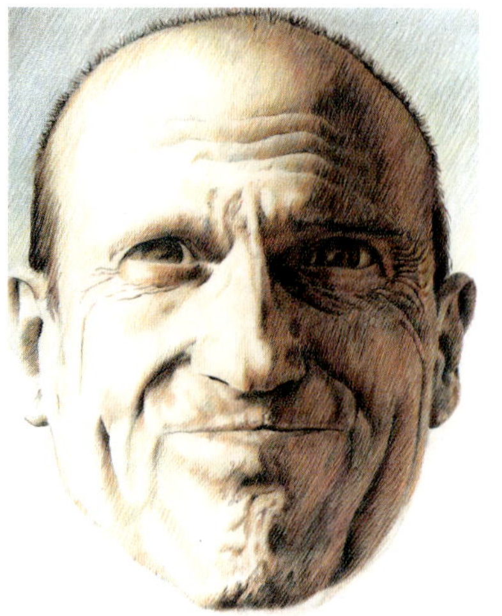

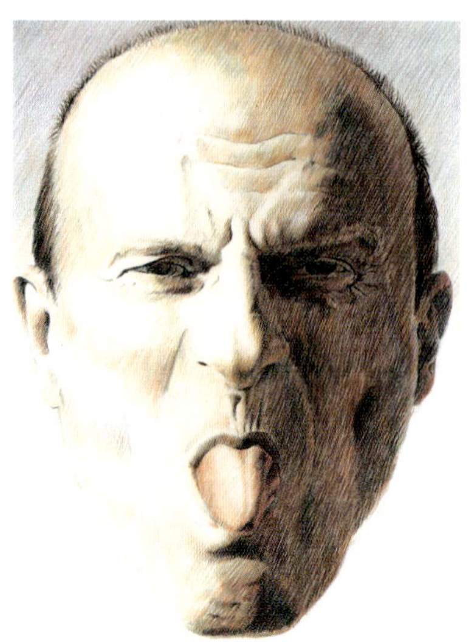

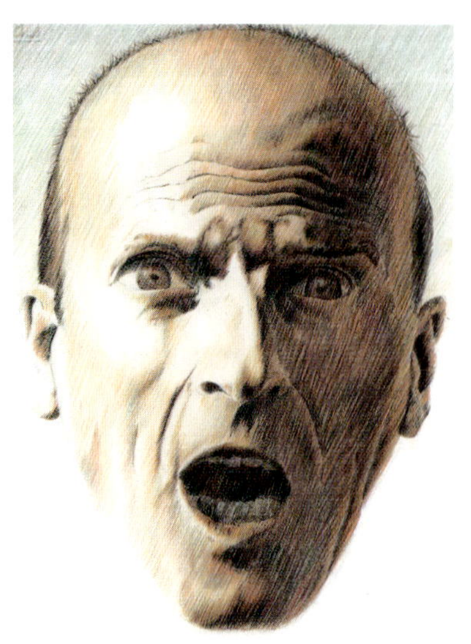

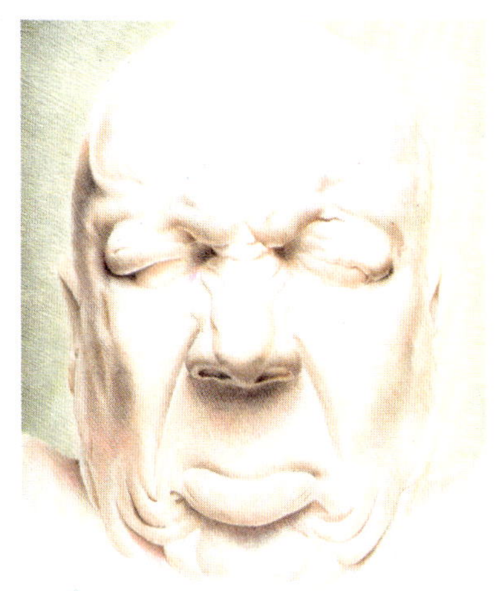

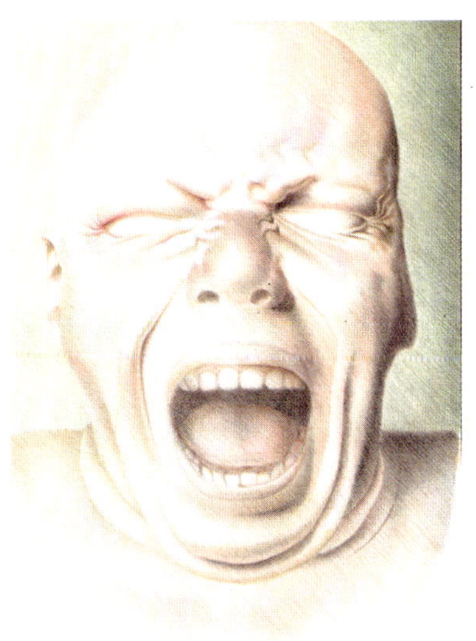

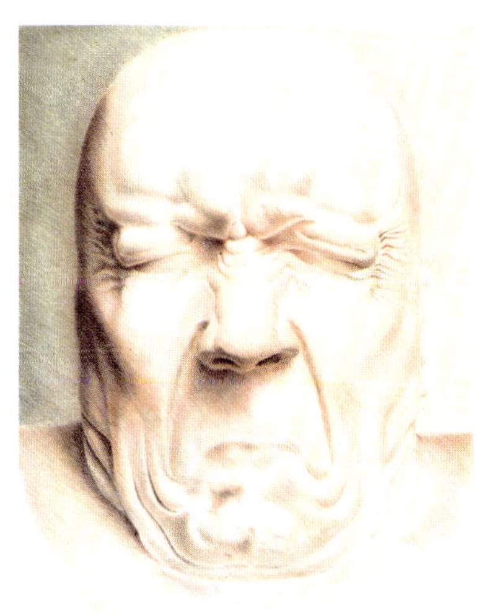

Gabriele Maschietti

Italy

Title of Work
Animals

Original Publisher and Date of Publication
Editoriale Giorgio Mondadori, 1995

Technique
Watercolour and pencil

Legend
. Portraits of reptiles
. Snowy owl

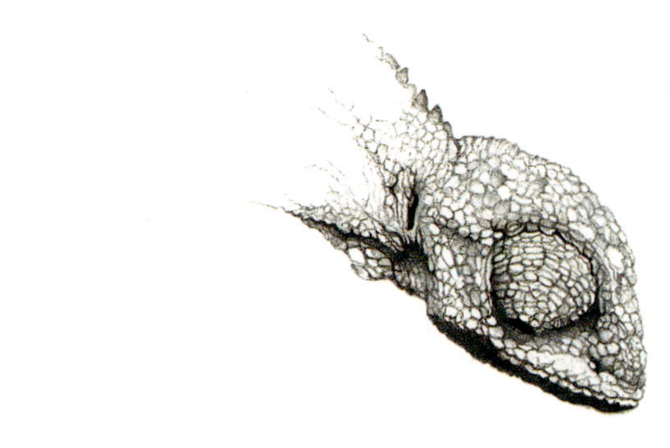

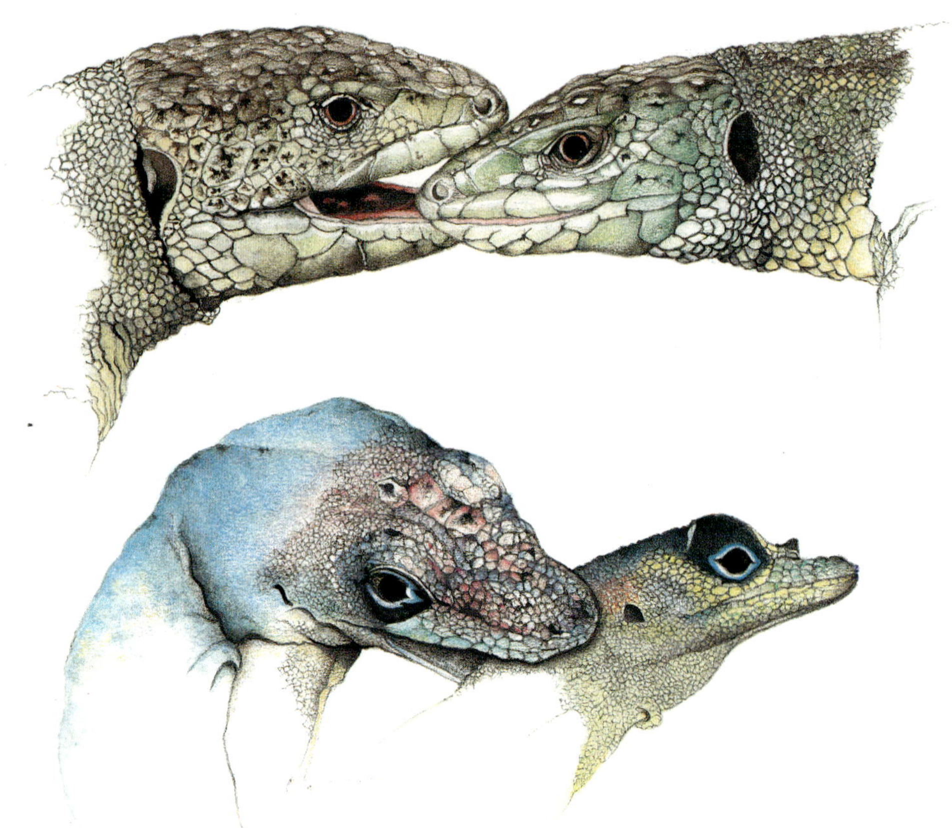

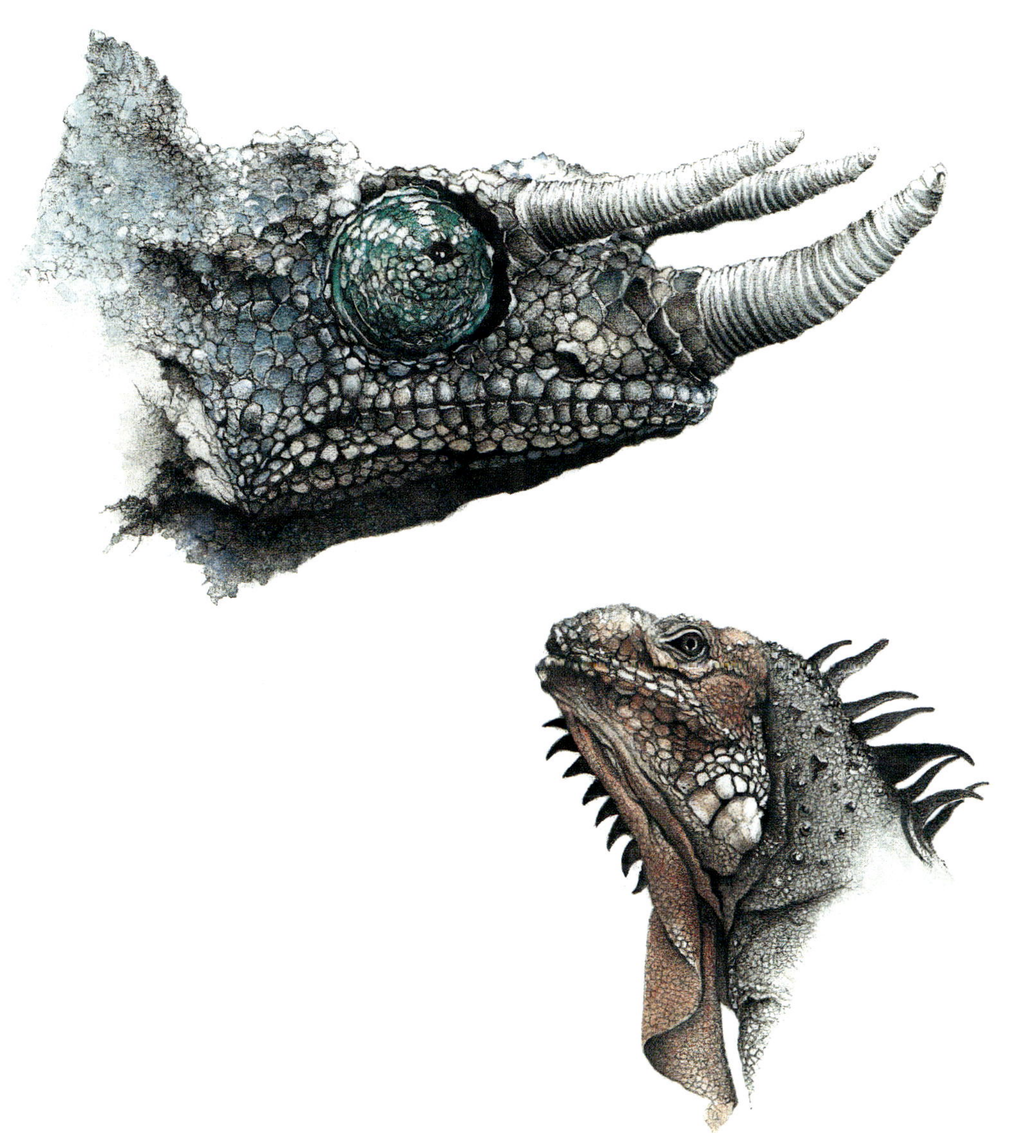

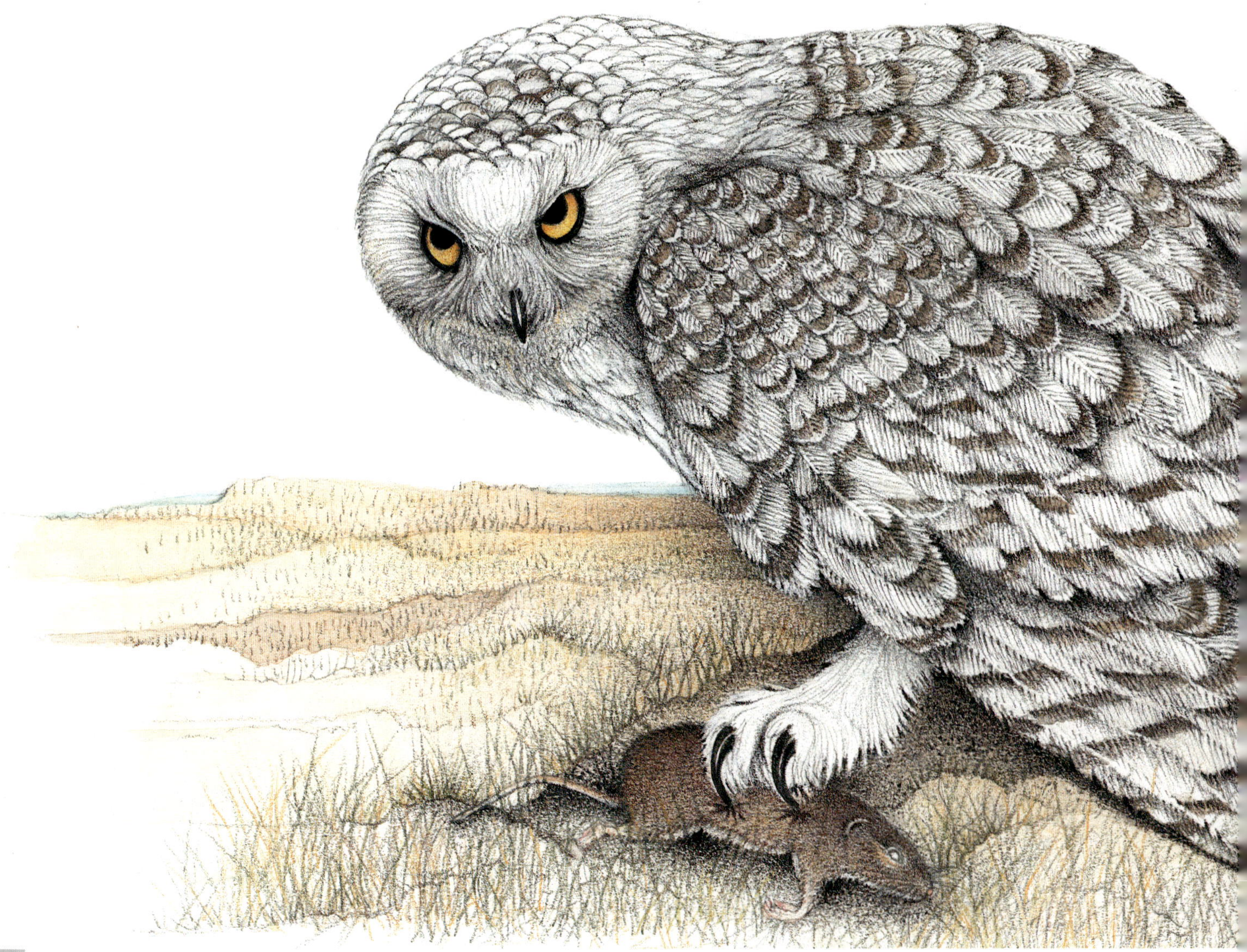

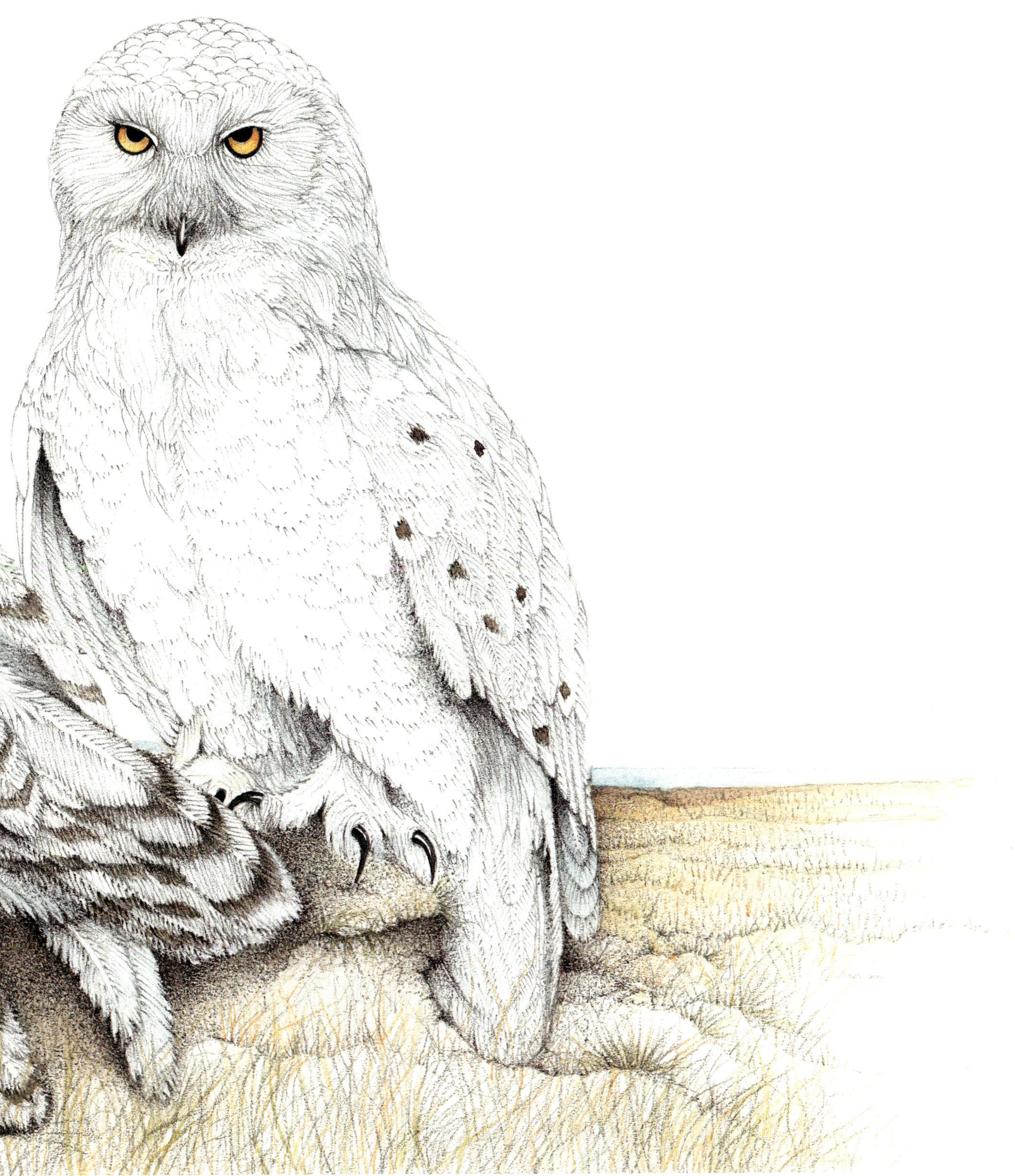

MARIA GAIA MASONI

Italy

Title of Work
Puppies in the garden

Technique
Tempera, watercolour,
coloured pencil

Legend
. Noises in the grass

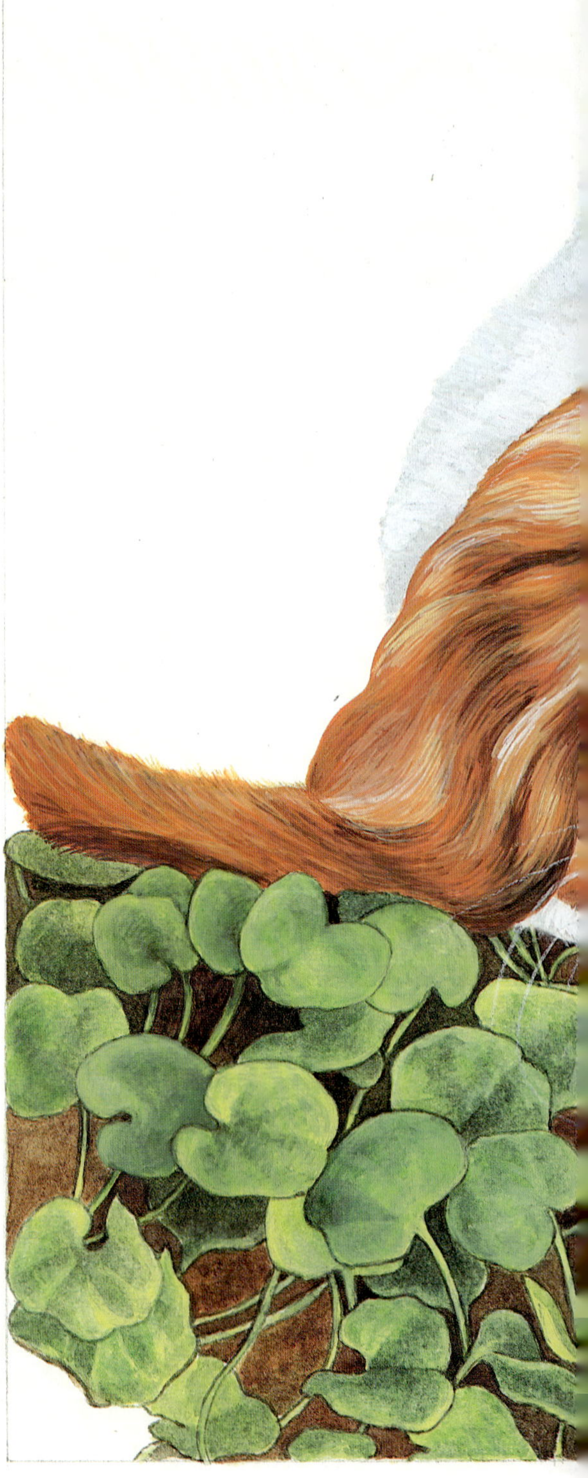

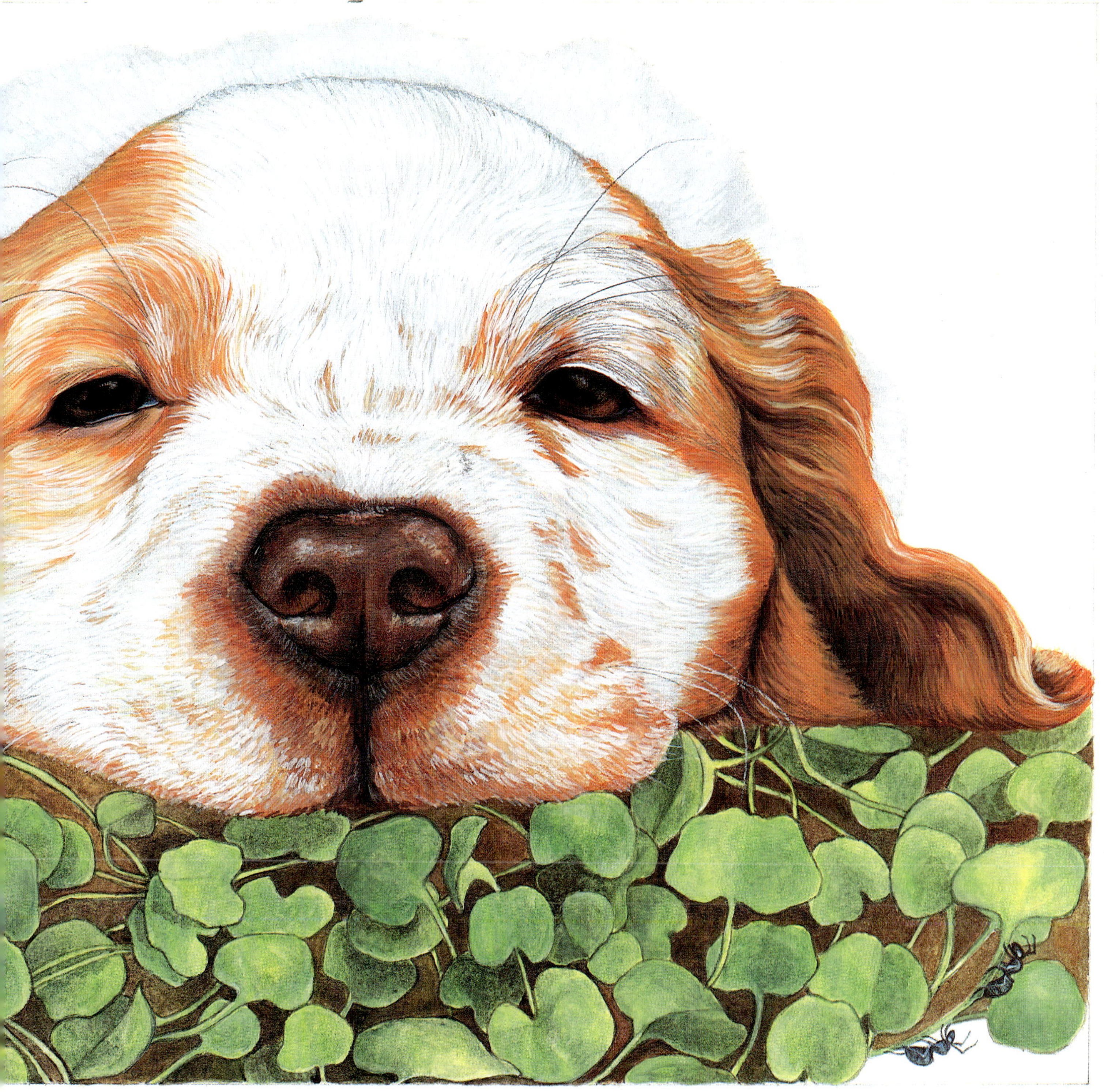

Stefano Maugeri

Italy

Titles of Works
De Rerum Natura
Dinosaurs from the Cretaceous Period

Original Publisher and Date of Publication
Edizioni Cogecstre, 1993
(De Rerum Natura)

Technique
Tempera, china ink, watercolour (plus pastel and/or air brush)

Legend
. The return of the black woodpecker to our woods
. The roar of the hadrosaurs in the forest

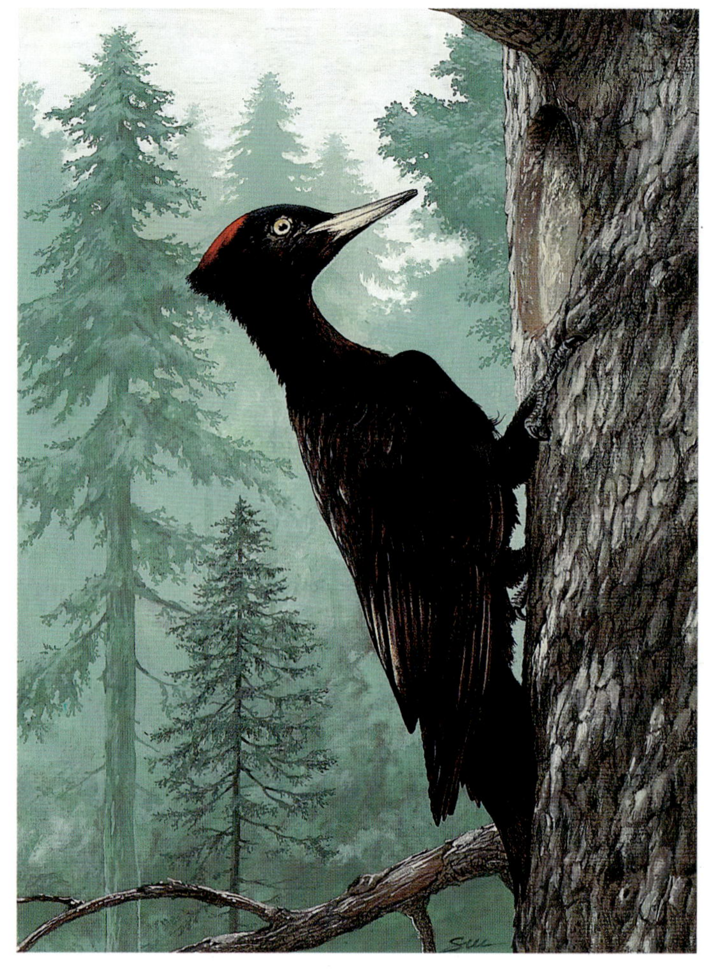

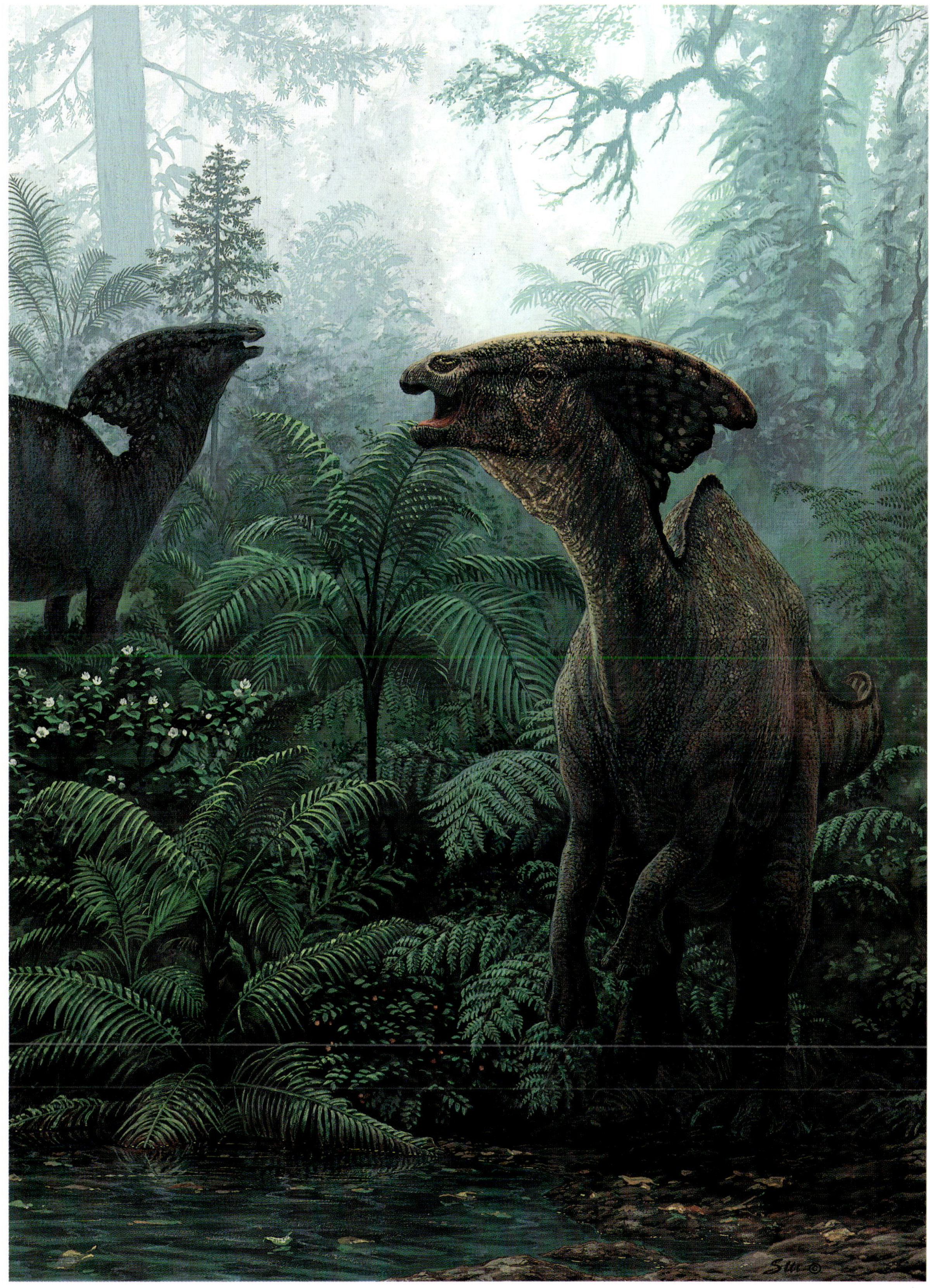

ALESSANDRA MICHELETTI

Italy

Title of Work
The works of man

Original Publisher and Date of Publication
Atlas, pending publication 1996

Legend
. The Lascaux cave paintings

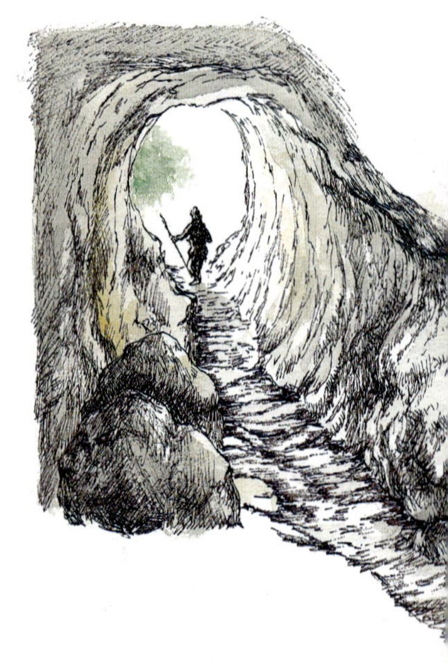

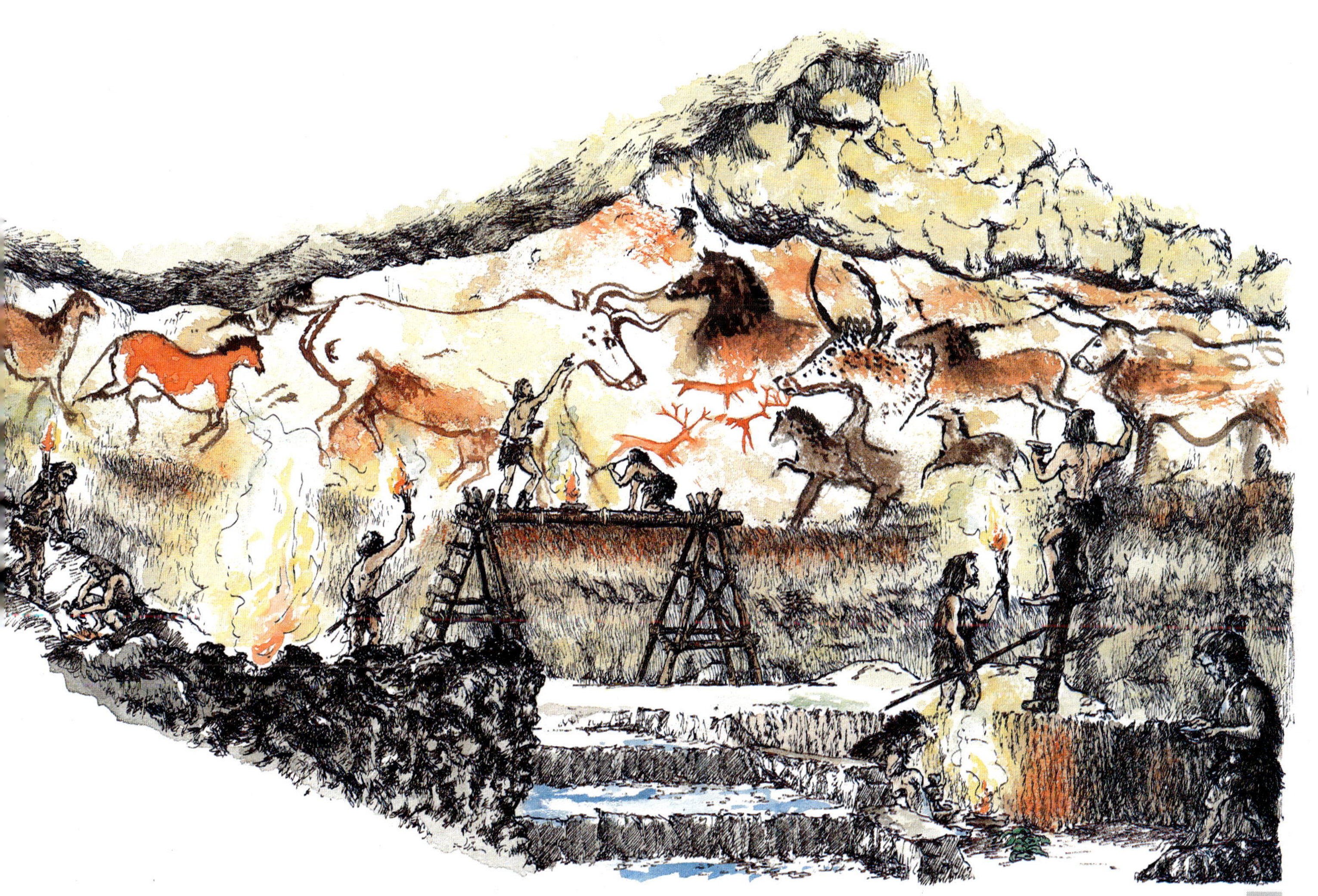

Philippe Munch

France

Title of Work
Guides Gallimard:
The Mayan World

Original Publisher and Date of Publication
Editions Gallimard, January 1995
ISBN 2-7424-0229-2

Technique
Acrylic

Legend
. Typical Mayan land in Guatemala
. Community centre

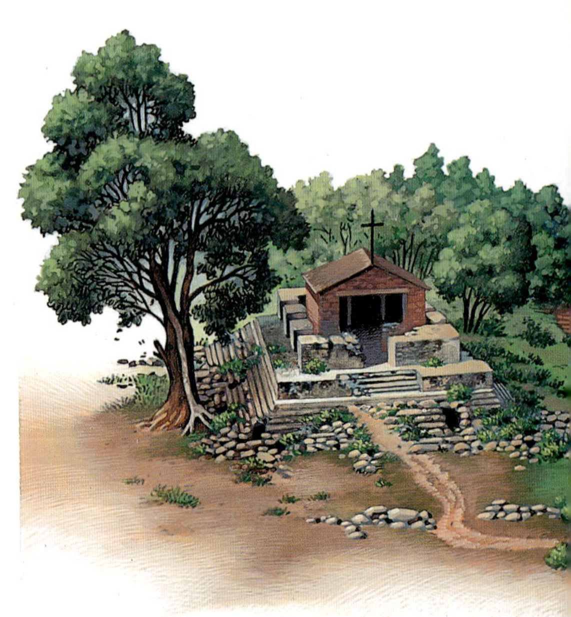

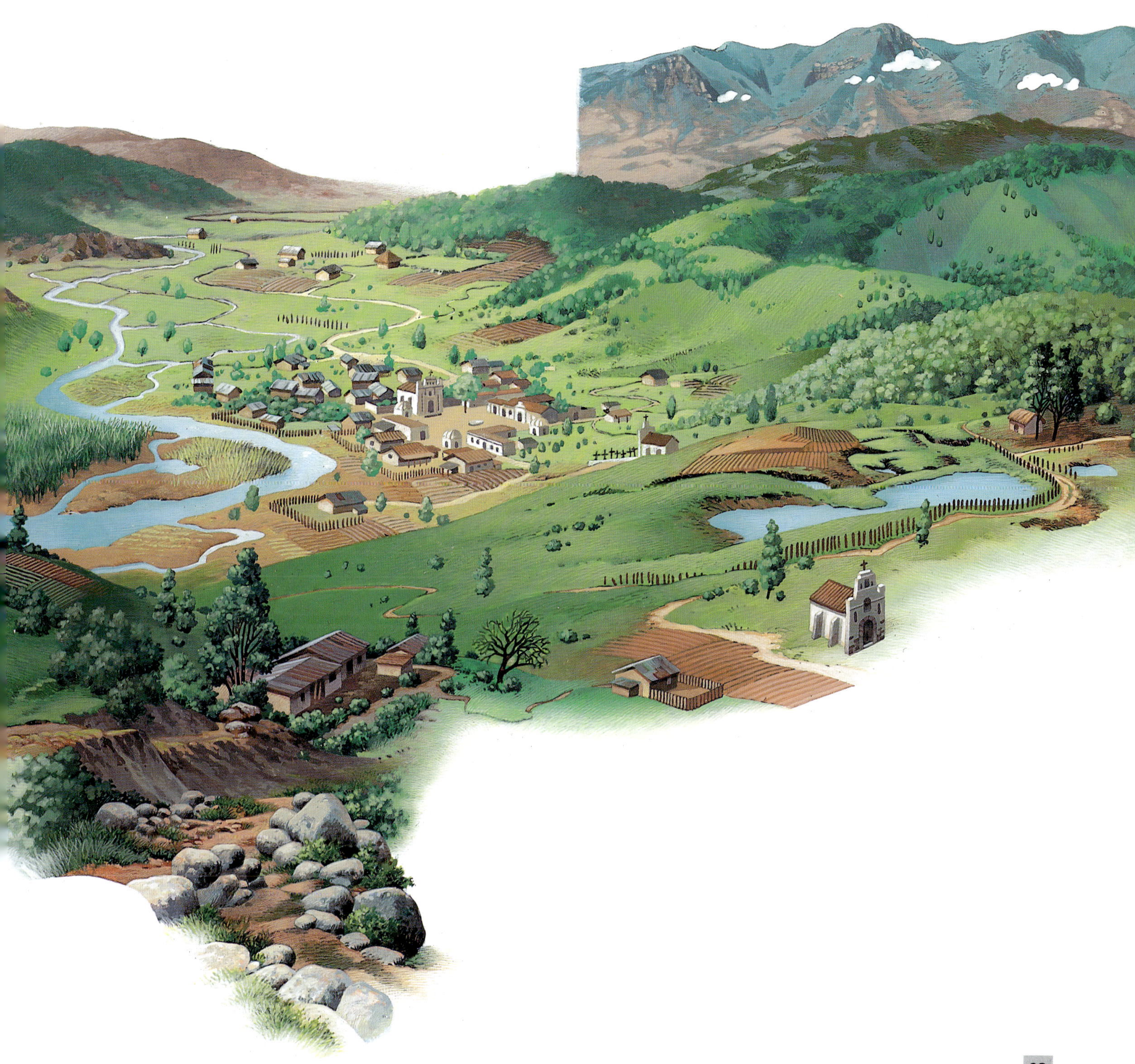

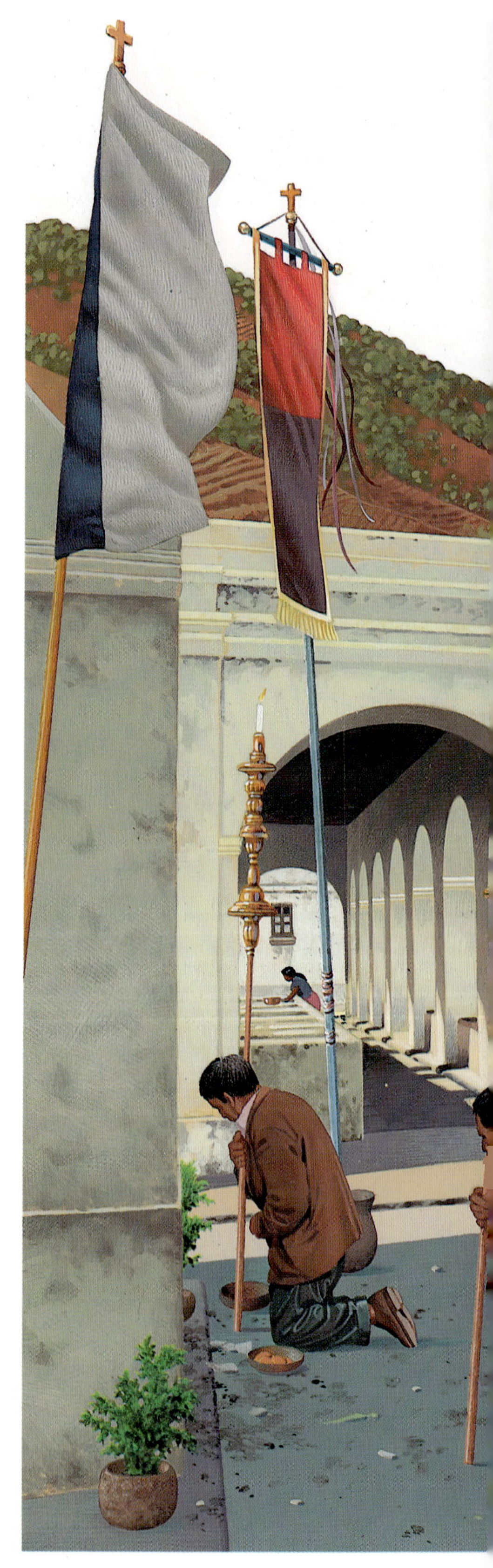

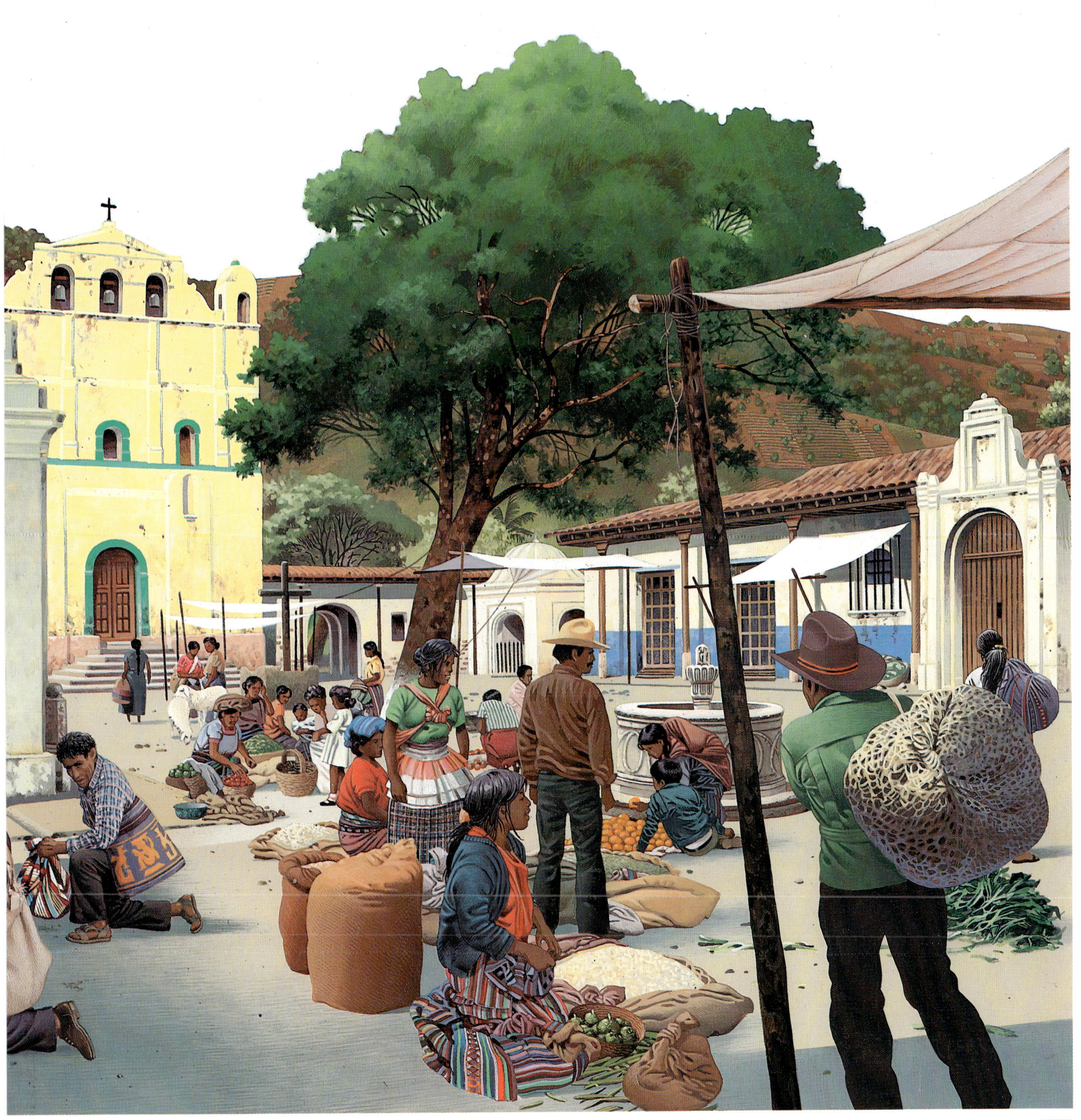

Monica Ottelli

Italy

Title of Work
Muscles of the human body

Technique
Acrylic, tempera

Legend
. Forearm muscles (front view)
. Hip and thigh muscles (rear view)

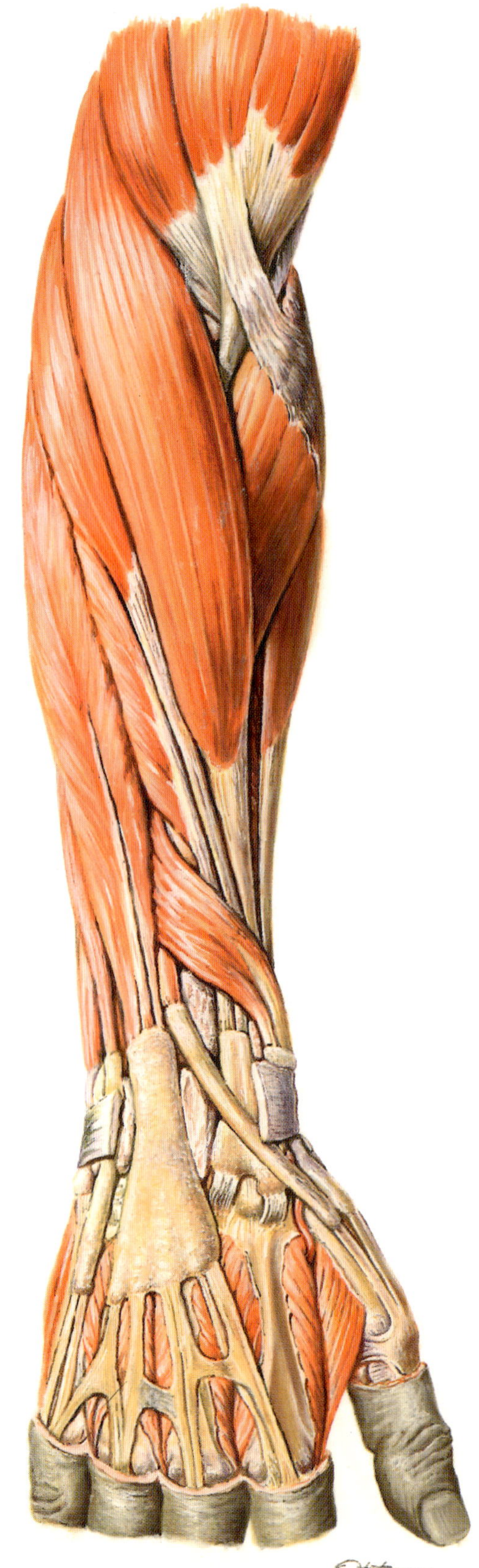

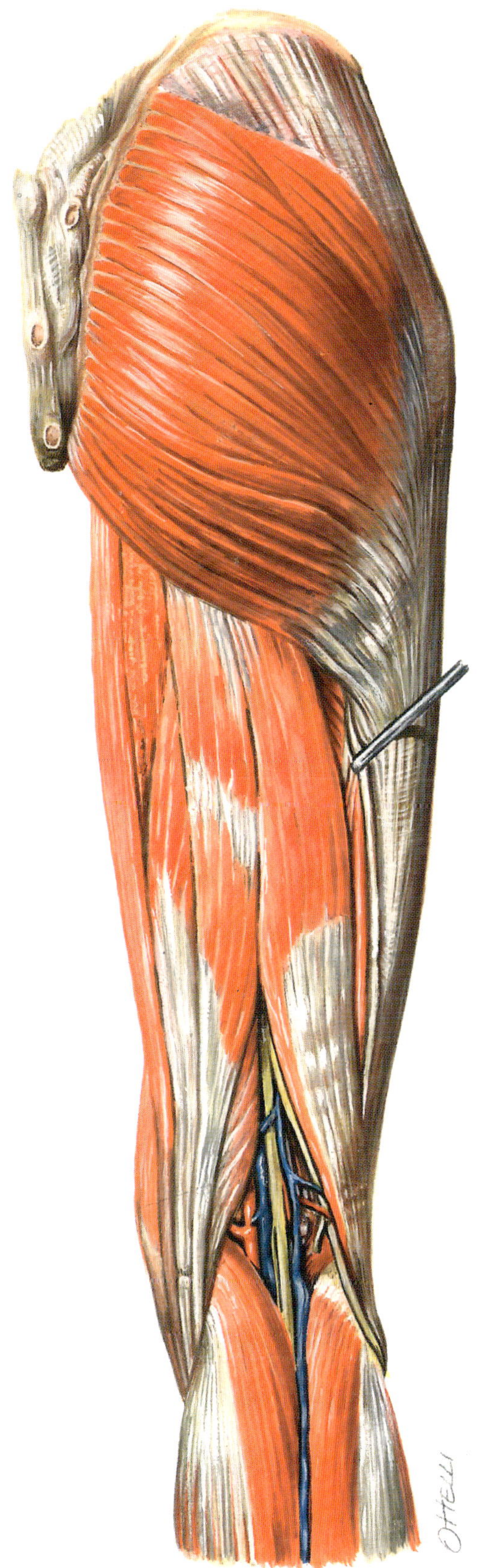

Jean Marc Pau

France

Title of Work
Ma première encyclopédie:
Peoples

Original Publisher and Date of Publication
Larousse S.A., 1994
ISBN 2-03-651-812-5

Technique
Watercolour

Legend
. *Gypsy festival*
. *Among the Greeks*
. *North of Europe*

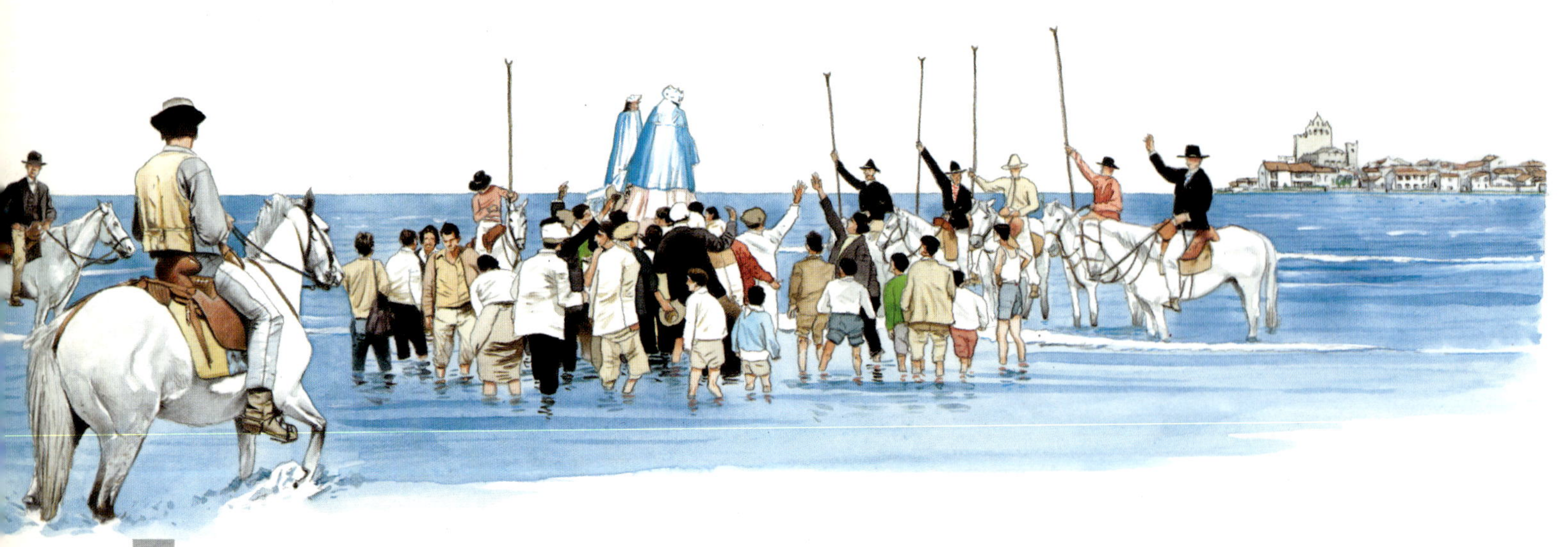

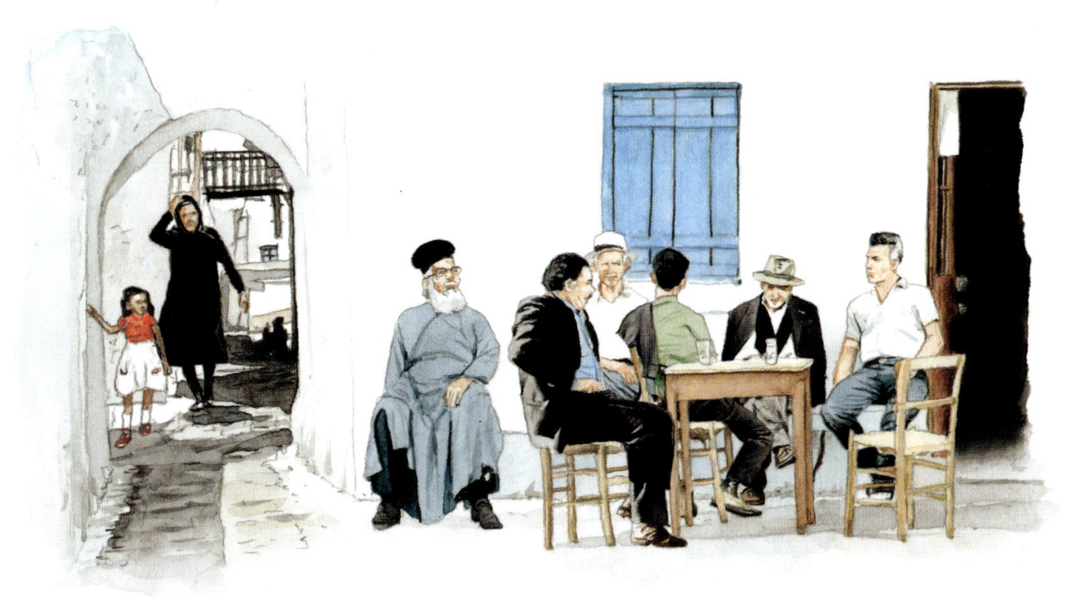

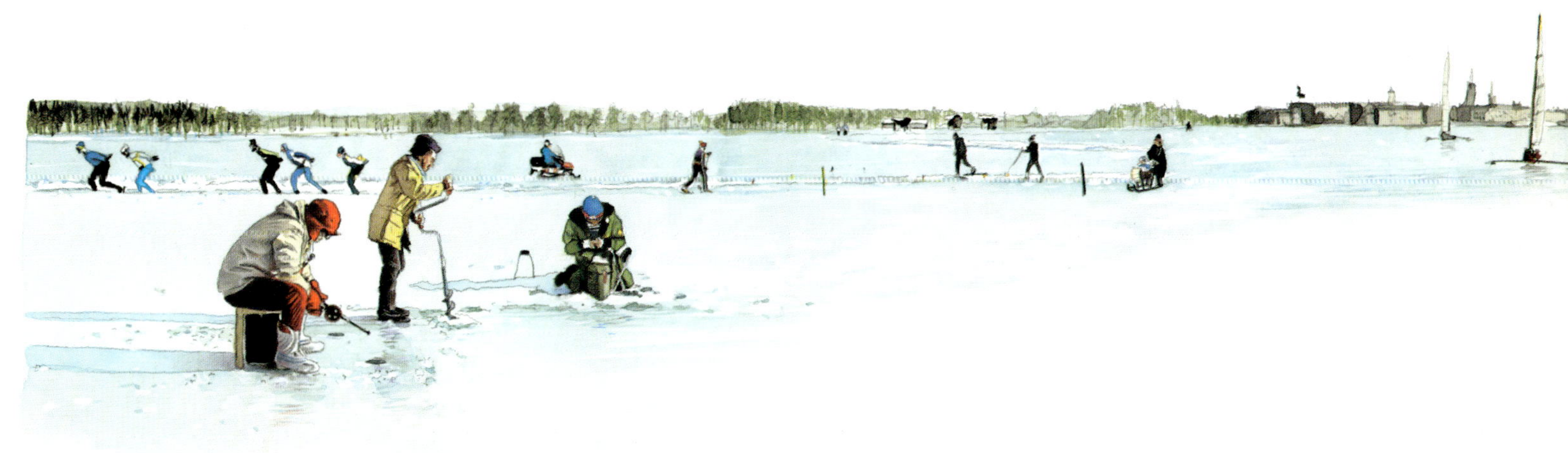

Daniela Perani

Italy

Title of Work
Birds

Technique
Coloured pencil

Legend
. *White cockatoo*
. *Hedge-sparrow*

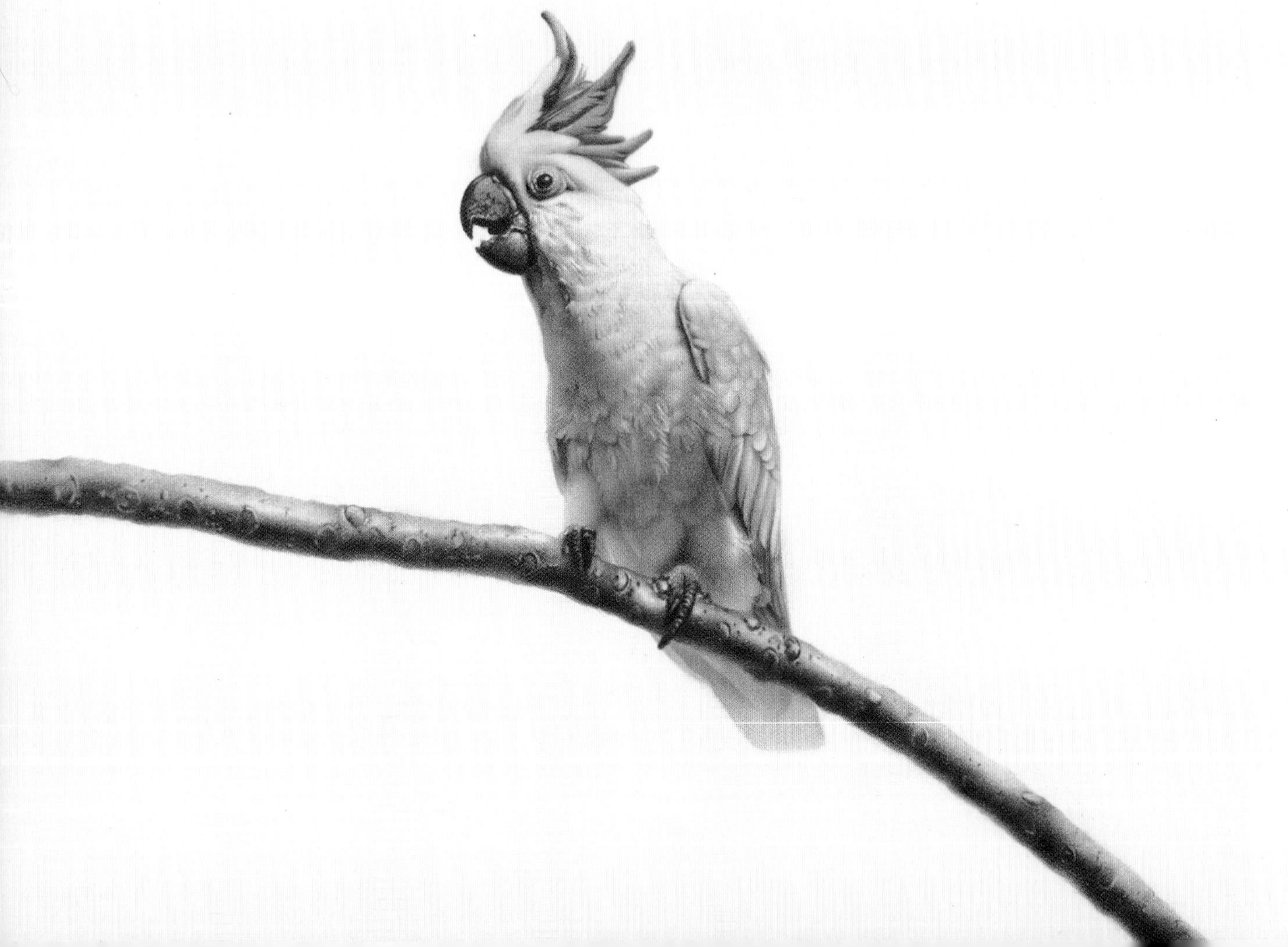

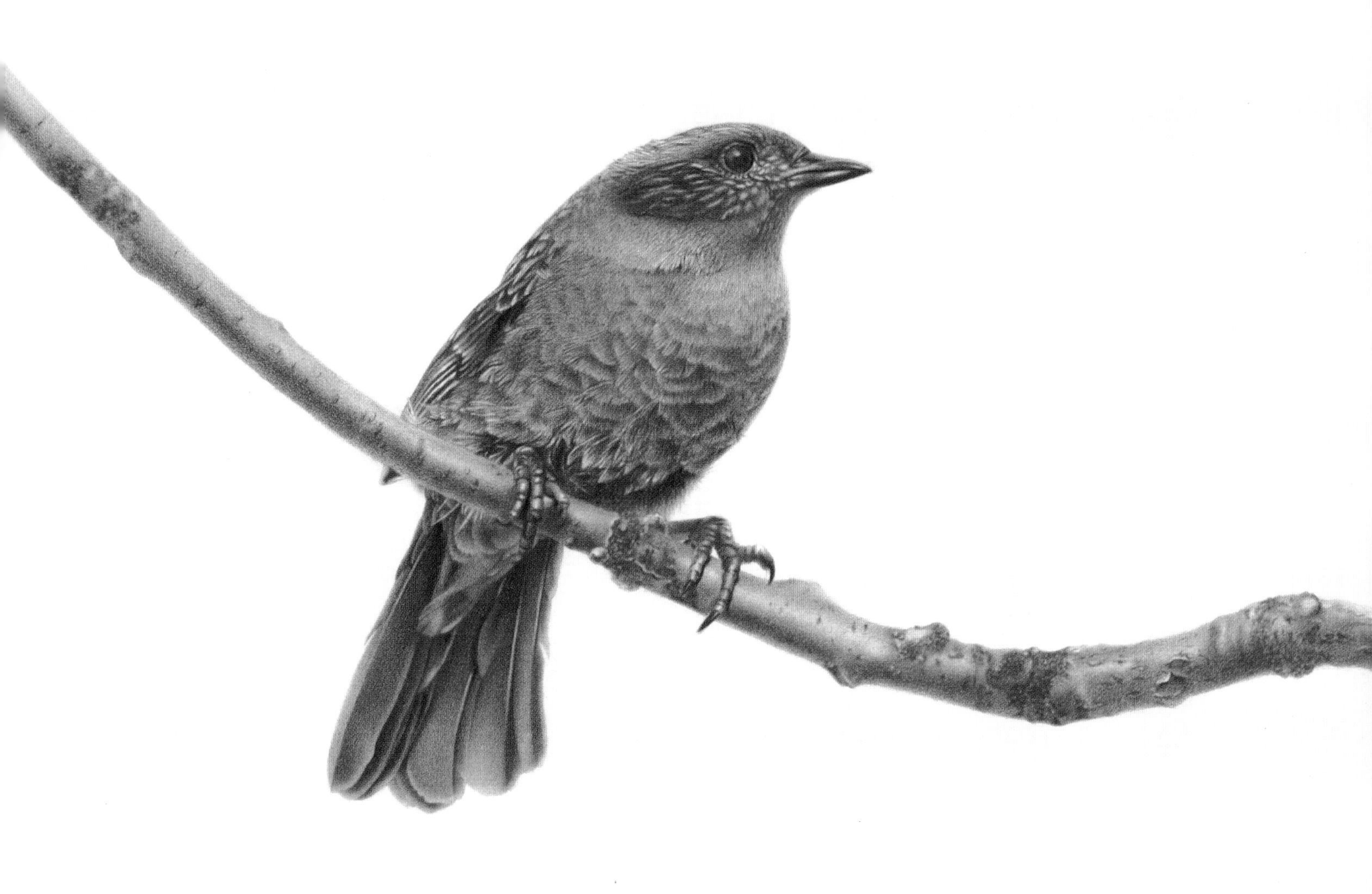

Sylvaine Perols

France

Title of Work
Premières Découvertes:
The beaver

Original Publisher and Date of Publication
Editions Gallimard,
October 1993
ISBN 2-0705-8143-8

Technique
Ink

Legend
. Beaver adapted anatomy
. Beaver building a dam
. Beaver architect

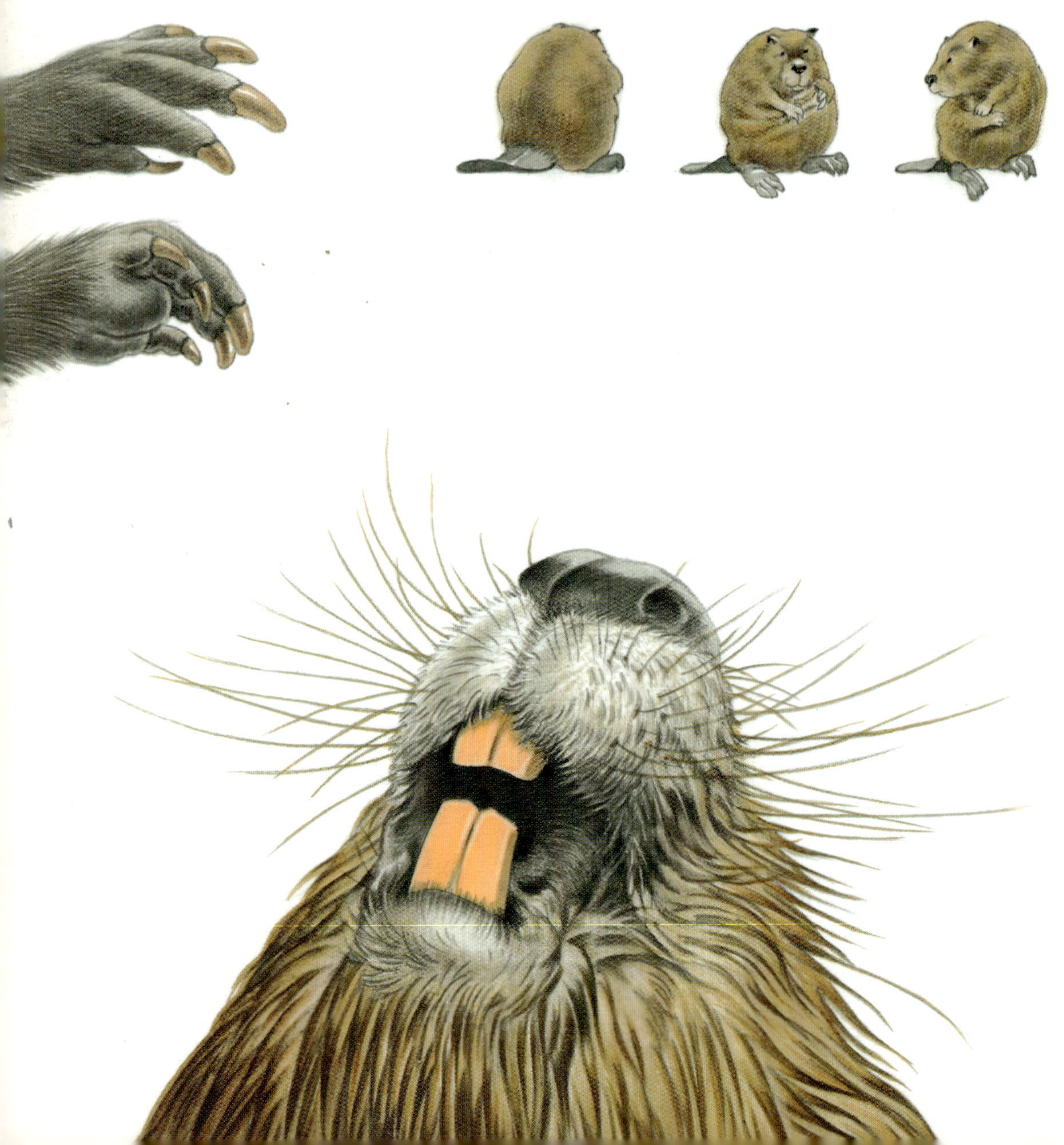

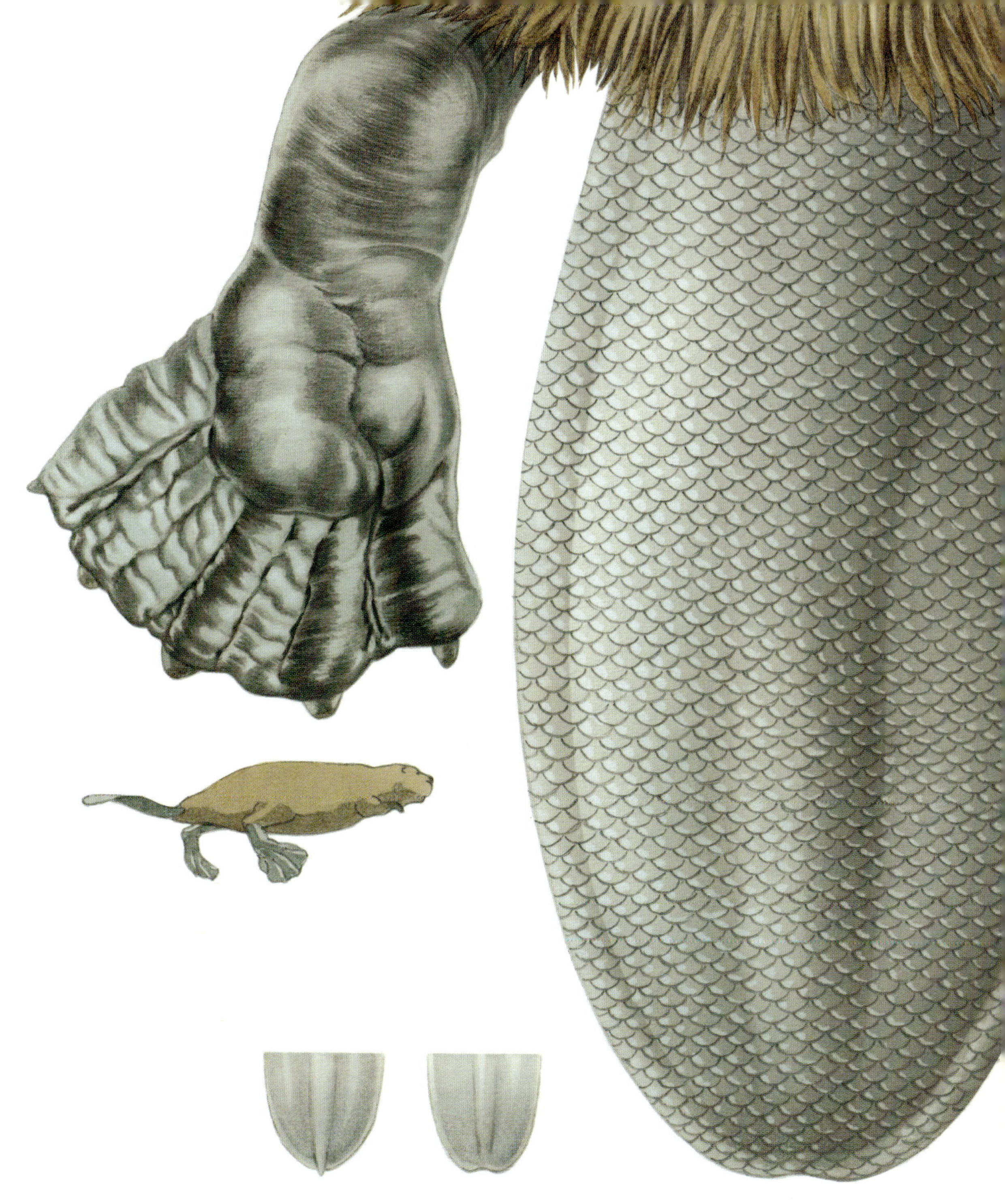

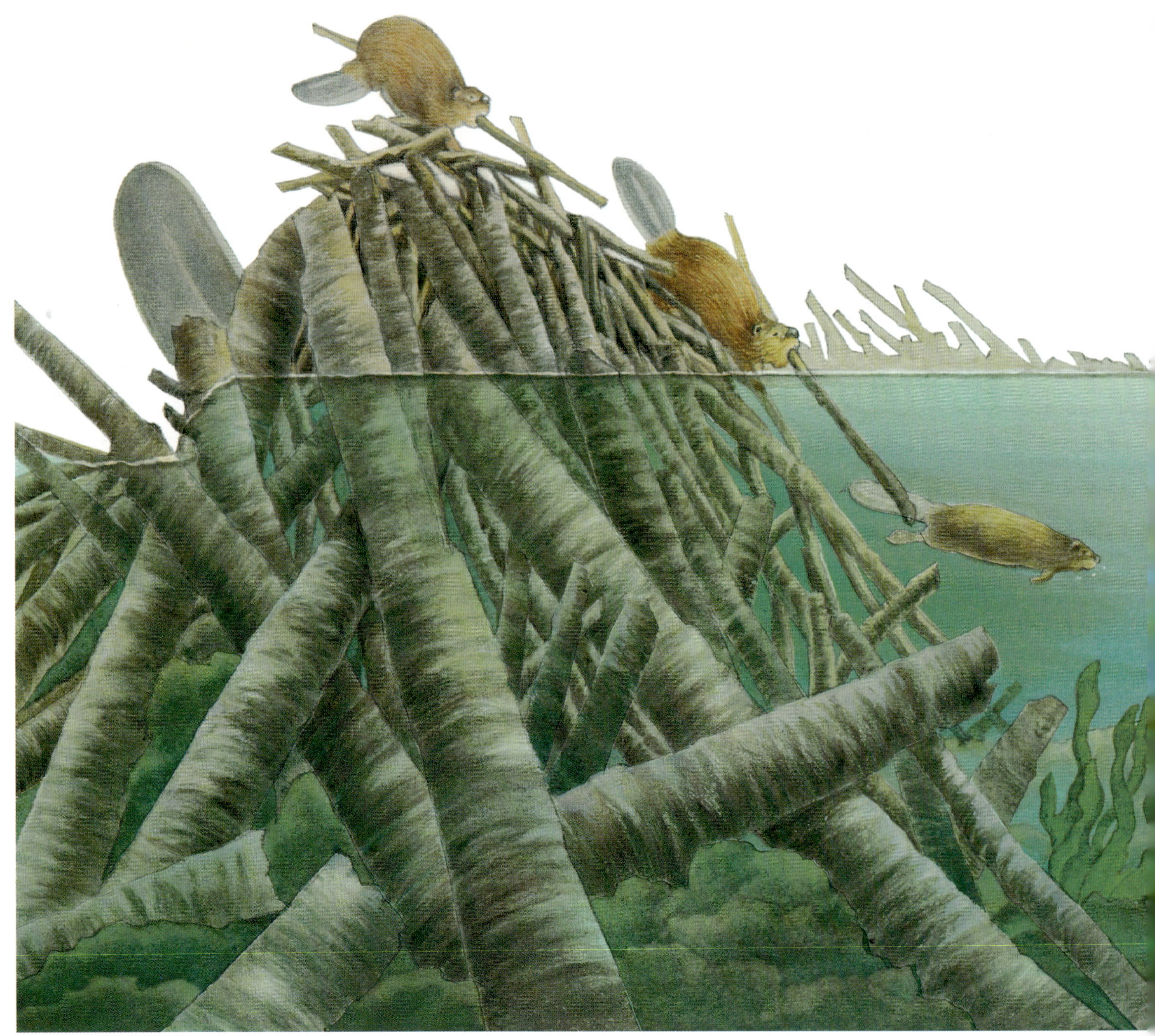

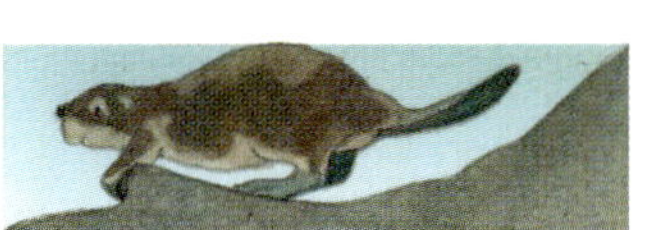

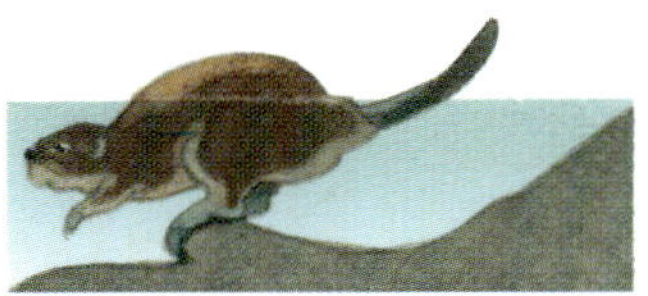

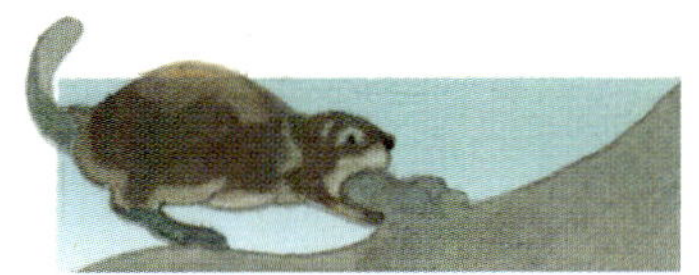

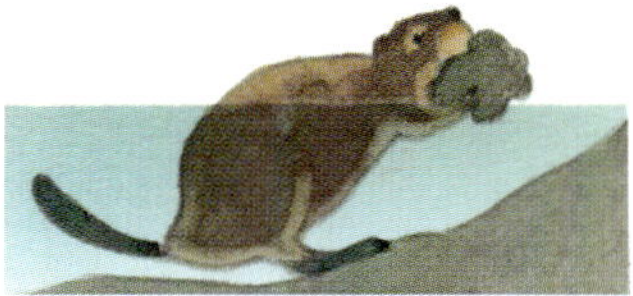

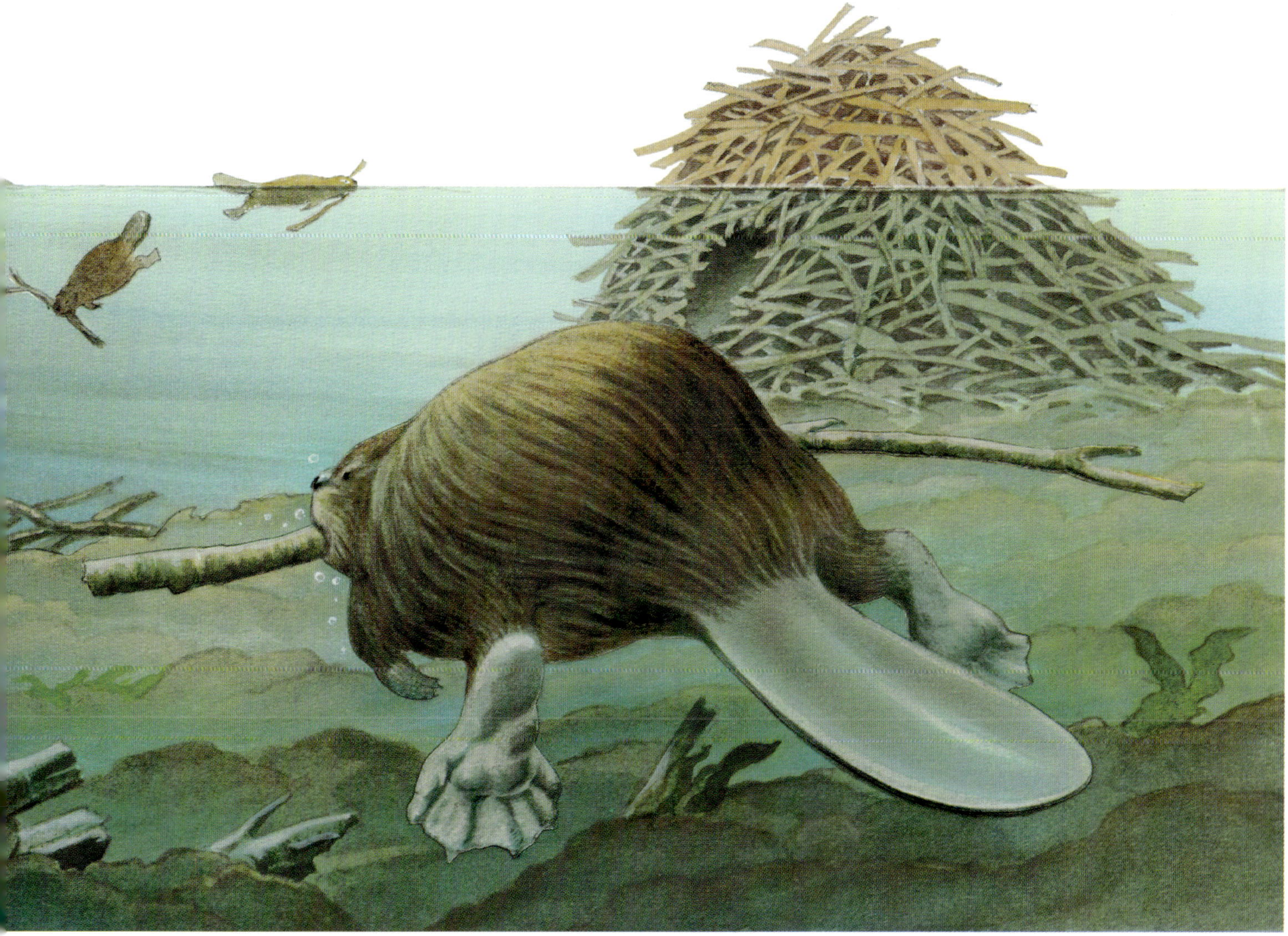

Maurice Pommier

France

Titles of Works
Guides Gallimard:
Prague
Premières Découvertes:
Cathédrales

Original Publisher and Dates of Publication
Editions Gallimard,
June 1994
ISBN 2-7424-0201-2
(Prague)
May 1995
ISBN 2-0705-9013-5
(Cathédrales)

Technique
Watercolour

Legend
. Chinese junk
. Construction of the cathédral spire

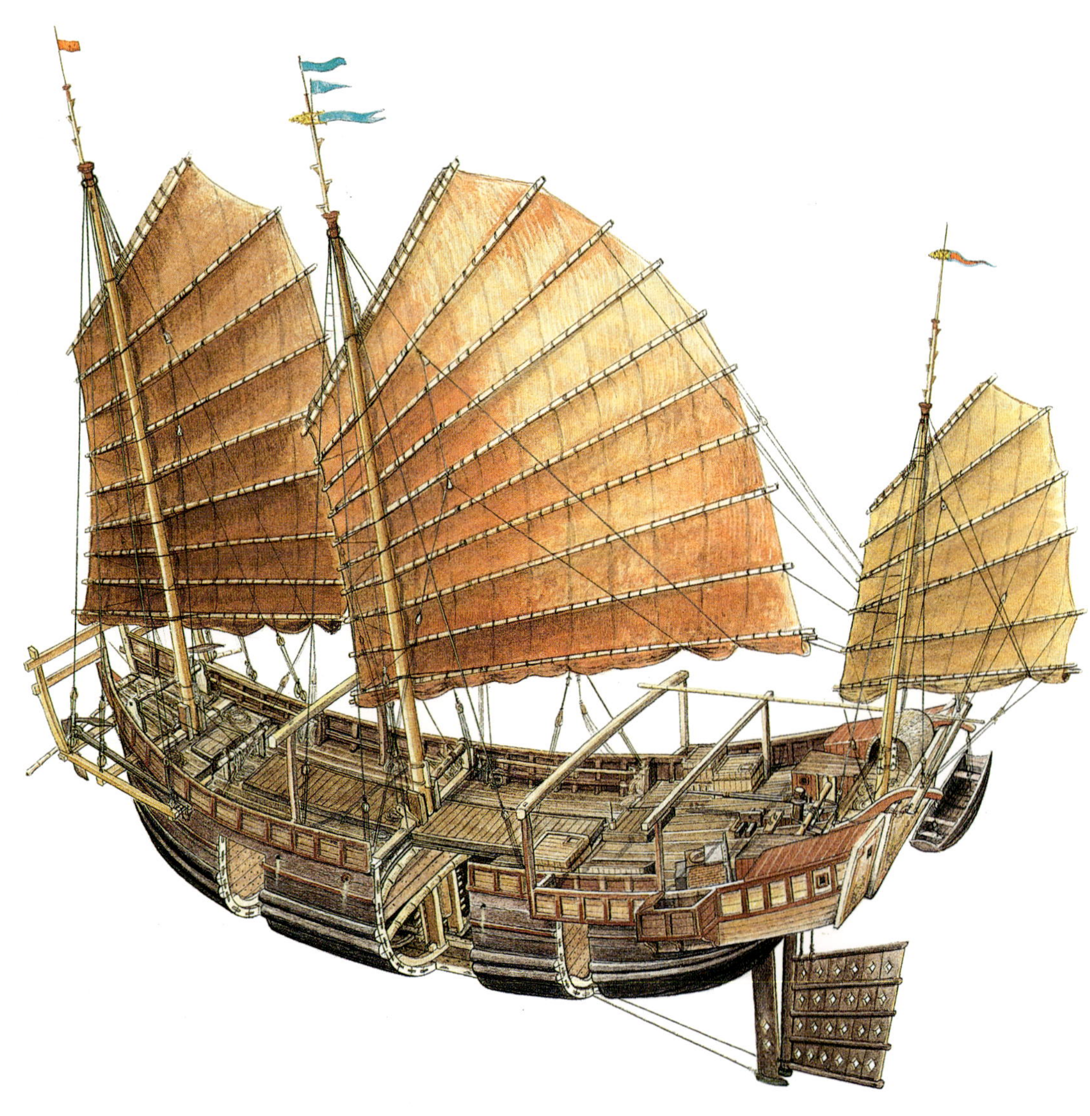

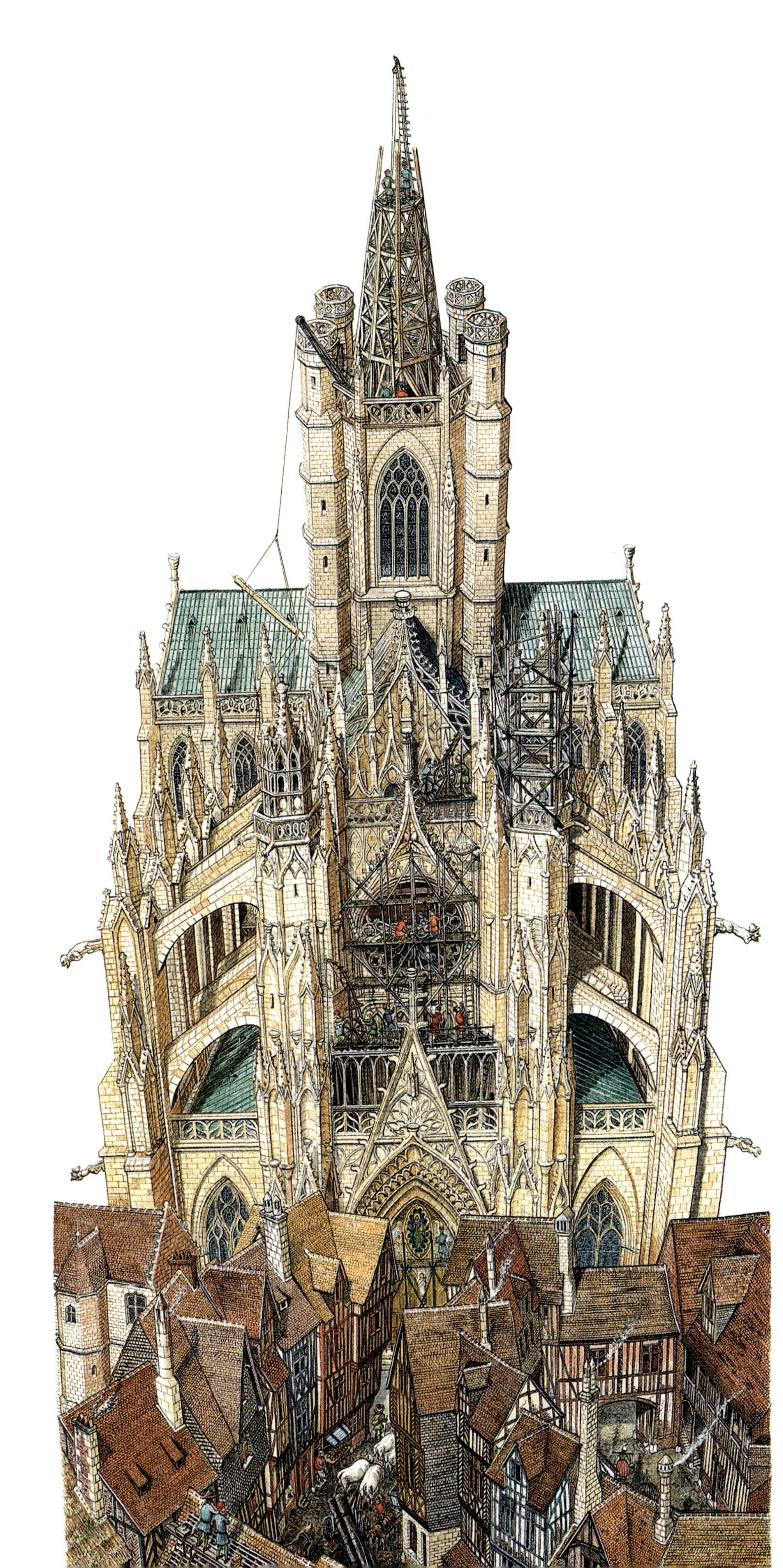

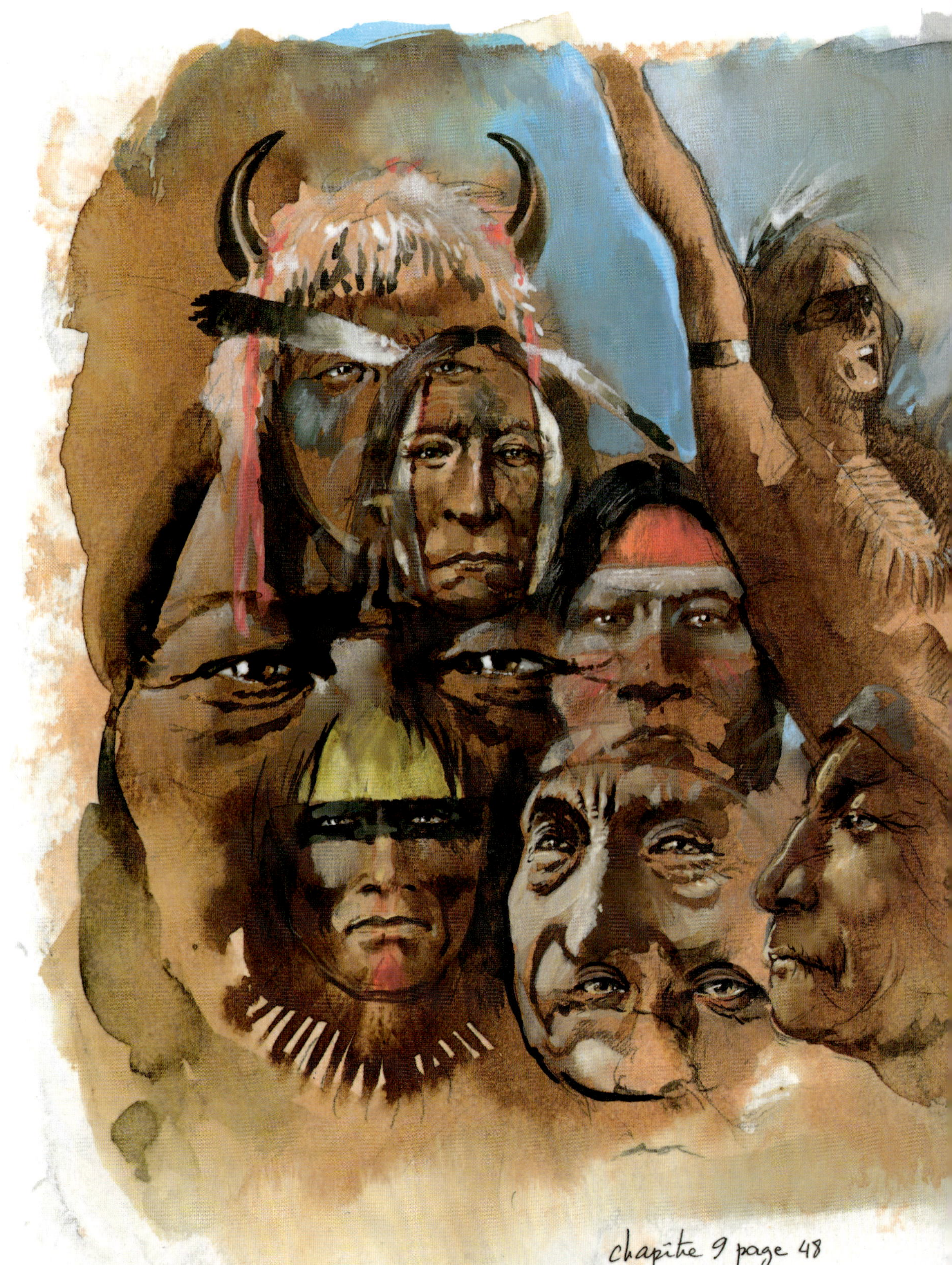

chapitre 9 page 48

les Oglalas de Cheval Fou, les Minniconjous de Lune Noire, les Cheyennes de Petit Cheval, des Arapahos, des Yanktonais, des Pieds Noirs, des Cheyennes du Sud... les indomptables Santees d'Inkpaduta et même des Brûlés qui ne reconnaissaient plus Queue Tachetée pour chef... Tous répondaient à l'appel de la guerre

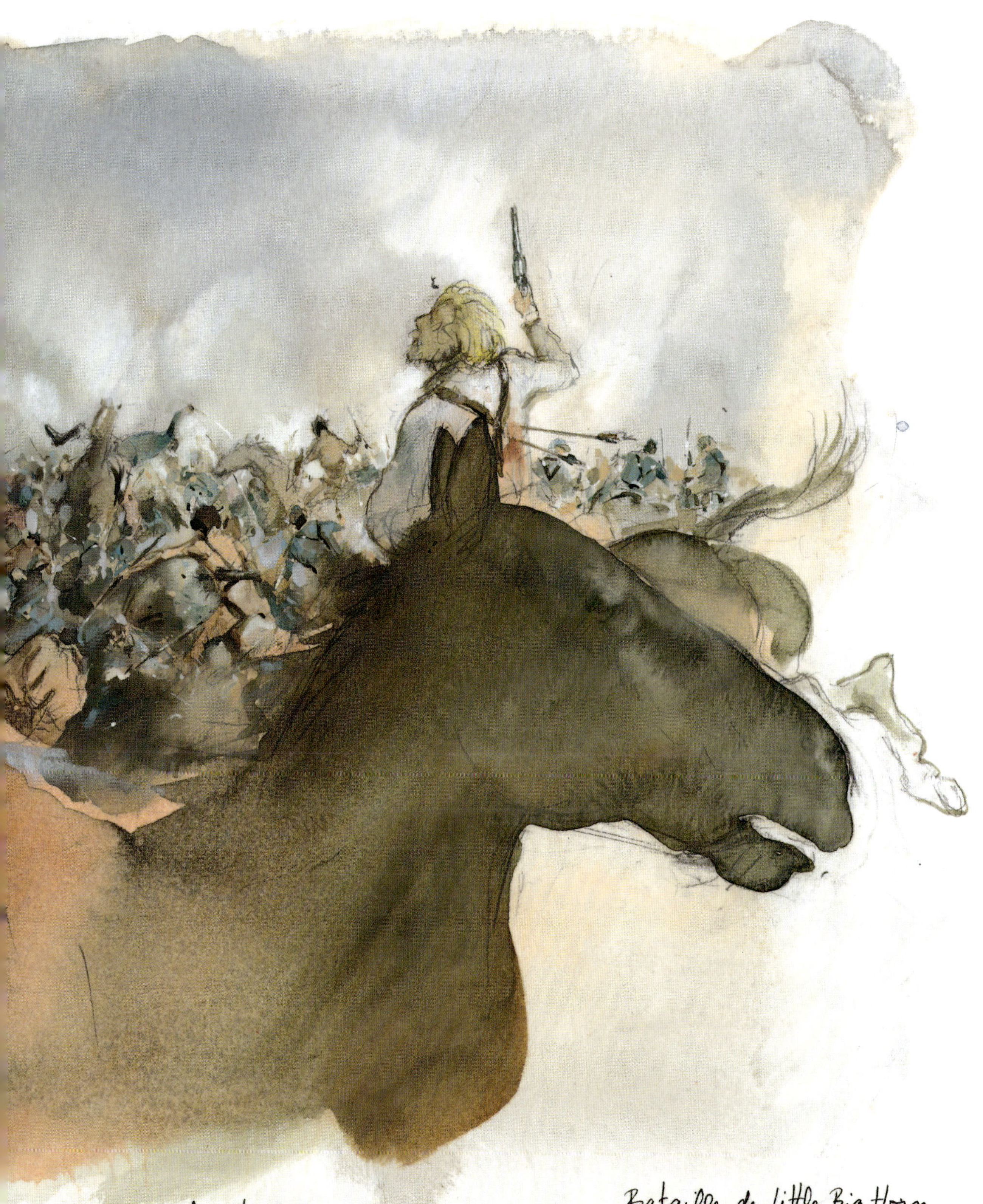

chapître 9 page 51

j'ai dansé tout au long de la
nuit et toute la journée qui suivit
jusqu'à l'heure où le Soleil se trouve droit au-
dessus des hommes. Mon esprit ne m'appartenait plus
voyageait par delà les nuages… j'ai vu des Tuniques
…ues qui arrivaient…

Bataille de little Big Horn
chapître 10 page 55

"Moi, Sitting Bull"
Michel Piquemal
274/19/18/21 Jame's Prunier II 95
Albin Michel

Pascal Robin

France

Title of Work
Carnets de la Nature:
High tide - Low tide

Original Publisher and Date of Publication
Editions Gallimard,
April 1995
ISBN 2-0705-8680-4

Technique
Watercolour

Legend
. Shrimp
. Various fish
. Mussels

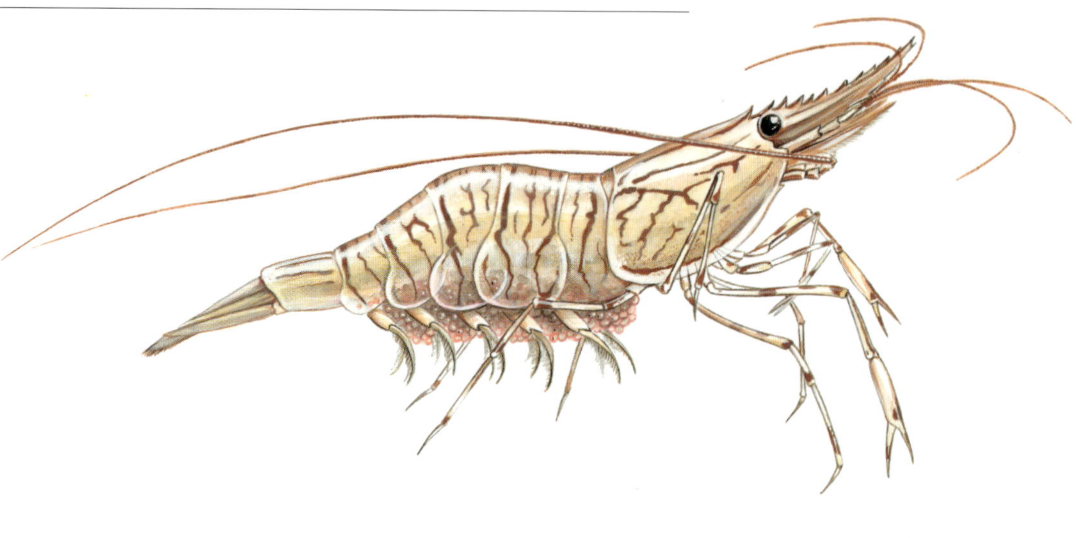

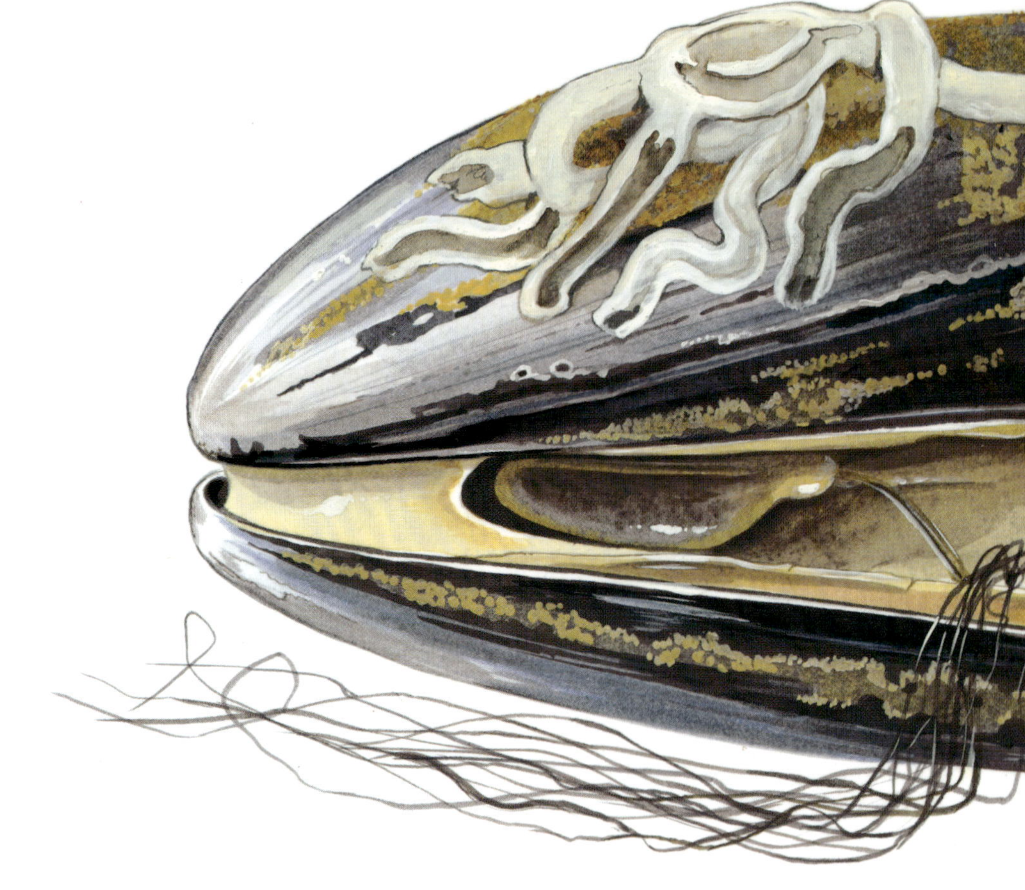

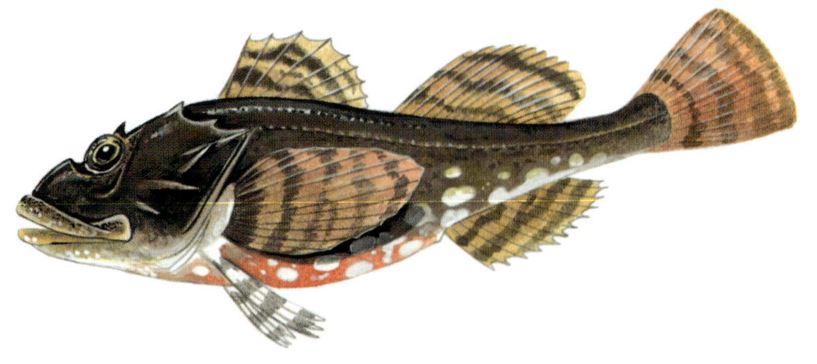

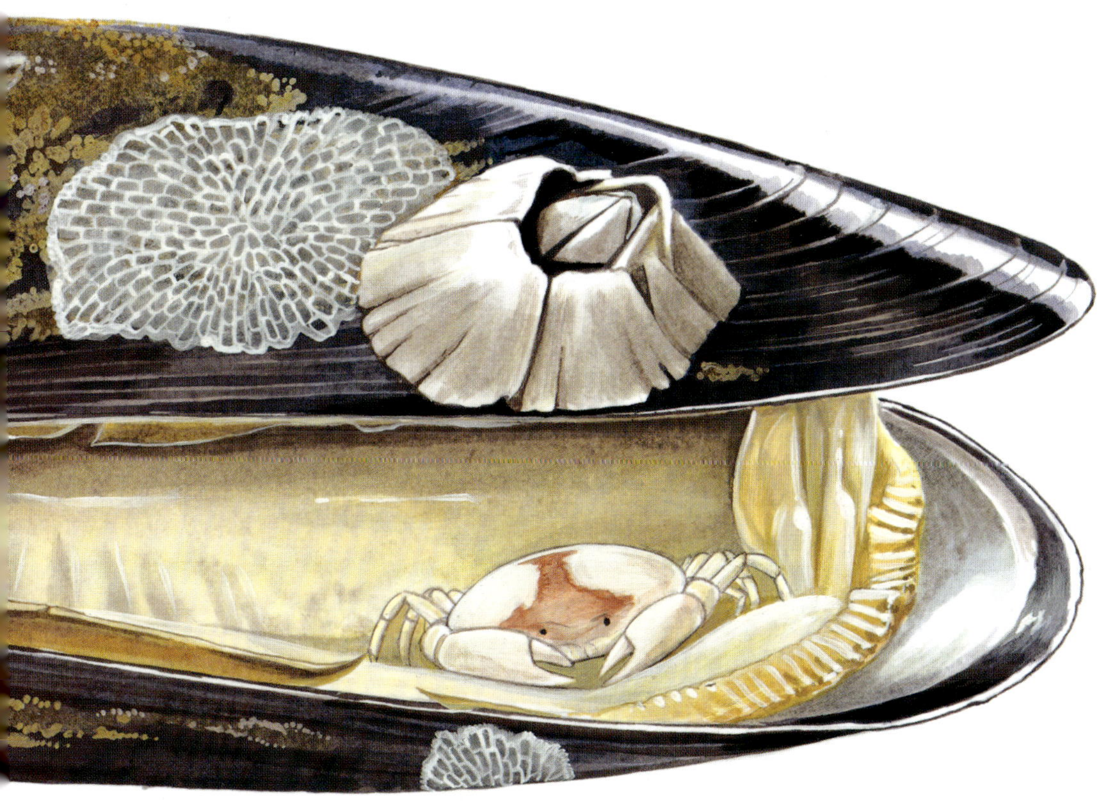

Frank Scímia

Italy

Title of Work
Ancient Rome

Technique
Tempera and gouache

Legend
. *Instruments of war*

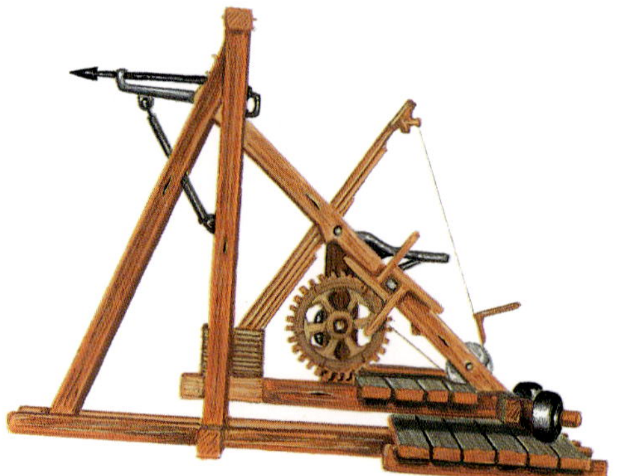

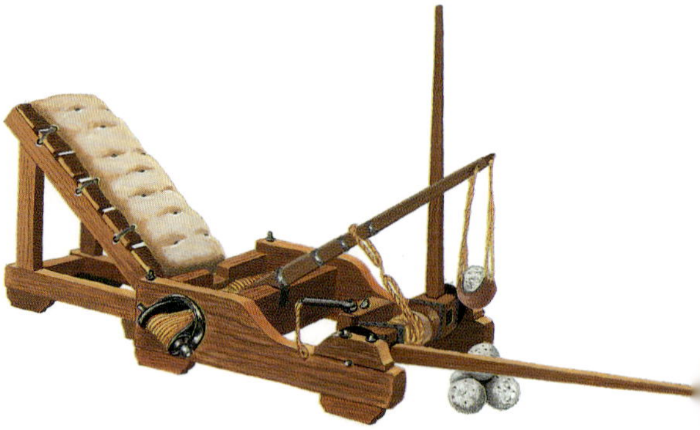

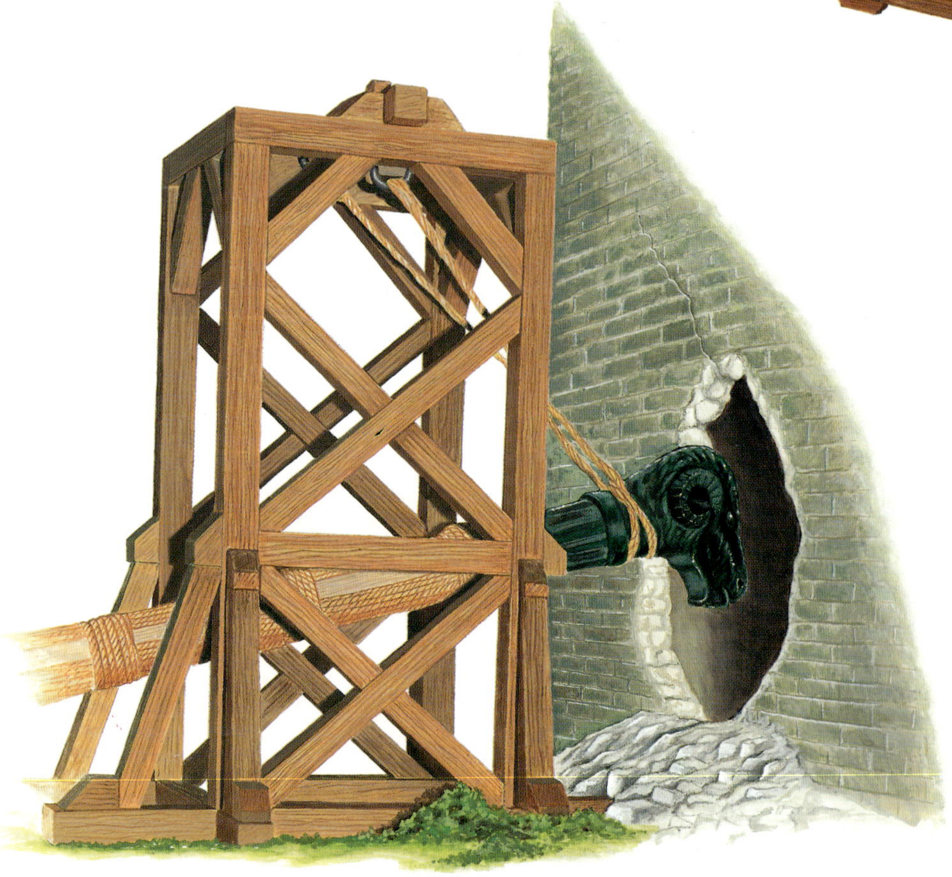

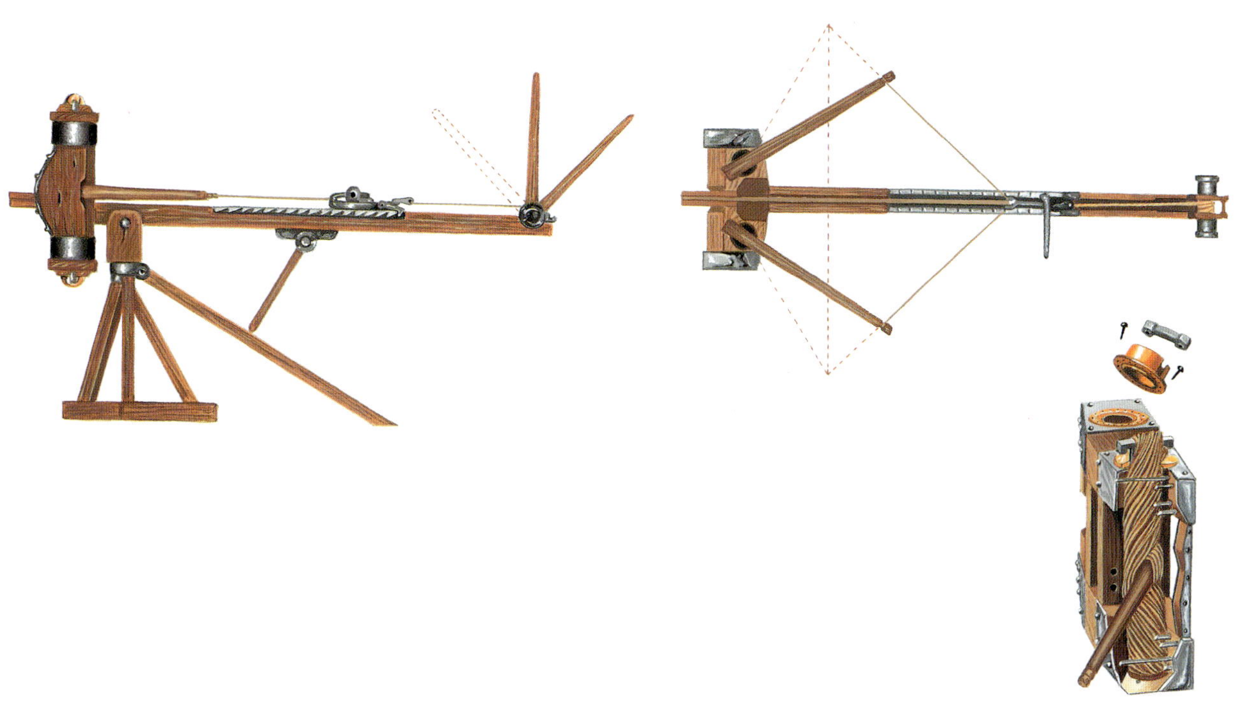

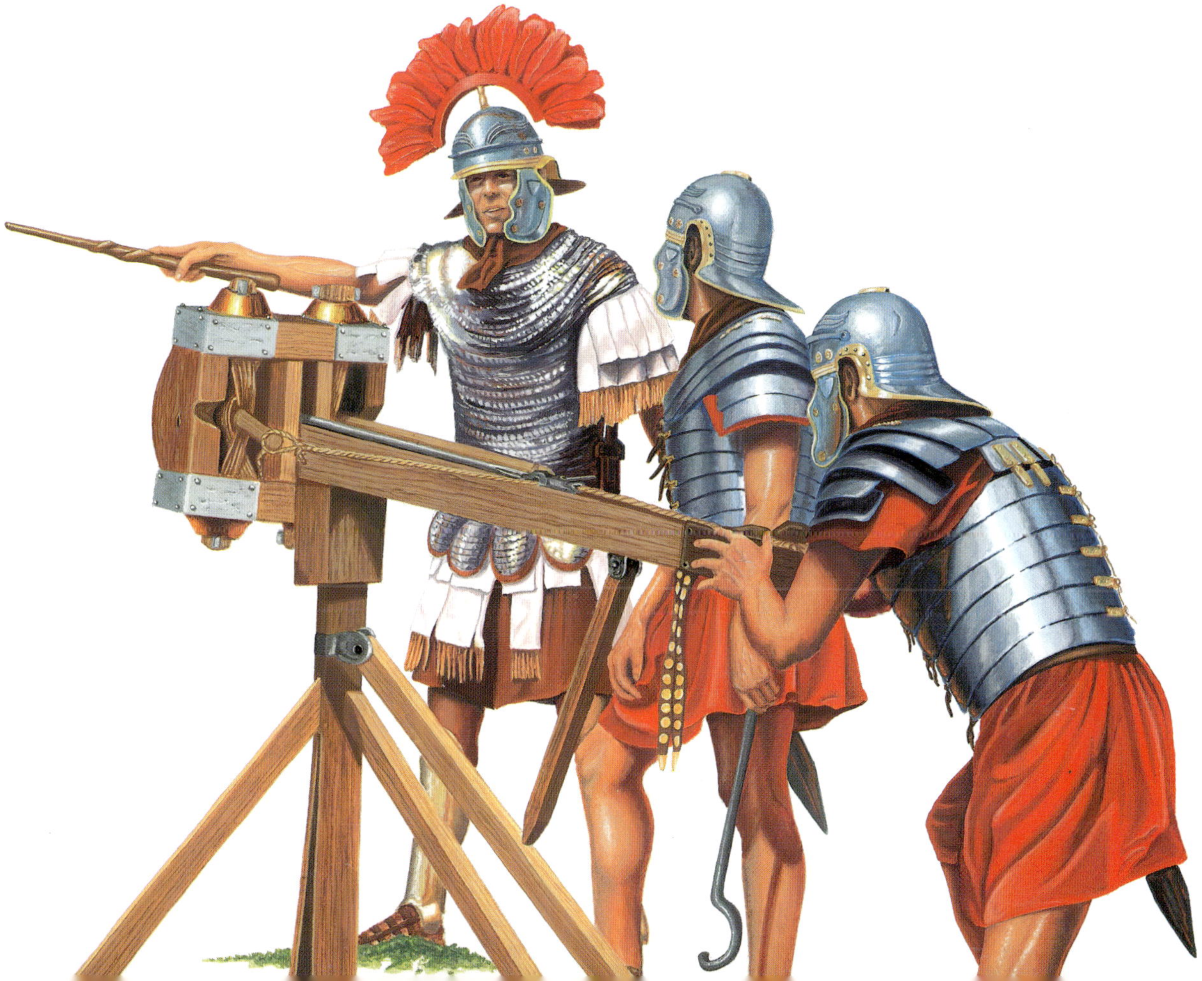

Valérie Stetten

France

Title of Work
Ma première encyclopédie: Peoples

Original Publisher and Date of Publication
Larousse S.A., 1994
ISBN 2-03-651812-5

Technique
Watercolour

Legend
. Life on the water in Benin
. A village in the African savannah

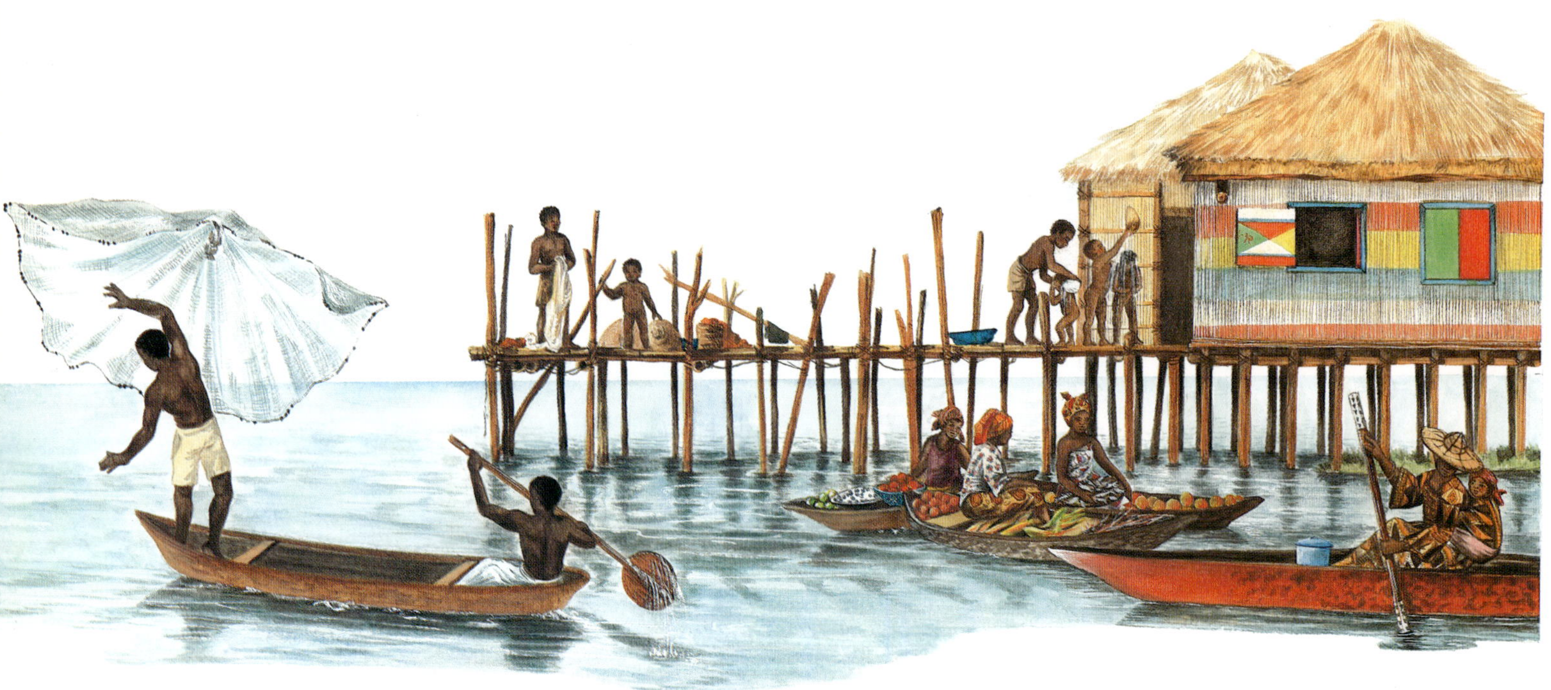

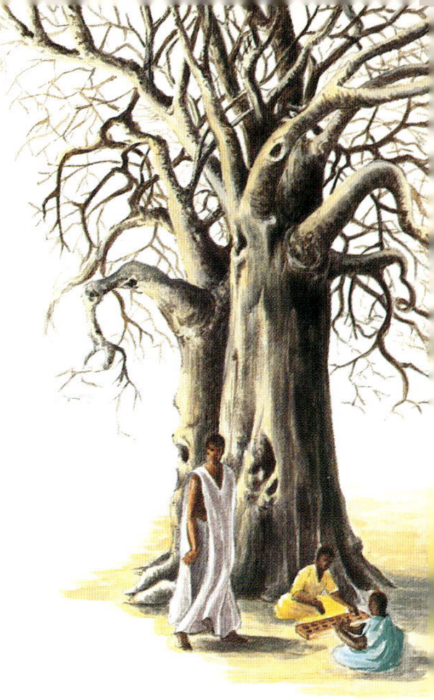

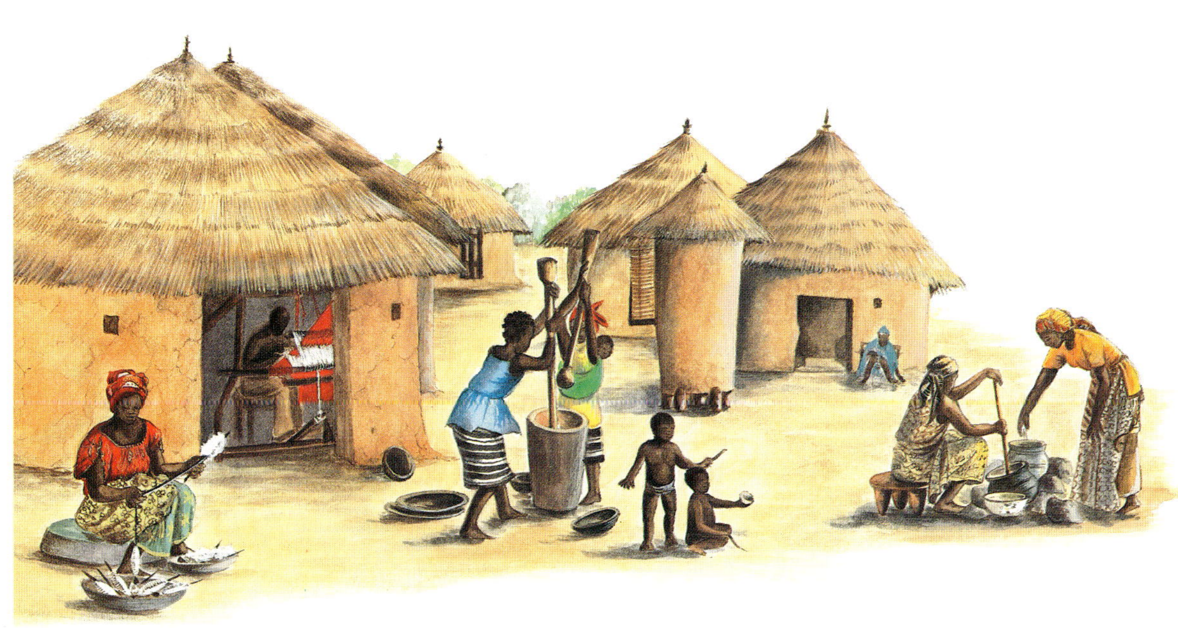

Gabor Szittya

Hungary

Titles of Works
Racines: Theatre
of the world
Dinosaurs

Original Publishers and Dates of Publication
Editions Gallimard,
October 1993
ISBN 2-07-058198-5
(Theatre)
Editions Fernand Nathan,
1993 (Dinosaurs)

Technique
Ink

Legend
. Interior of the Globe Theatre
. Dinosaurs

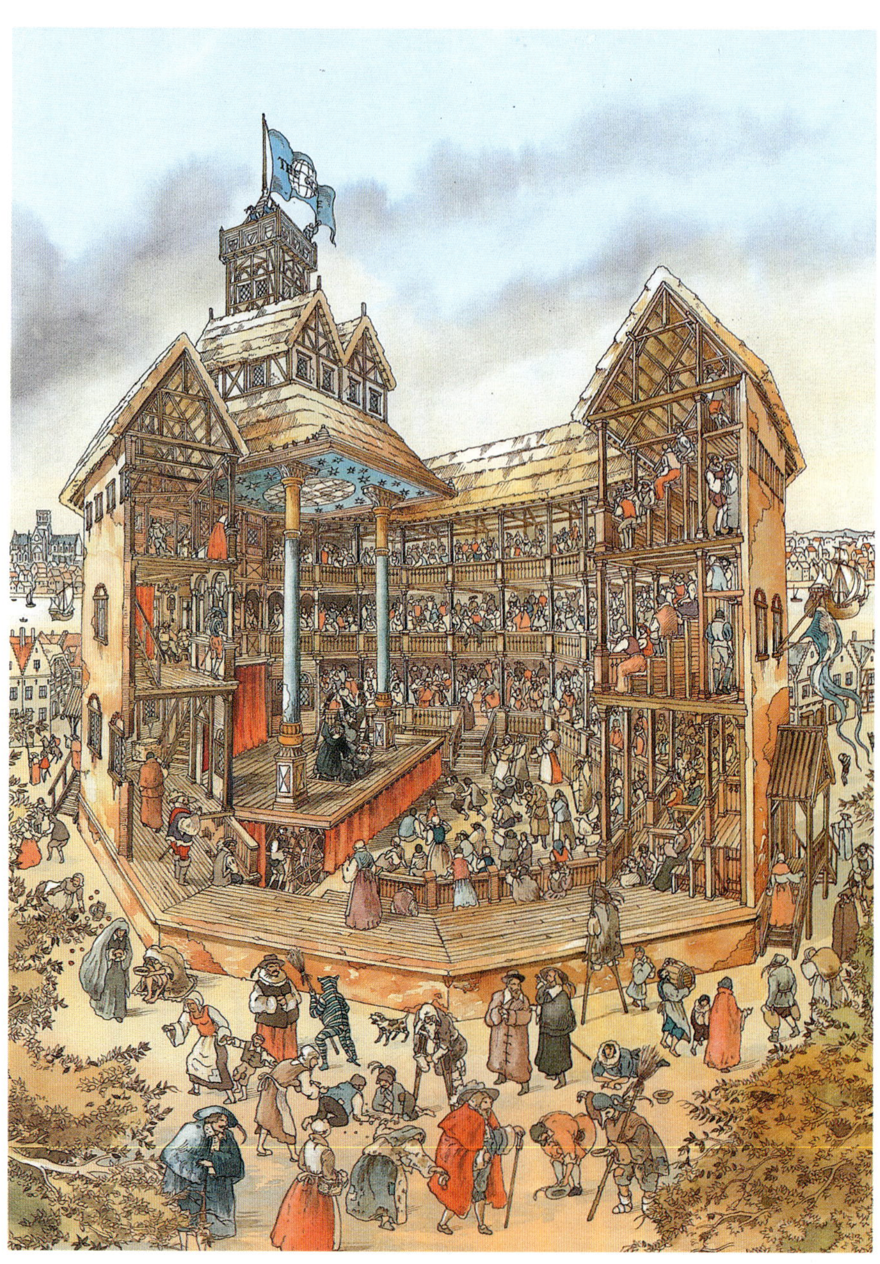

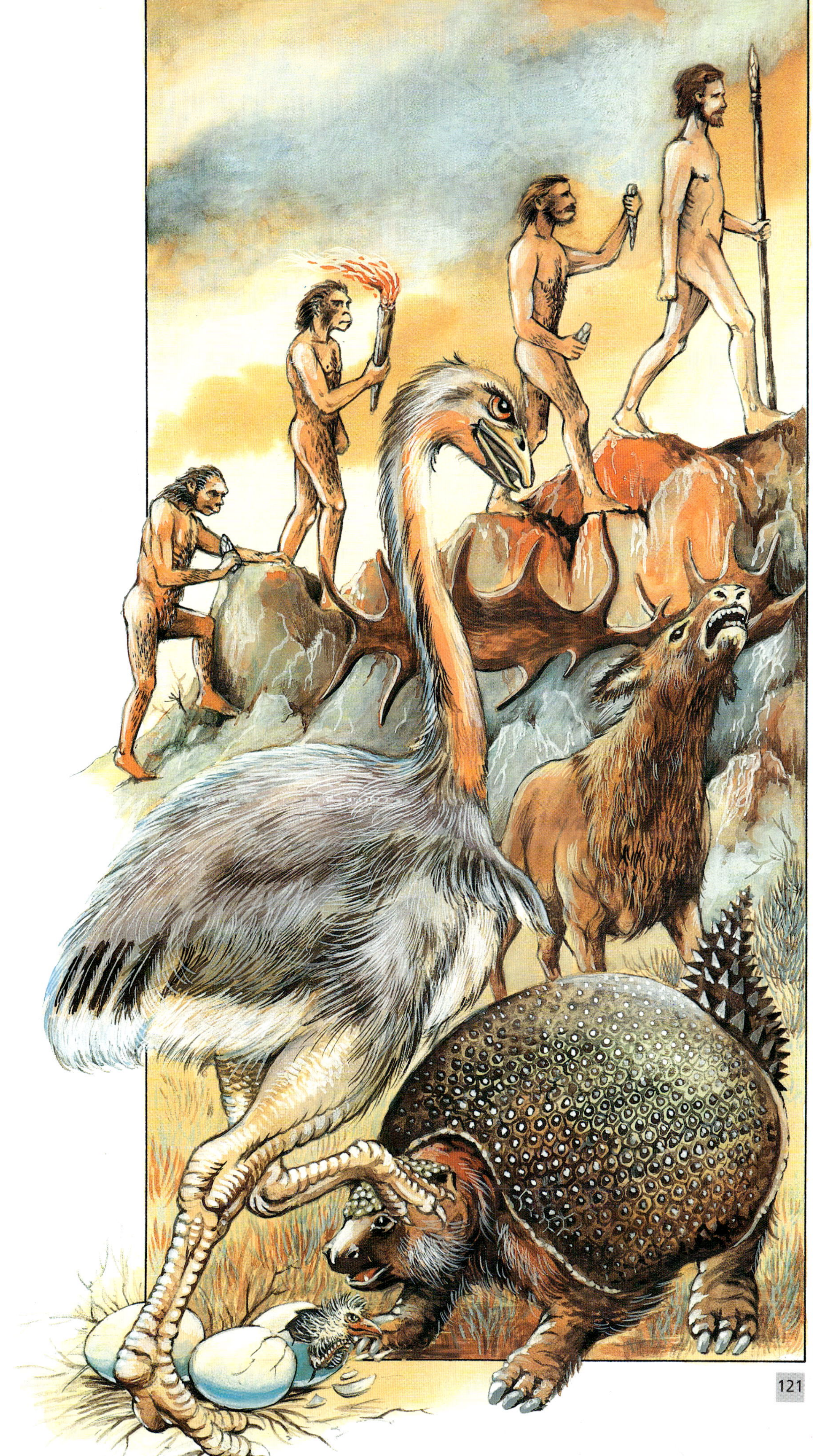

Nicolas Winz

France

Titles of Works
Guides Gallimard:
Tahiti
Martinique

Original Publisher and Dates of Publication
Editions Gallimard,
June 1994
ISBN 2-7424-0164-4
(Martinique)
July 1995
ISBN 2-7424-0236-5
(Tahiti)

Legend
. *Construction of the Tapa*
. *Creole garden*

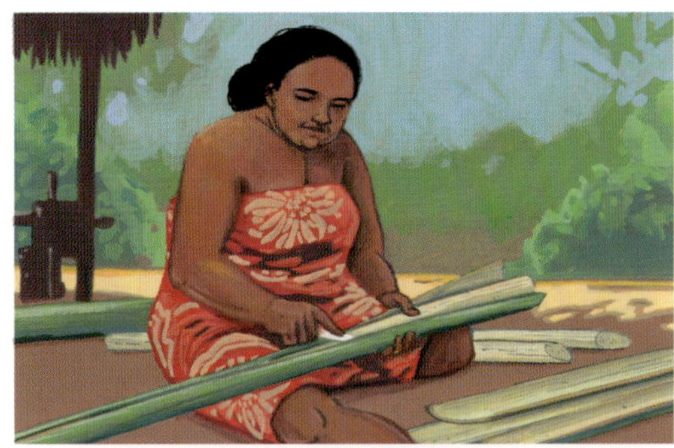

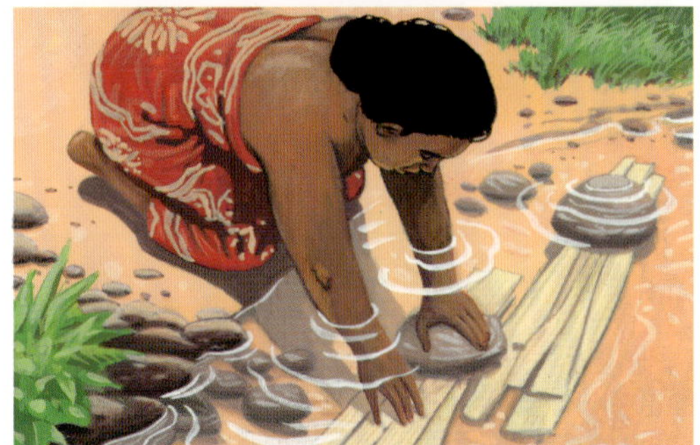

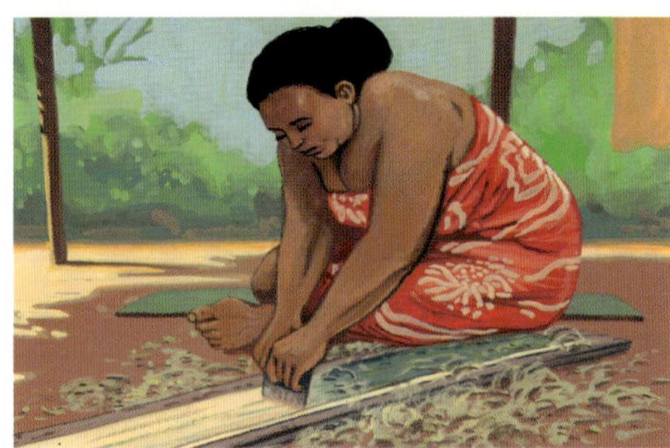

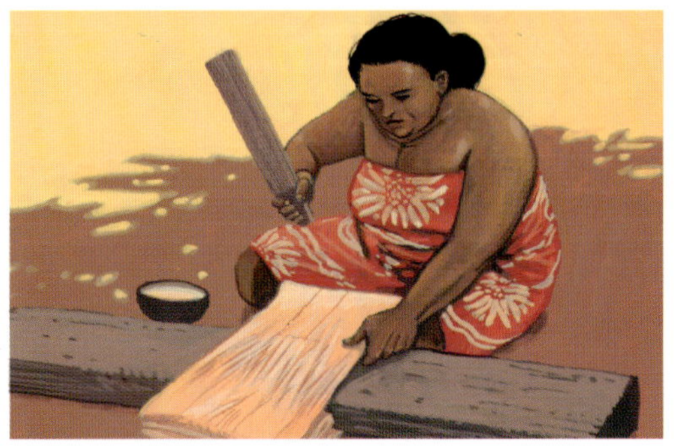

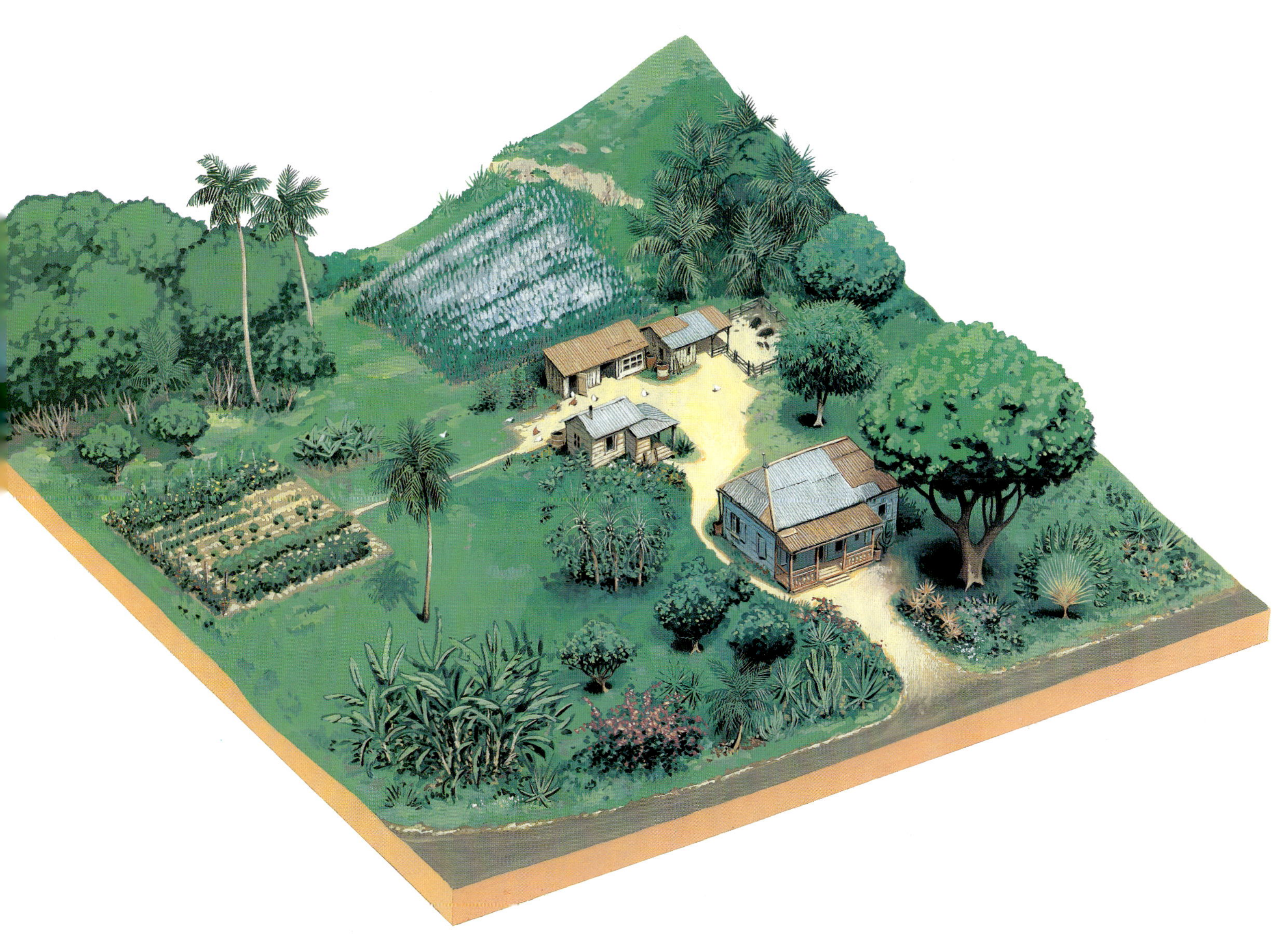

Marek Zawadzki

Poland

Title of Work
Ahajute and the cloud-eater

Original Publisher and Date of Publication
Verlag J.F. Schreiber, 1995
ISBN 3-215-13003-3

Technique
Acrylic, coloured pencil, gouache

Legend
. The cloud eater

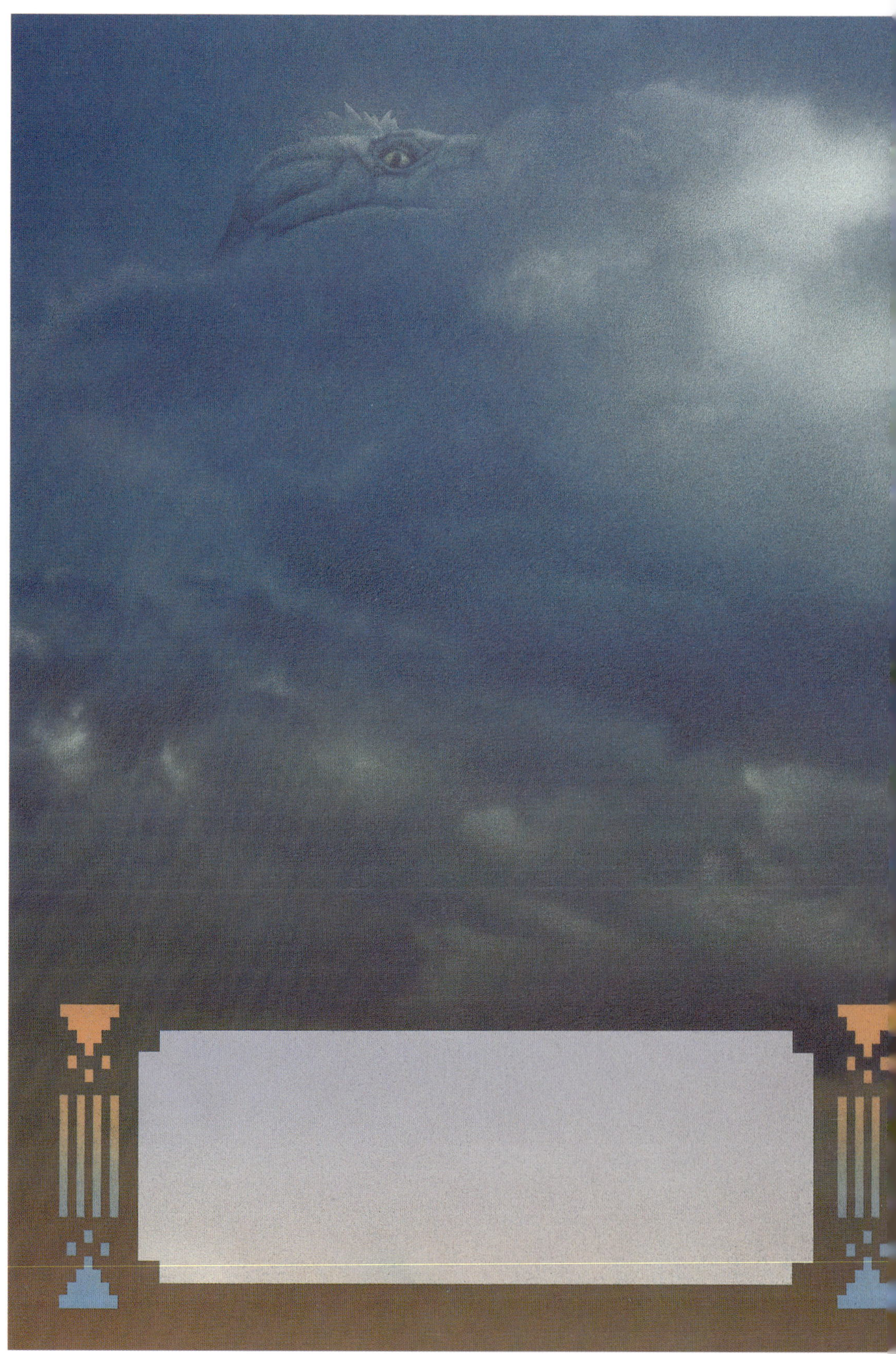

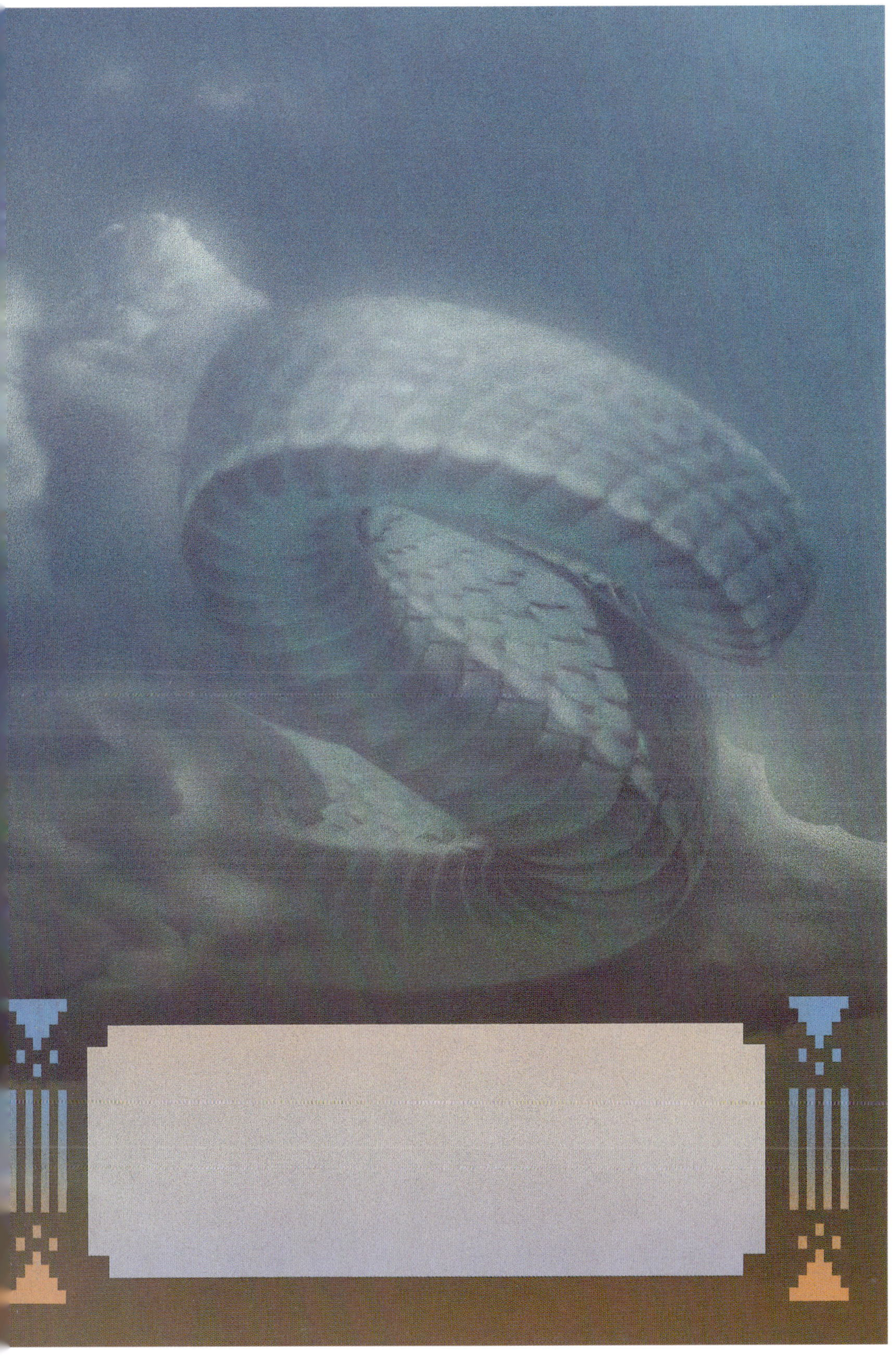

Mona Zimen

Germany

Title of Work
The world at the end of the world

Original Publisher and Date of Publication
C. Bertelsmann Verlag, September 1995
ISBN 3-570-12130-5

Technique
Watercolour

Legend
. Travelling is difficult in the spring ice
. Old Inuit woman from the small village of Chaplino

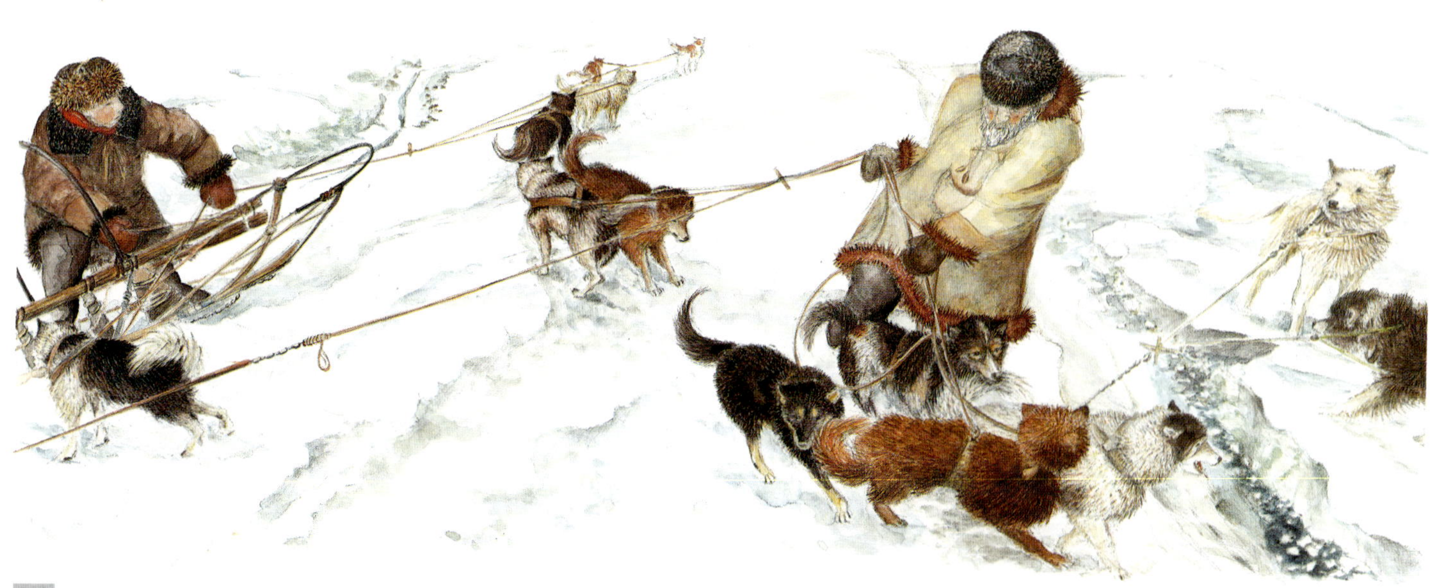

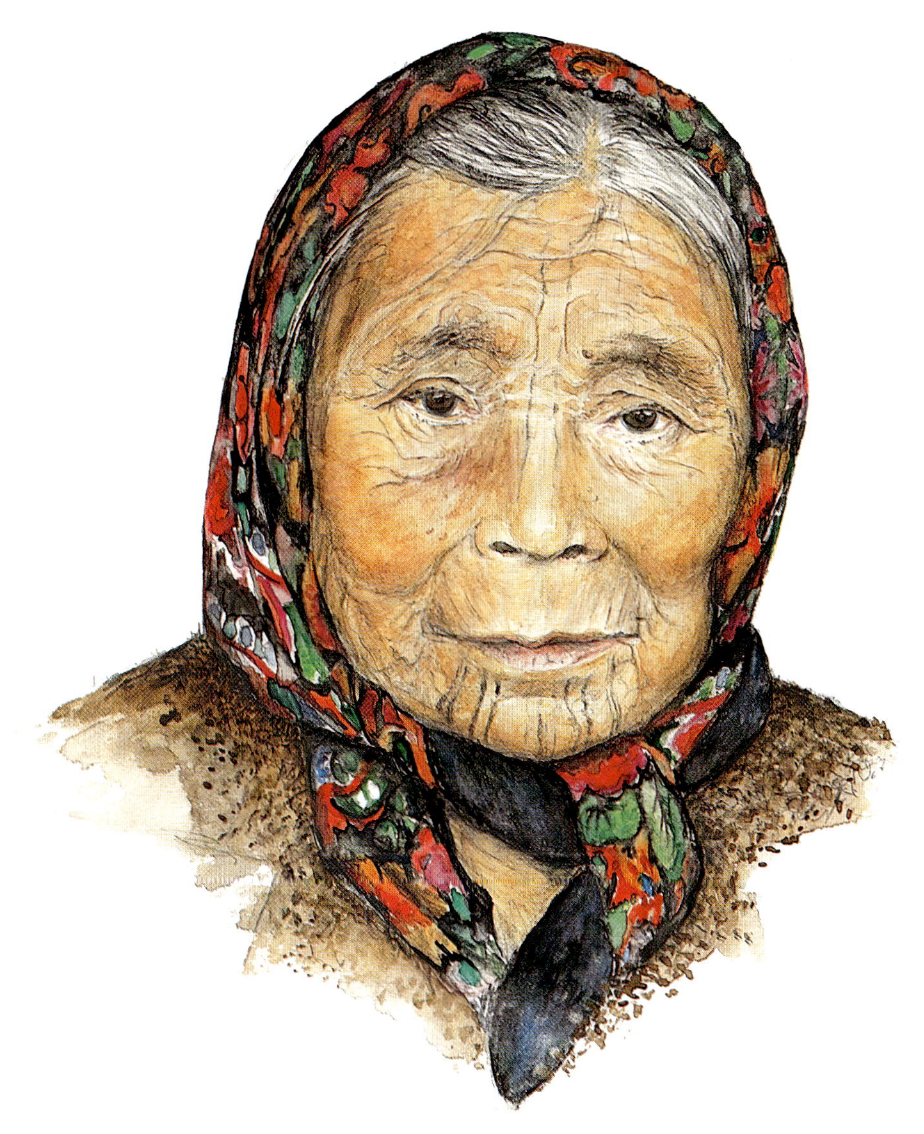

ANNUAL'97

BOLOGNA ILLUSTRATORS OF CHILDREN'S BOOKS · ILLUSTRATORI DI LIBRI PER RAGAZZI

FICTION
NON FICTION

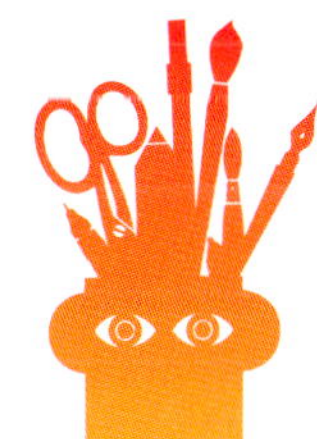

Mostra degli
Illustratori
Illustrators
Exhibition
BOLOGNA
10-13/4/'97

ANNUAL'95

BOLOGNA **ILLUSTRATORS OF CHILDREN'S BOOKS** · ILLUSTRATORI DI LIBRI PER RAGAZZI

NON FICTION

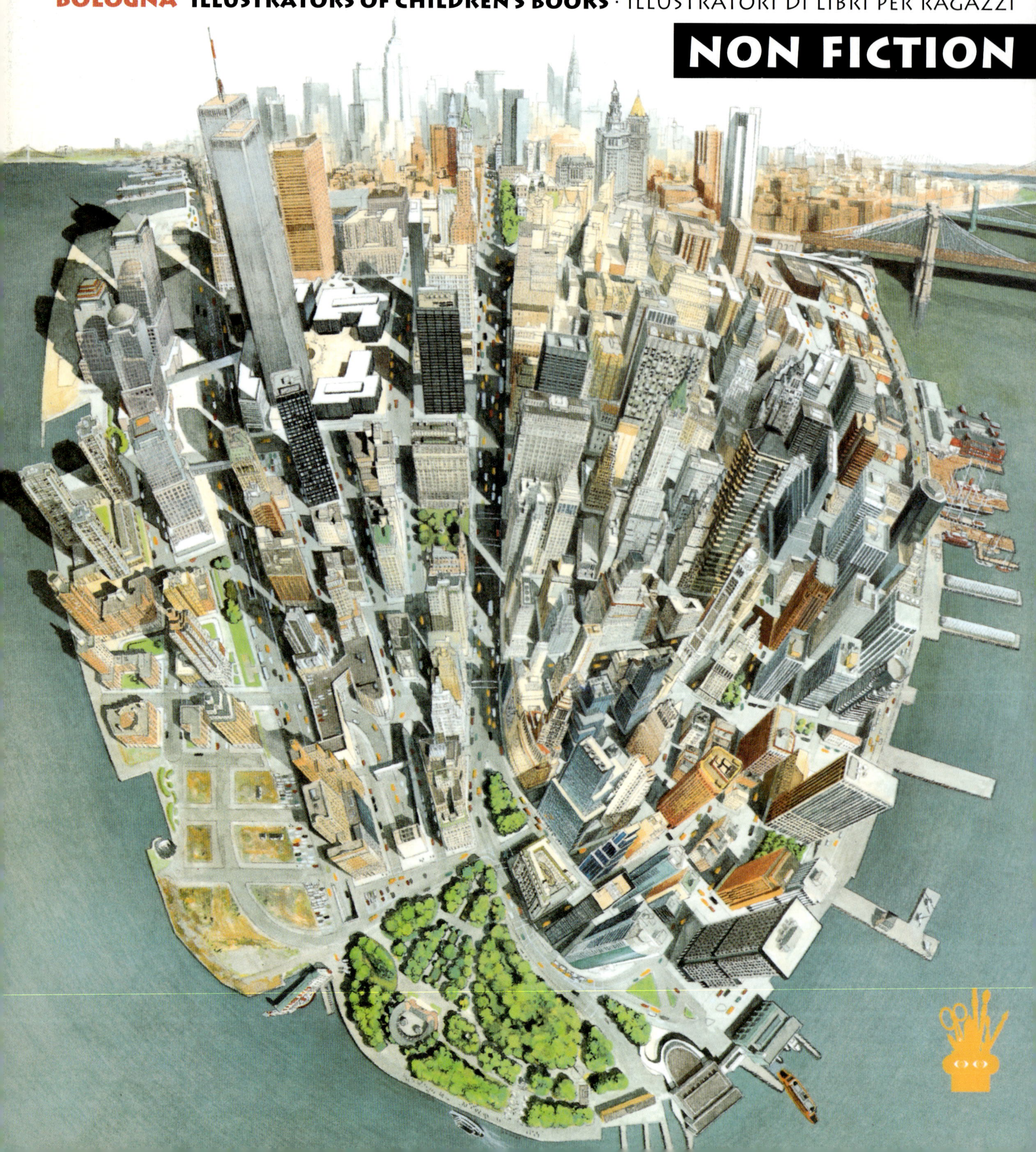

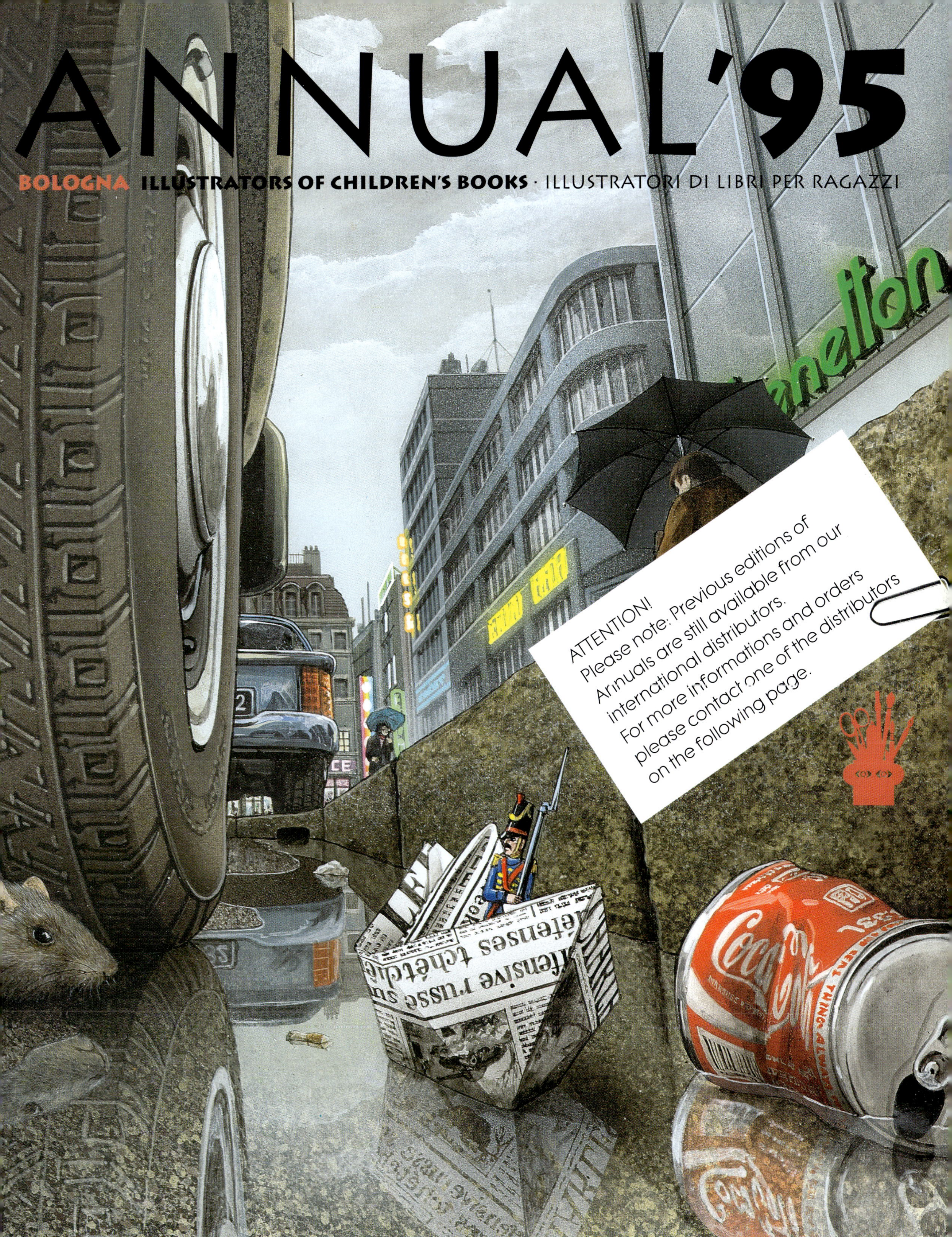
ANNUAL'95
BOLOGNA ILLUSTRATORS OF CHILDREN'S BOOKS · ILLUSTRATORI DI LIBRI PER RAGAZZI
ATTENTION!
Please note: Previous editions of Annuals are still available from our international distributors.
For more informations and orders please contact one of the distributors on the following page.

Copyright © 1996
Fiera del Libro per Ragazzi
Piazza Costituzione 6
40128 Bologna, Italy

Distributed in Italy only, by
BolognaFiere
Piazza Costituzione 6
40128 Bologna, Italy

Copublished with and distributed by:

Michael Neugebauer Verlag AG
Industriestrasse 837
CH-8625 Gossau Zürich
Tel. (1) 936 6969
Fax (1) 9366900

Australia:
North-South Books
c/o CIS Educational Pty. Ltd.
245 Cardigan Street
Carlton, Victoria 3053
Tel. (3) 349 1211
Fax (3) 347 0175

Austria and Germany:
Michael Neugebauer Verlag AG
c/o Vertriebsbüro Hamburg
Poppenbütteler Chaussee 53
D-22397 Hamburg
Tel. (40) 607 909 06
Fax (40) 607 23 26

Canada:
Editions Nord-Sud
c/o Diffusion Dimedia Inc.
539, Lebeau blvd
Ville St-Laurent, Québec H4N 1S2
Tel.(514) 336 39 41
Fax (514) 331 39 16
North-South Books
c/o Vanwell Publishing Ltd.
1, Northrup Crescent
St. Catharines, Ont L2M 6P5
Tel. (905) 937 31 00
Fax (905) 937 17 60

France:
Editions Nord-sud
c/o SOFEDIS
29, rue Saint-Sulpice
F-75006 Paris
Tel. (143) 29 09 60
Fax (146) 33 71 59

Great Britain:
North-South Books
c/o Ragged Bears Ltd.
Ragged Appleshaw
Andover
Hampshire SP11 9HX
Tel. (264) 772 269
Fax (264) 772 391

Japan
North-South Books Japan
Enshu Bldg. 3-3, Otsuka 3-Chome
Bunkyo-ku
Tokyo 112
Tel. (3) 3942 3986
Fax (3) 3942 1523

Netherlands
De Vier Windstreken
Industrieweg 7
NL-2254 AE Voorschoten
Tel. (71) 617 642
Fax (71) 619 741

Taiwan
Chinese edition only:
Ta Chien Publishing Co., Ltd
No. 19, Sin Ho Heng Road,
Tainan, Taiwan, R.O.C.
Tel. (06) 291 7489
Fax (06) 292 1618

USA
North-South Books Inc.
1123 Broadway, Suite 800
New York, N.Y. 10010
Tel.(212) 463 97 36
Fax (212) 633 10 04

Also available from above addresses:
BOLOGNA ANNUAL 96
FICTION catalogue
Consultant Non Fiction
Illustrators Exhibition:
Paola Vassalli

Graphic Designer:
G.Lanzi, Bologna
Litographed films:
Fotocrom, Udine
Printer:
La Editoriale Libraria SpA,
Trieste

Per informazioni
For information:

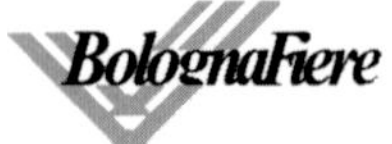

Mostra degli Illustratori
Piazza Costituzione 6
40128 Bologna (Italy)
Tel. 051-282111
Telex 511248 FIERBO I
Teefax 051-282333

Illustrators

Biographies

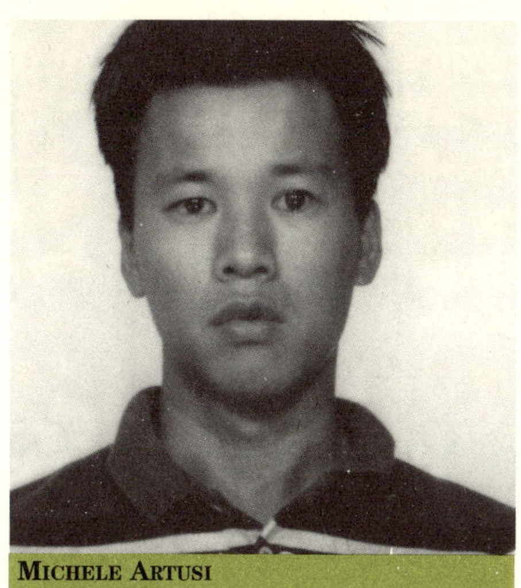

Michele Artusi

Address
Via Palestro 44
00187 Roma
Italy

Place and Date of Birth
Saigon, 8 March 1972

Art School Attended
European Institute of Design, Rome

School Director
Francesco Moschini

Coordinators of the Illustration Department
Giovanni Mazzoleni
Luciano Crovato

▲ UNPUBLISHED ▲

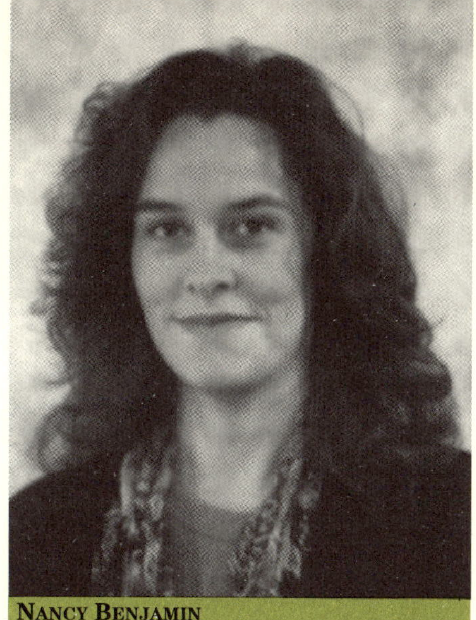

Nancy Benjamin

Address
Viale Le Corbusier 129
04100 Latina
Italy

Place and Date of Birth
Rome, 22 February 1958

Art Schools Attended
European Institute of Design, Rome
Academy of Fine Arts, Rome

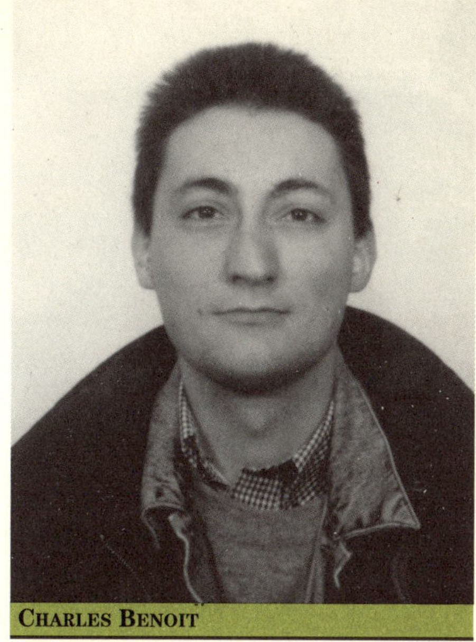

Charles Benoit

Address
2, rue Frederic
67100 Strasbourg
France

Place and Date of Birth
Compiègne, 10 June 1972

Art School Attended
School of Decorative Arts, Strasbourg

School Director
Jean Pierre Greff

Coordinator of the Illustration Department
Pierre Kuentz

▲ UNPUBLISHED ▲

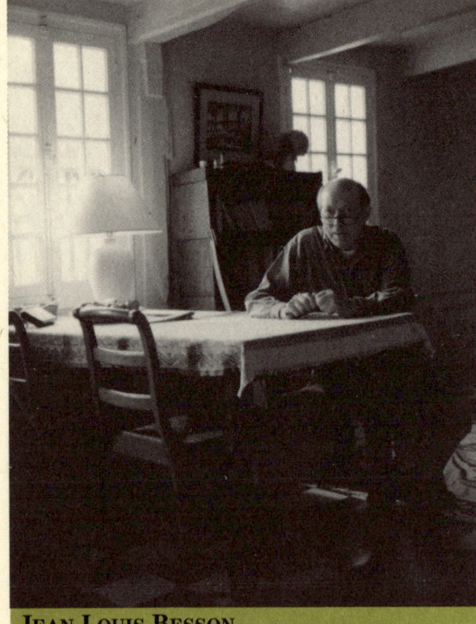

Jean Louis Besson

Address
35, rue d'Assas
75006 Paris
France

Place and Date of Birth
Paris, 9 July 1932

Art School Attended
School of Applied Arts, Paris

Published Titles
Le livre des découvertes et des inventions, Editions Gallimard
Le livre de l'histoire de France, Editions Gallimard
Le livre du costume, Editions Gallimard
Faites des mères, faites des pères!, Editions Gallimard

Techniques
Watercolour, coloured pencil

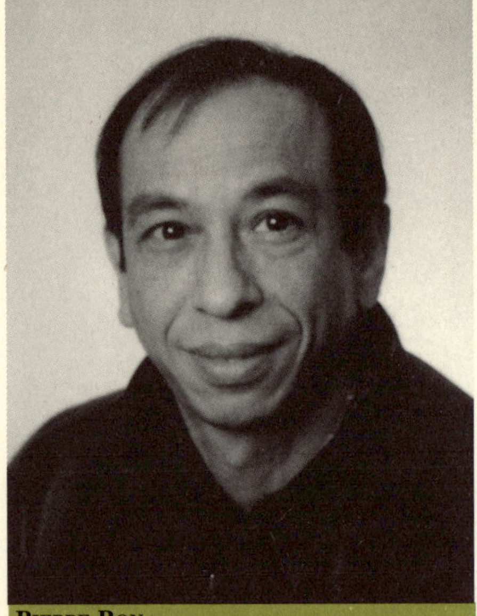

Pierre Bon

Address
144, Boulevard Voltaire
75011 Paris
France

Place and Date of Birth
Nhatrang, 18 May 1948

Art School Attended
School of Fine Arts, Department of Architecture, Paris

Published Titles
Les trains, Editions Fleurus
Plus haut, plus loin, L'Ecole des Loisirs/Archimede

Techniques
Airbrush

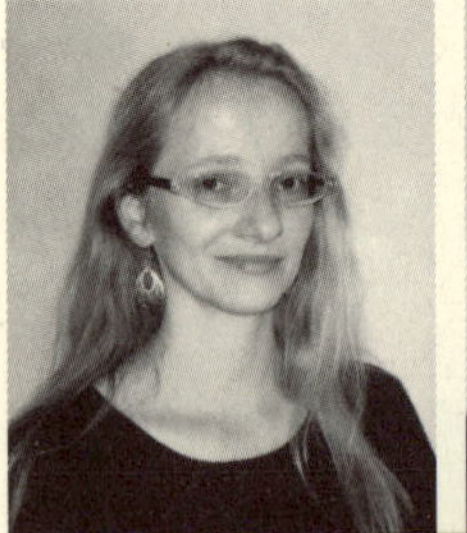

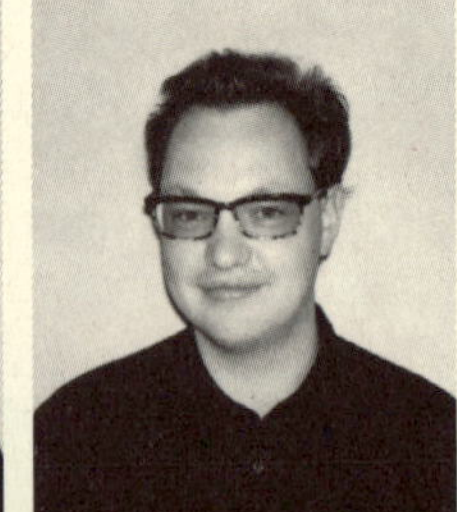

Susanne Bräunig - Harald Vorbrugg

Address
Stuntzstrasse 25
81677 München
Germany

Places and Dates of Birth
Bayreuth, 25 July 1965 (S. Bräunig)
Munich, 27 January 1965 (H. Vorbrugg)

Art Schools Attended
School and Academy of Art, Munich
Mountain College of Art and Design, Denver (S. Bräunig)

Schoool of Art, Munich
(H. Vorbrugg)

Published Titles
Haustiere Bei uns und Anderswo, Franckh-Kosmos Verlags
Tierkinder aus aller welt, Franckh-Kosmos Verlags
Das Buch vom Klima, Ravensburger Buchverlag Otto Maier
Das Buch vom Müll, Ravensburger Buchverlag Oto Maier
Deutschland Atlas für Kinder, Schönberger's Verlag
Europa Atlas für Kinder, Schönberger's Verlag
Weltatlas für Kinder, Schönberger's Verlag

Techniques
Watercolour

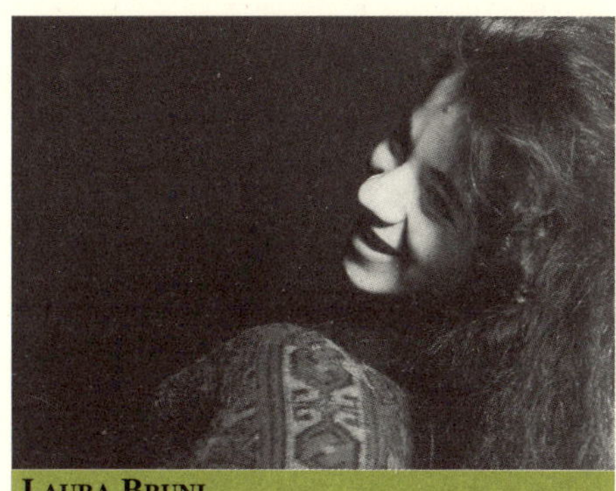

Laura Bruni

Address
Via San Benedetto 57
09129 Cagliari
Italy

Place and Date of Birth
Cagliari, 13 August 1968

Art School Attended
European Institute of Design

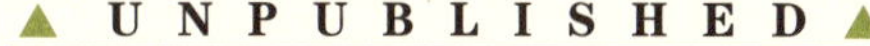

▲ UNPUBLISHED ▲

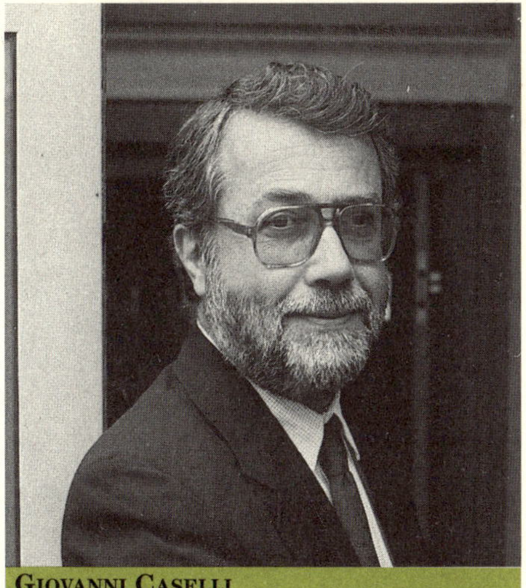

Giovanni Caselli

Address
P.O. Box 22
St. Paul's Bay
Malta

Place and Date of Birth
Bagno a Ripoli, 14 April 1939

Published Titles
Il primo uomo, Vallardi Industrie Grafiche
La storia del mondo, Dorling Kindersley Childrens
Le sette meraviglie del mondo, Dorling Kindersley Childrens

Techniques
Mixed

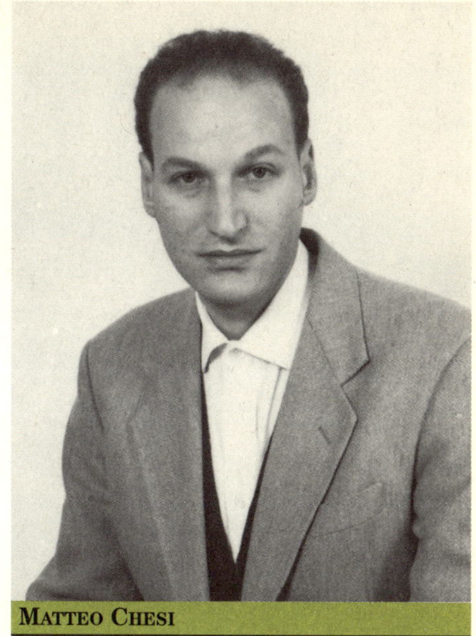

Matteo Chesi

Address
Via del Serraglio 89
50047 Prato
Italy

Place and Date of Birth
Florence, 7 November 1964

Art Schools Attended
School of Art, Florence
Academy of Fine Arts, Florence

Published Titles
Gli antichi cinesi, Giunti Publishing Group
Racconti inediti, Editrice Piccolo
La grande storia di Firenze, Ponte delle Grazie Editore
Il mio primo vocabolario illustrato, Editoriale Giorgio Mondadori
Dentro la lettura, Minerva Italica
L'albero delle parole, La Nuova Italia Editrice
La valigetta delle parole, La Nuova Italia Editrice
L'antica civiltà romana, Gemini/Larousse S.A.
Il mio primo libro dei contrari, Editoriale Giorgio Mondadori

Techniques
Acrylic colours

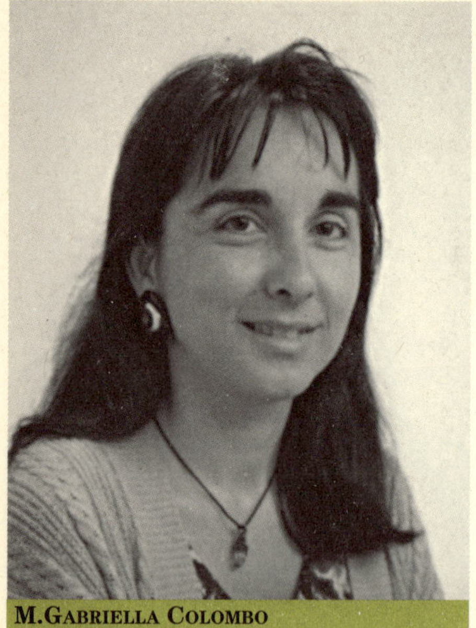

M.Gabriella Colombo

Address
Via Sabotino 12
20048 Carate/Milano
Italy

Place and Date of Birth
Besana in Brianza, 28 September 1959

Art School Attended
School of Cartoon Design

▲ U N P U B L I S H E D ▲

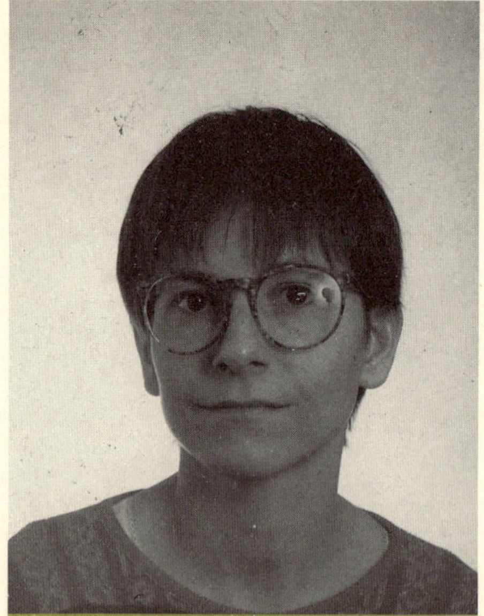

Isabelle Courmont

Address
21, Boulevard Carnot
59800 Lille
France

Place and Date of Birth
Courniéres, 14 December 1962

Art School Attended
E.S.A.T.T.

Published Titles
1492 en Mediterranée, Alif/Hatier
Mille et un nil, Alif/Hatier

Being Published Titles
Le cirque, Mango

Techniques
Watercolour and gouache

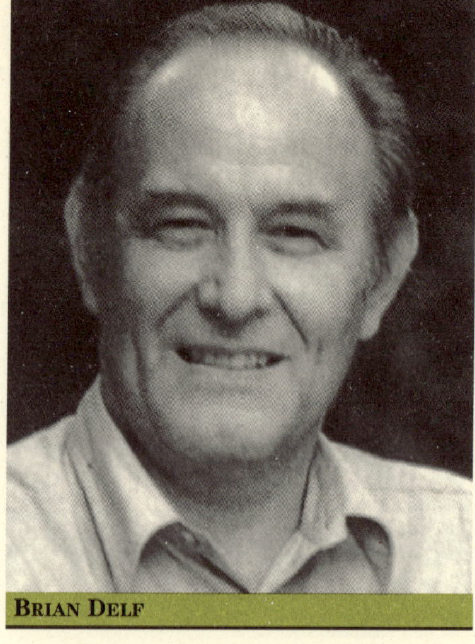

Brian Delf

Address
c/o Dorling Kindersley Children's Books
9 Henrietta Street
WC2E 8PS London
Great Britain

Place of Birth
Abington

Published Titles
The picture Atlas of the world, Dorling Kinderstley Childrens

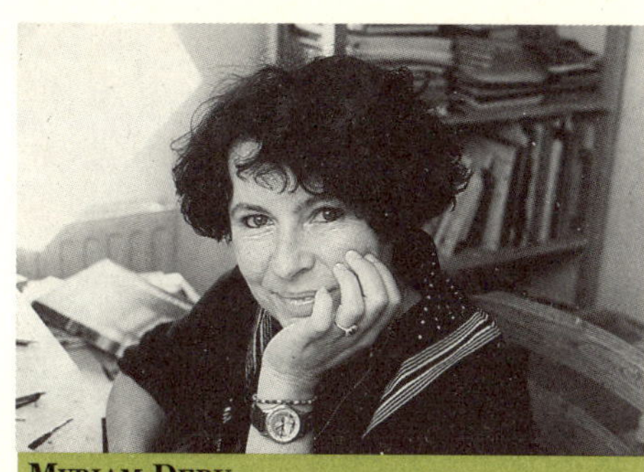

Myriam Deru

Address
75, rue du Tilleul
1332 Genval
Belgium

Place and Date of Birth
Libengé, 23 November 1954

Art School Attended
St. Luc Institute of Graphic Arts, Brussels

Published Titles
Le petit nuage pris de vertige, Gautier Languereau Deux Coqs d'Or
Le lutin pâtissier, Gautier Languereau Deux Coqs d'Or
Une toute petite taupe, Gautier Languereau Deux Coqs d'Or
Un anniversaire surprise, Gautier Languereau Deux Coqs d'Or
Aglaé au pays des couleurs, Casterman
Aglaé au pays des animaux, Casterman
Aglaé au pays des chiffres, Casterman
Aglaé au pays des arbres, Casterman
Aglaé au pays des fruits, Casterman
Aglaé au pays des heures, Casterman
Premier jour d'école, Gautier Languereau Deux Coqs d'Or
Pomme et Ananas, Gautier Languereau Deux Coqs d'Or
Victor va en Afrique, Gautier Languereau Deux Coqs d'Or
Le méchant loup, Gautier Languereau Deux Coqs d'Or
L'imagier des animaux, Editions Lito-Jesco
L'archipel des Tuamoutus, je vous prie, Livres du Dragon d'Or
Charlie fait du sport, Gautier Languereau Deux Coqs d'Or
Dix histoires de lutins, Editions Lito-Jesco
Le beaux jours, Editions Fernand Nathan
Après la pluie, Editions Fernand Nathan

Techniques
Watercolour, pastel, pencil

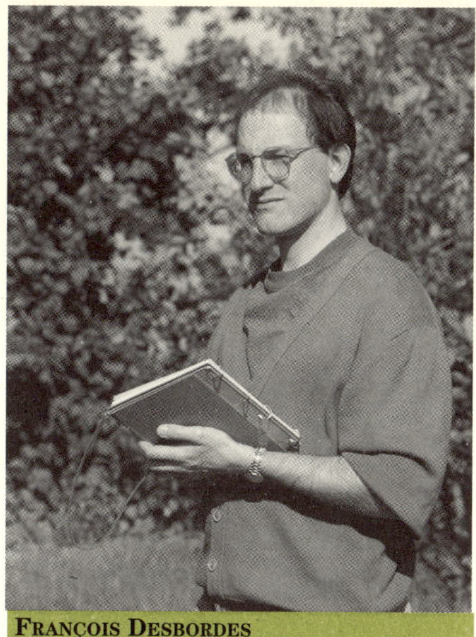

François Desbordes

Address
12, rue Saint Germain/Serny
62145 Enquin les Mines
France

Place and Date of Birth
Gueret, 11 July 1962

Art School Attended
Duperré School of Applied Arts, Paris

Published Titles
Carnets de la Nature:
Les mammifères marins, Editions Gallimard

Techniques
Watercolour

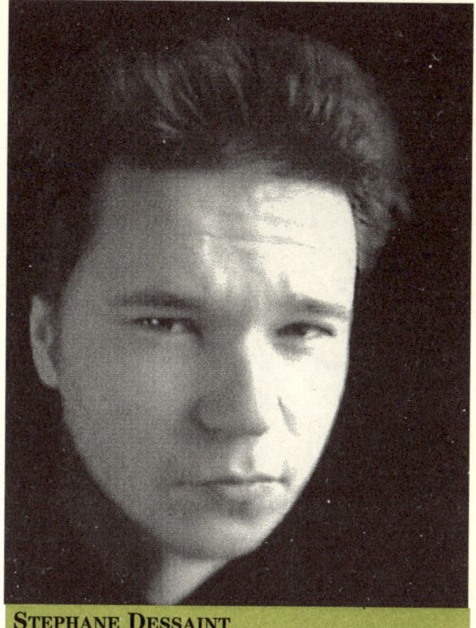

Stephane Dessaint

Address
12, rue de Rome
67000 Strasbourg
France

Place and Date of Birth
Istres, 6 August 1973

Art School Attended
School of Decorative Arts, Strasbourg

School Director
Jean Pierre Greff

Coordinator of the Illustration Department
Pierre Kuentz

▲ UNPUBLISHED ▲

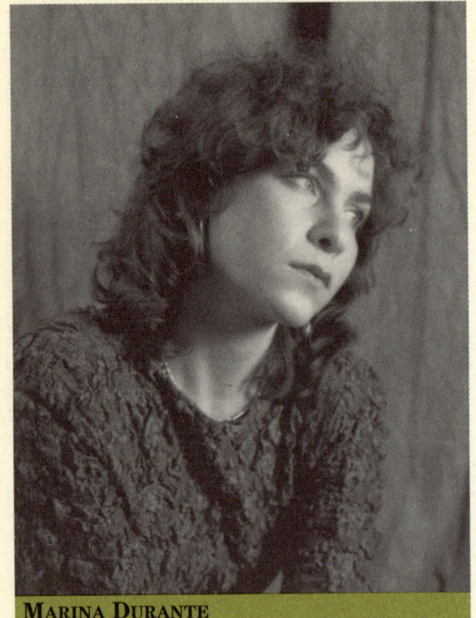

Marina Durante

Address
Via dei Gracchi 9
20146 Milano
Italy

Place and Date of Birth
Milan, 12 June 1964

Art Schools Attended
School of Applied Industrial Art, Milan
University of Milan, Faculty of Architecture

Published Titles
Giardini e terrazzi, Gruppo Editoriale Fabbri
Alberi amici miei, Edizioni San Paolo
Grideranno le pietre, Edizioni San Paolo
La geografia degli animali, Edizioni San Paolo
Benvenuti, bentornati, Edizioni San Paolo
Agenda natura, Edizioni San Paolo
Rubrica natura, Edizioni San Paolo
Magico tris, Edizioni San Paolo
Le vie della scienza, Carlo Signorelli
Cuaderno de la naturaleza, Editorial Everest, S.A.
Il giornale del birdwatch, Pubblinova Edizioni Negri
My feet are just right, Wendy Pye Limited
Jahreszeiten, SKV
Unsere freunde, SKV
Lied der Jahreszeiten, SKV

Techniques
Watercolour, acrylic, airbrush

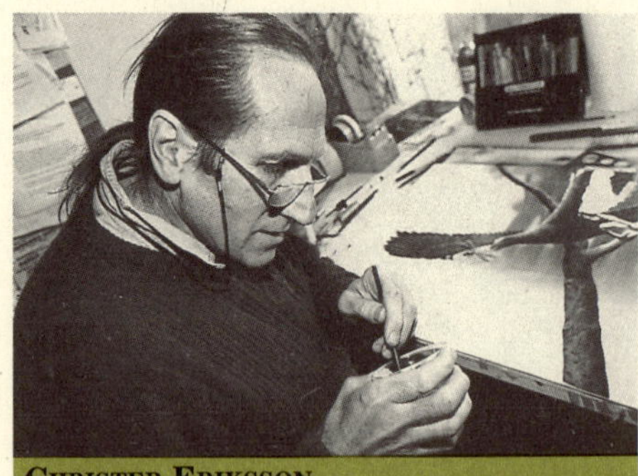

Christer Eriksson

Address
5, Gilbert Place
2086 Frenchs Forest
Australia

Place and Date of Birth
Stockholm, 20 September 1942

Art School Attended
School of Art, Stockholm

Published Titles
Discoveries, Weldon Owen Pty Ltd:
Dangerous animals
Under the sea
The human body
Games and sports
Mammals
How things work
Our neighbourhood

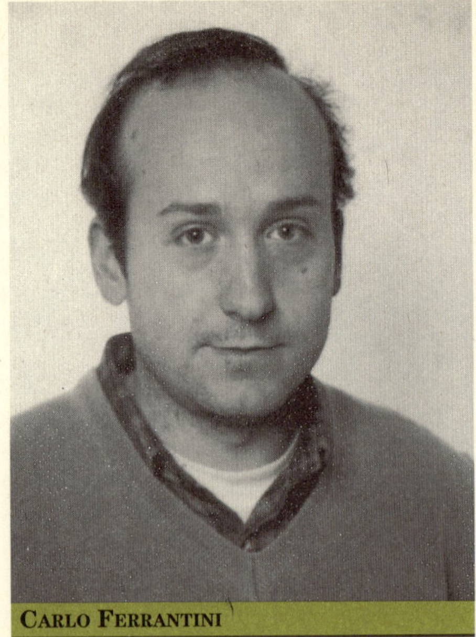

Carlo Ferrantini

Address
Via Aretina 108
50136 Firenze
Italy

Place and Date of Birth
Florence, 26 October 1967

Art Schools Attended
School of Anatomic Drawing, Bologna
Course on Technical Illustrations, Florence

Published Titles
I Maya, Vallardi Industrie Grafiche
Gli Arabi in Italia, Vallardi Industrie Grafiche
I Giapponesi, Vallardi Industrie Grafiche
I Fenici, Vallardi Industrie Grafiche
Il mondo capovolto, Einaudi Ragazzi
L'Odissea, I Dioscuri
L'Iliade, I Dioscuri

Techniques
Airbrush, mixed

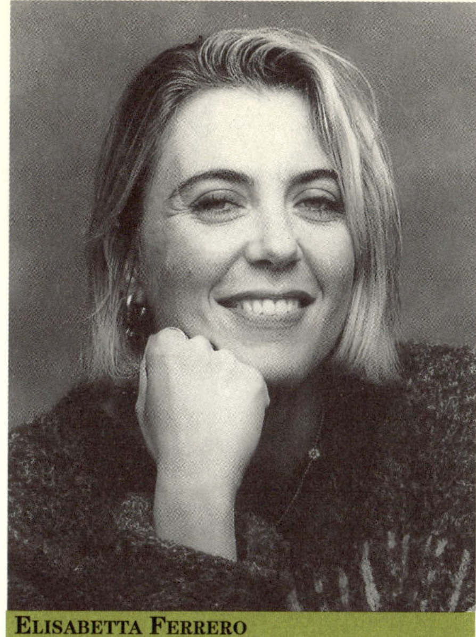

Elisabetta Ferrero

Address
Via Francesco Borgogna 8
13100 Vercelli
Italy

Place and Date of Birth
Vercelli, 8 September 1960

Art School Attended
European Institute of Design, Milan

Published Titles
Fiabe classiche per il Giappone, Gruppo Editoriale Fabbri - Gakken Co.
Heidi, Gruppo Editoriale Fabbri
Where in the world, Orpheus Books
Record holders, Orpheus Books
Under the sea, Orpheus Books
Mon chat, Fleurus Presse - Tardy
Sharks, Ravensburger Buchverlag Otto Maier
Animali in casa, Giunti Publishing Group

Techniques
Coloured pencil

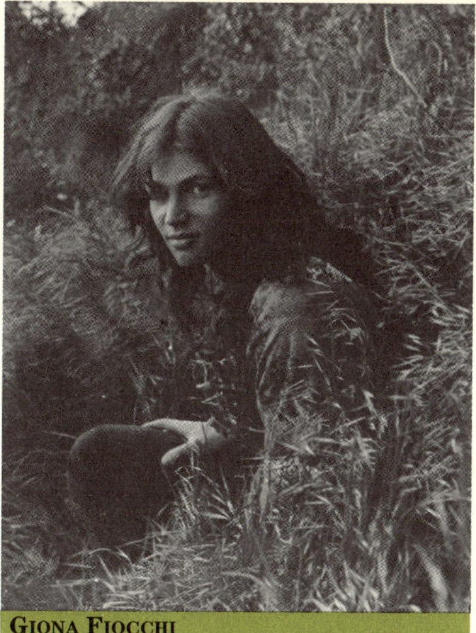

Giona Fiocchi

Address
Via Dante 256
21030 Cassano Valcuvia/Varese
Italy

Place and Date of Birth
Varese, 6 June 1969

Art Schools Attended
School of Art, Varese
Academy of Fine Arts, Brera
Academy of Art, Vienna
Academy of Applied Art, Vienna

Published Titles
The poet, Grimm Press
Detective novels, Grimm Press
The Bible, Ottenheimer Publishers

Techniques
Pencil on transparent polyester radex paper, ink pen and watercolour

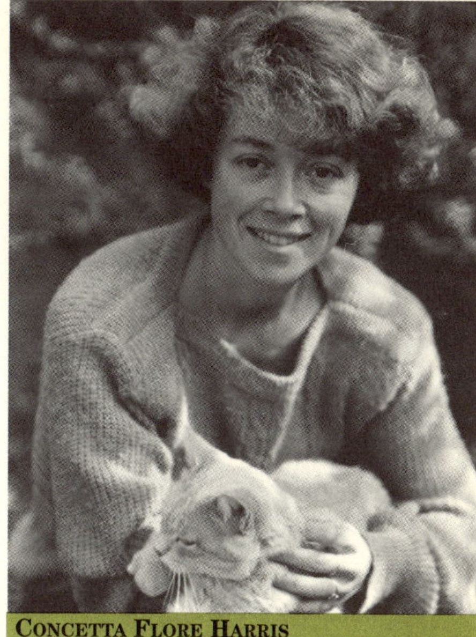

Concetta Flore Harris

Address
Via Pietro Venturi 21
00149 Roma
Italy

Place and Date of Birth
Rome, 26 November 1962

Art School Attended
Academy of Fine Arts, Rome

Published Titles
Guida ai parchi d'Europa, Giorgio Mondadori
Primo manuale: animali intorno a noi, Istituto Geografico De Agostini - Happy Books
Pieren om ons heen, J. Mulder & Zoon B.V. - Happy Books
Primo manuale: animali amici miei, Istituto Geografico De Agostini - Happy Books
Autour de nous: mes amis les animaux, Piccolia - Happy Books

Techniques
Watercolour, china, mixed

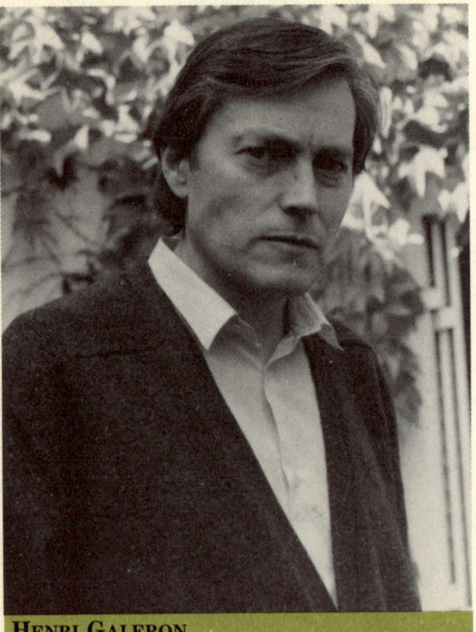

Henri Galeron

Address
45, rue Racine
92120 Montrouge
France

Place and Date of Birth
Saint-Etienne du Grès, 4 December 1939

Art School Attended
School of Fine Arts, Marseille

Published Titles
The kidnapping of the coffee pot, Harlin Quist
When!, Harlin Quist
Roll call, Harlin quist
L'oublide Noé, Harlin Quist
Voyage au pays des arbres, Editions Gallimard
Le doigt magique, Editions Gallimard
Le pêche à la baleine, Editions Gallimard
Le pont, Editions Gallimard
Lettre d'anniversaire, Editions Gallimard

Techniques
Ink, watercolour, pencil, acrylic

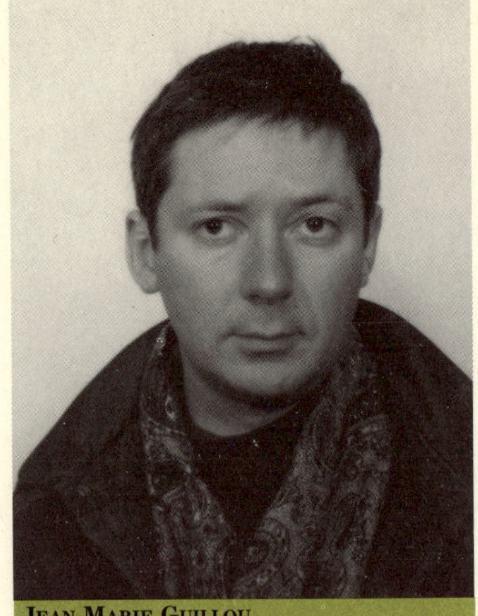

Jean-Marie Guillou

Address
2, rue Poullain du Parc
35000 Rennes
France

Place and Date of Birth
Brest, 7 March 1965

Art School Attended
School of Fine Arts, Rennes

Matthias Haab

Address
Im Thal
8714 Feldbach
Switzerland

Place and Date of Birth
Zurich, 26 January 1958

Art School Attended
School of Art, Zurich

▲ UNPUBLISHED ▲

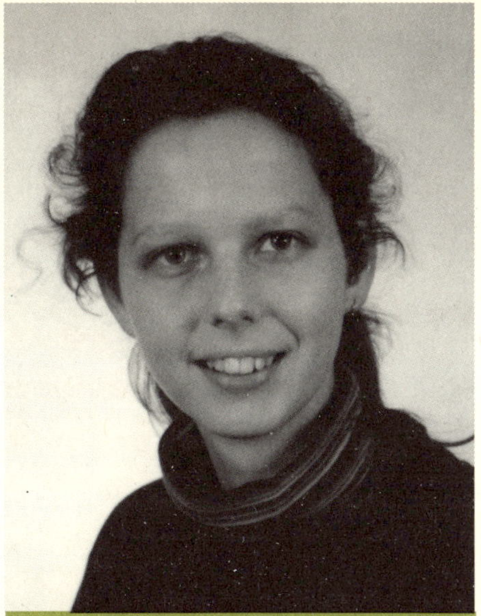

Andrea Hebrock

Address
Argartstrasse 24
22087 Hamburg
Germany

Place and Date of Birth
Herford, 12 August 1971

Art School Attended
College of Figurative Arts, Hamburg

School Director
Gero Flurschütz

Coordinator of the Illustration Department
Gero Flurscütz

Published Titles
So lonely, Verlag Friedrich Oetinger
Karin Schwing erzählt von den Eskimos, Verlag Friedrich Oetinger

Techniques
Watercolour, coloured pencil, tempera

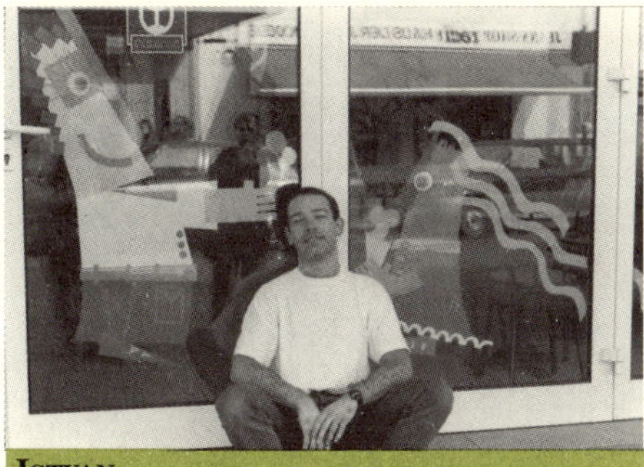

Istvan

Address
Saavedra 1549
1623 Ingeniero Maschwitz/Buenos Aires
Argentina

Place and Date of Birth
Madrid, 8 October 1968

Published Titles
¿Asmalegrético o Asmatristón?, Ediciones Astro
Les murs nets ne disent rien, Ediciones Quirquincho
Espagnol comme langue étrangère, Institut du Professorat à langues vives
Histoire 4me année, Espagnol 3me année, Intégral 1er année, Université Pédagogique National
L'histoire qu'ont vécu les mathématiques, Ediciones Letra Buena
J'experimente et j'apprends, Ediciones Lugar
En pensant à choisir, Ediciones El Hacedor
Lire et connaître, Ediciones Aique
El nuevo escriturón, Ediciones El Hacedor
Ta-te-titeres, Ediciones Estrada

Techniques
China ink, collage

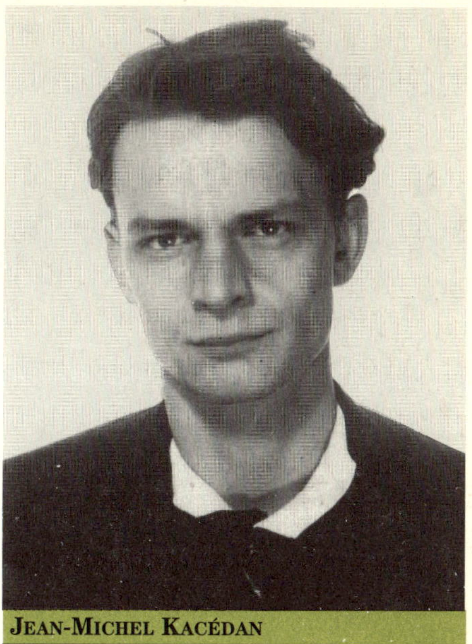

Jean-Michel Kacédan

Address
8, Impasse des Gendarmes
78000 Versailles
France

Place and Date of Birth
Versailles, 30 April 1965

Art School Attended
ENSAD, Paris

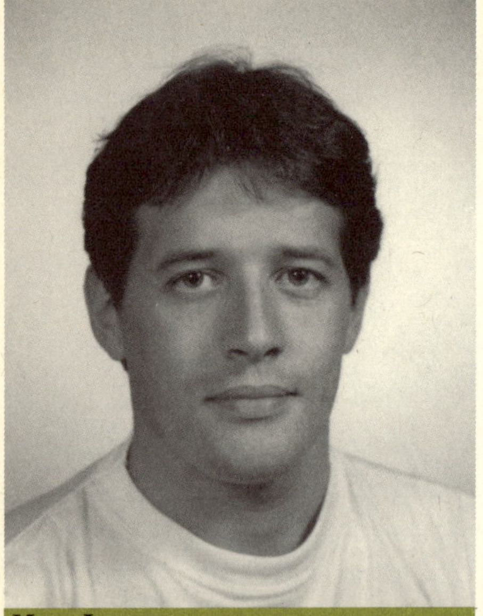

Marc Lagarde

Address
46, rue D'Orsel
75018 Paris
France

Place and Date of Birth
Bordeaux, 23 March 1965

Art School Attended
School of Decorative Arts, Paris

Published Titles
Ma Première Encyclopédie: L'histoire, Larousse S.A.
Encyclopédie des Jeunes, Larousse S.A.:
L'atlas des pays du monde
Geologie
Découvertes Junior: Le sport, Editions Gallimard
Lecture Junior: L'homme de vagues, Editions Gallimard
Les Racines du savoir, Editions Gallimard:
L'architecture
L'eau
La musique
Le cinema
Vivre sur l'eau

Techniques
Watercolour

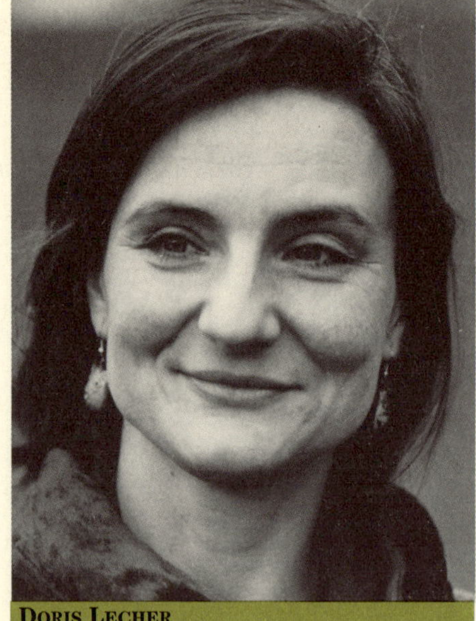

Doris Lecher

Address
15, Grabenmattweg
4123 Allschwil
Switzerland

Place and Date of Birth
Zurich, 25 May 1962

Art School Attended
Parsons School of Design, New York

Published Titles
Angelita's magic yarn, Farrar, Straus & Giroux
Das Bunte ABC - Such Bilder Buch, Verlag Herder AG

Techniques
Watercolour

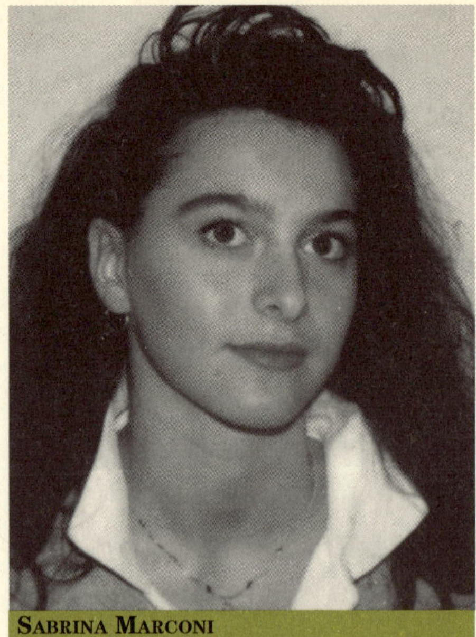

Sabrina Marconi

Address
Via Calimno 49
00141 Roma
Italy

Place and Date of Birth
Rome, 8 June 1974

Art School Attended
European Institute of Design, Rome

School Director
Francesco Moschini

Coordinators of the Illustration Department
Giovanni Mazzoleni
Luciano Crovato

▲ UNPUBLISHED ▲

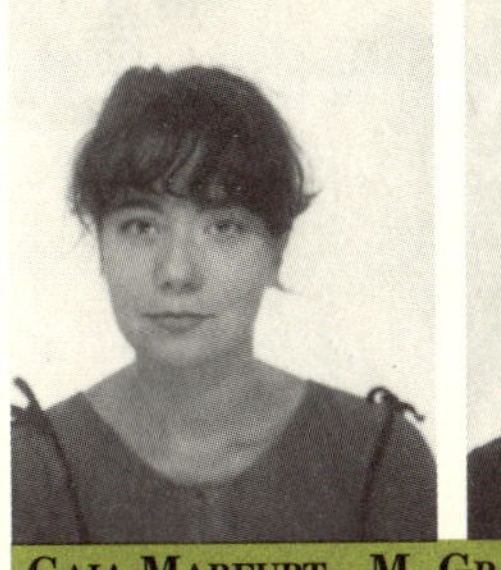
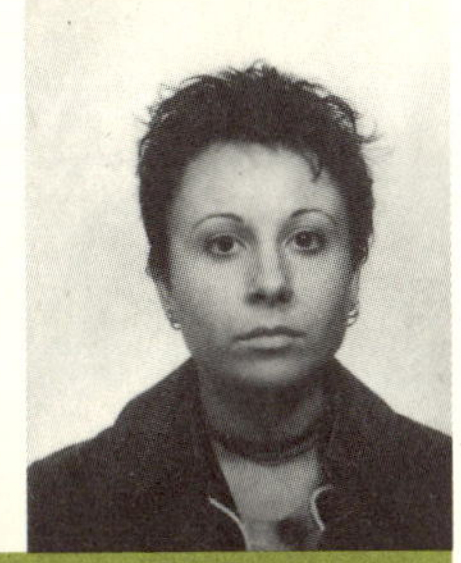

Gaia Marfurt - M. Grazia Di Bernardo

Address
G.Marfurt
Via A. Bertolotto 65
00122 Roma

M.G.Di Bernardo
Via Cesare Battisti 144
65100 Roma
Italy

Places and Dates of Birth
Rome, 5 June 1974 (G.Marfurt)
Pescara, 25 August 1975 (M.G.Di Bernardo)

Art School Attended
European Institute of Design, Rome

School Director
Francesco Moschini

Coordinator of the Illustration Department
Patrizia Di Sciullo

▲ UNPUBLISHED ▲

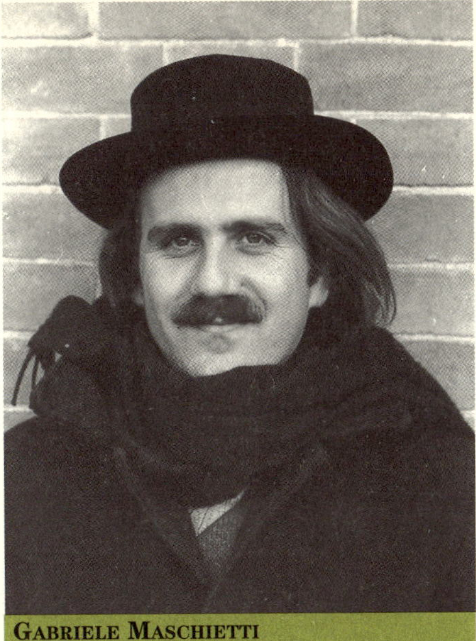

Gabriele Maschietti

Address
Via Condove 11
10129 Torino
Italy

Place and Date of Birth
Milan, 12 June 1954

Art Schools Attended
School of Art
University of Turin, Faculty of Architecture

Published Titles
Serragli e menagerie, Umberto Allemandi & C.
Giardini zoologici, Umberto Allemandi & C.

Being Published Titles
Aesopo and us, Lutterworth Press James Clarke & Co.
Fly,fly, Lutterworth Press James Clarke & Co.

Techniques
Watercolour, pencil

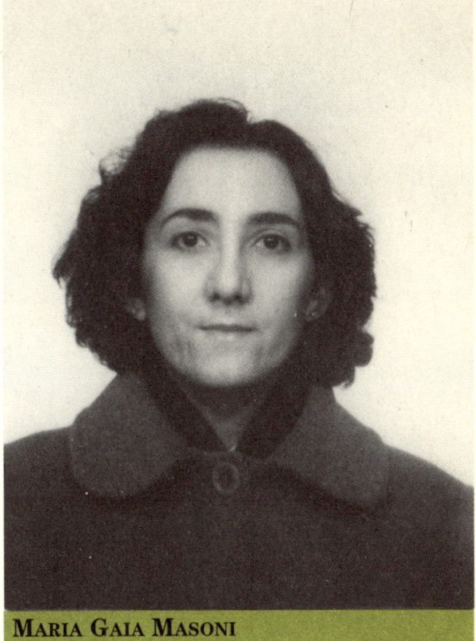

Maria Gaia Masoni

Address
Via Vecchia S. Alberto 10
16154 Genova
Italy

Place and Date of Birth
Genoa, 5 August 1971

Art Schools Attended
Paul Klee School of Art
Academy of Fine Arts

▲ UNPUBLISHED ▲

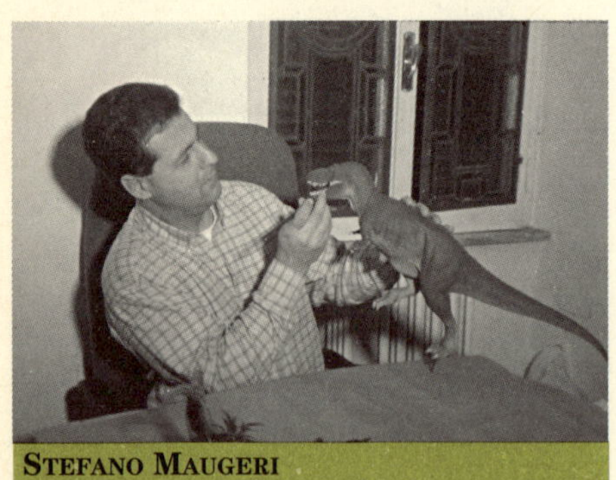

Stefano Maugeri

Address
Via Adriano Tilgher 41, Pal. 8/A
00137 Roma
Italy

Place and Date of Birth
Rome, 7 October 1052

Art School Attended
Art Institute, Rome

Published Titles
Le isole della saggezza, Gastaldi
Rettili d'Italia, Giunti Publishing Group
Il popolo delle rocce, R.C.S.Libri & Grandi Opere S.P.A. Rizzoli
Orso vivrai!, Editoriale Giorgio Mondadori
Serpenti d'Europa, Editoriale Giorgio Mondadori
Animali a rischio, Editoriale Giorgio Mondadori
Nel parco nazionale d'Abruzzo, K & B

Techniques
Pastel, tempera, watercolour, acrylic

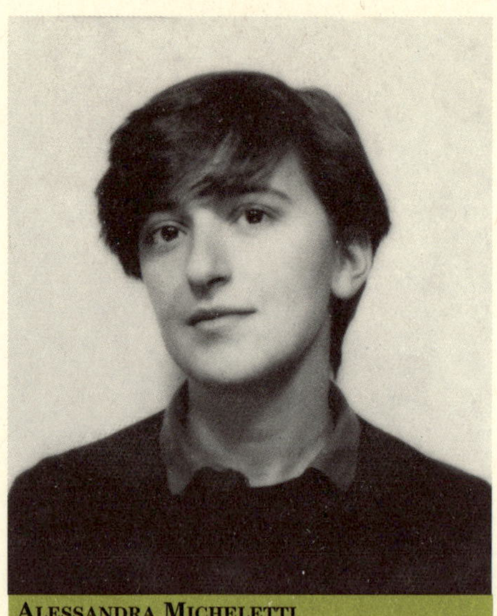

Alessandra Micheletti

Address
Via Tagliabue 419
24030 Pontida/Bergamo
Italy

Place and Date of Birth
Santa Margherita Ligure, 27 June 1958

Art School Attended
Carrara Academy of Fine Arts, Bergamo

Published Titles
Il libro della giungla, Mursia Ugo Editore
Pattini d'argento, Mursia Ugo Editore
Pollicino, Mursia Ugo Editore
Il richiamo della foresta, Mursia Ugo Editore
La bella addormentata nel bosco, Lucchetti Editore
Story time - Two easy stories, Minerva Editrice
Storie d'ombra, Edizioni Scolastiche Bruno Mondadori
Le avventure di Tom Sawyer, Edizioni Piccoli
Piccole donne, Edizioni Piccoli
La foresta tropicale, Editoriale Jaca Book
Cenerentola, Istituto Geografico de Agostini

Techniques
Pencil, china, watercolour, acrylic, oil, tempera, chalk, engraving

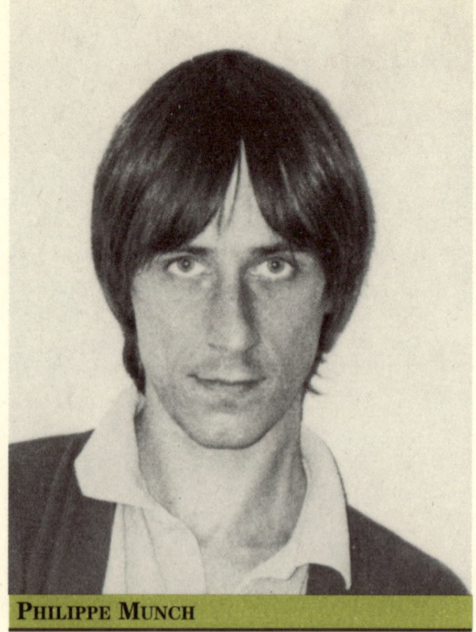

Philippe Munch

Address
1, rue Fritz
67000 Strasbourg
France

Place and Date of Birth
Colmar, 1 March 1959

Art School Attended
School of Decorative Arts, Strasbourg

Published Titles
Folio Cadet, Editions Gallimard:
Le géant de fer / Madame Curie.
Folio Junior, Editions Gallimard:
L'habitant des étoiles / Youg / Les pirates de l'espace / Terreur sur la planète / L'invasion des Androïdes / Grite.
Le seigneur des anneaux:
La communauté de l'anneau, Livres 1 et 2 / Les deux tours, Livres 3 et 4 / Le retour du roi, Livres 5 et 6 / Les clandestins / L'île de docteur Moreau / Le mystère de la chambre jaune / Le parfum de la dame en noir / Les cinq pépins d'orange / Le grizzly.
Aventures à construire, Casterman:
Odamok / Diego / Mahil / Olle, les voyages du cormoran.
Passé Composé, Casterman:
L'auberge des trois tambours / L'esclave d'Athenes.
Mystère, Casterman:
Blues pour Marco / Sonnez les matines.
Editions Milan:
Les aventures du Mouton Marcel / Monsieur Fantastico / Le vol du faucon / Diabolo S.O.S. Terre.
Bayard Presse:
L'escrocoeur / Petit guerrier / Le maître du bronze.
Plon:
Terre Humaine - Les lances du crépuscule

Techniques
Acrylic

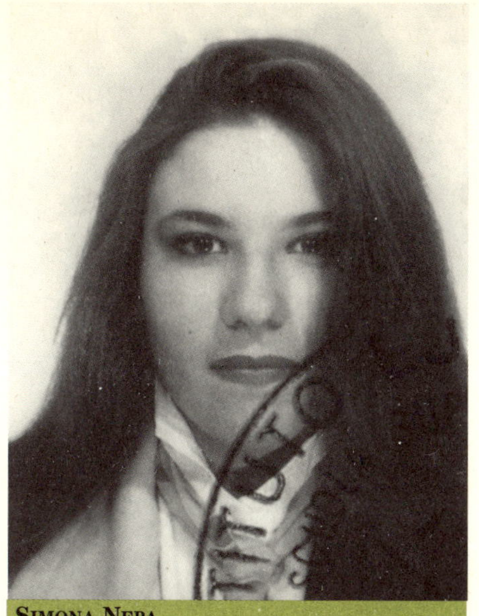

Simona Nepa

Address
Contrada Foro int. 5
Francavilla al Mare/Chieti

Place and Date of Birth
Pescara, 26 August, 1974

Art School Attended
European Institute of Design, Rome

School Director
Francesco Moschini

Coordinator of the Illustration Department
Antonello Cuccu

▲ UNPUBLISHED ▲

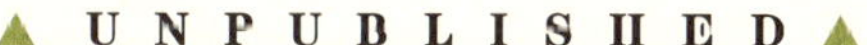

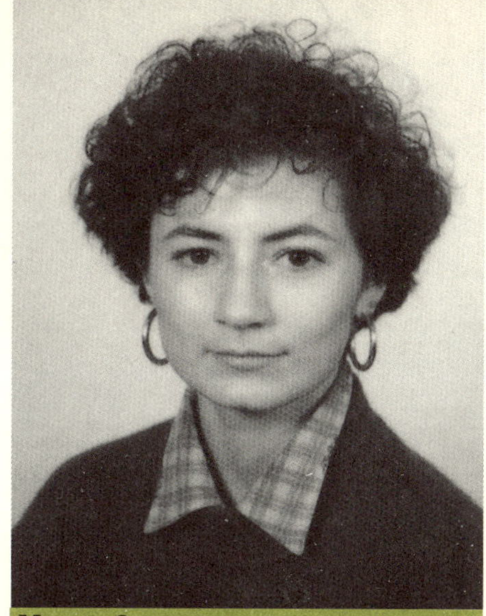

Monica Ottelli

Address
Via Vivaldi 12
46043 Castiglione delle Stiviere/Mantova
Italy

Place and Date of Birth
Castiglione delle Stiviere, 1 September 1969

Art Schools Attended
Institute of Art
G.B.Cignaroli Academy of Fine Arts

▲ UNPUBLISHED ▲

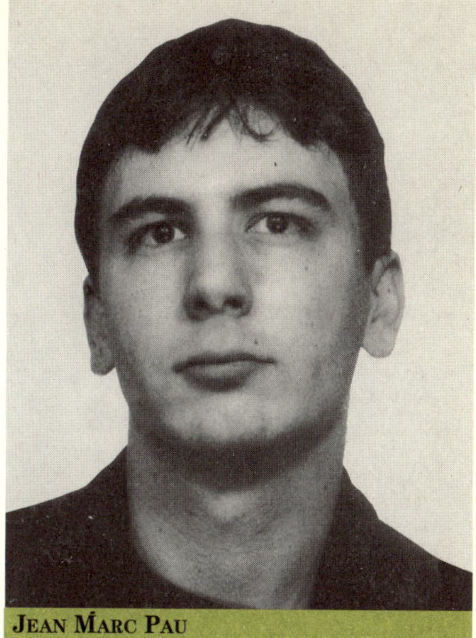

Jean Marc Pau

Address
17, rue Alfred de Musset
94310 Orly
France

Date of Birth
30 September 1965

Art School Attended
E.M.S.A.T., Paris

Published Titles
Pasteur, bataille contre les microbes,
Editions Fernand Nathan
Les Racines du savoir: Sur les traces des mammifères, Editions Gallimard

Techniques
Coloured pencil, watercolour, ink, markers

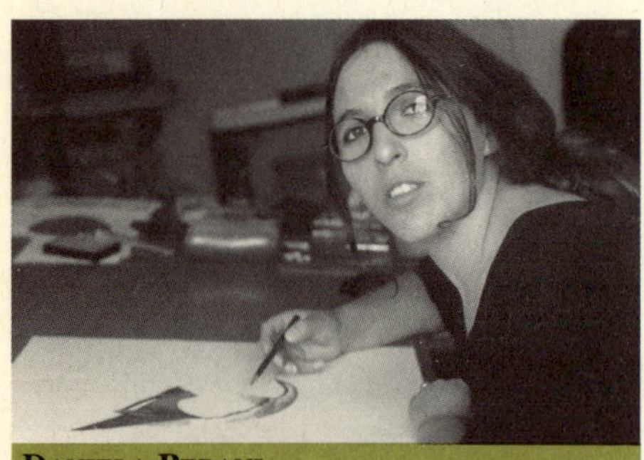

DANIELA PERANI

Address
Strada Molino 4
46040 Birbesi di Guidizzolo/Mantova
Italy

Place and Date of Birth
Castelgoffredo, 6 February 1969

Art Schools Attended
Art Institute, Guidizzolo
Academy of Fine Arts, Brera

▲ UNPUBLISHED ▲

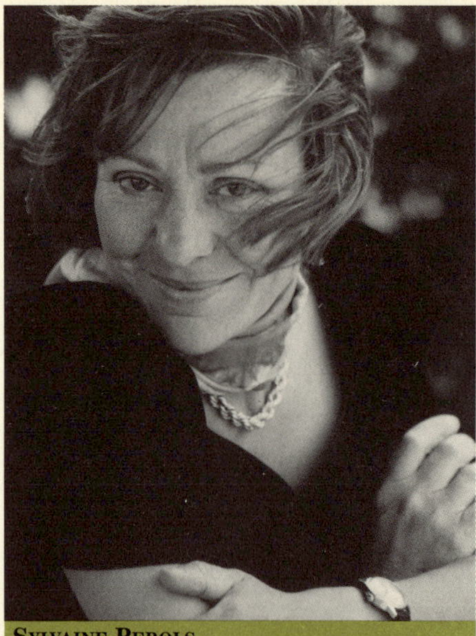

SYLVAINE PEROLS

Address
35 rue Labat
75018 Paris
France

Place and Date of Birth
Angers, 11 November 1959

Art School Attended
Art Institute, Angers

Published Titles
Mes Premières Découvertes, Editions Gallimard:
La chouette
Le corps
Atlas des animaux en danger
Atlas de plantes
La coccinelle
Le ciel et la terre
La souris
La ferme

Techniques
Ink

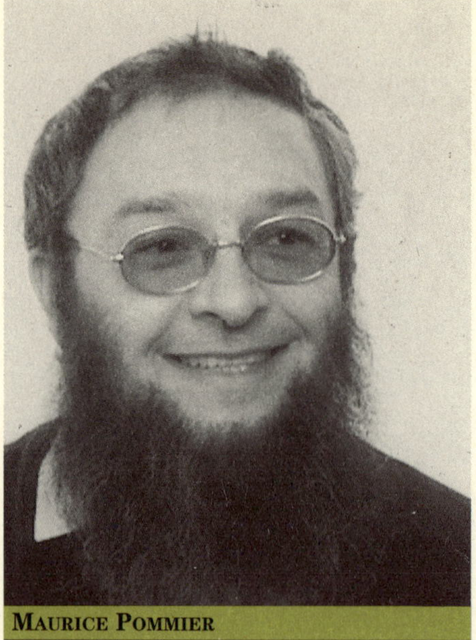

MAURICE POMMIER

Address
5, rue Sébastien Bottin
75007 Paris
France

Place and Date of Birth
Bellac, 9 December 1946

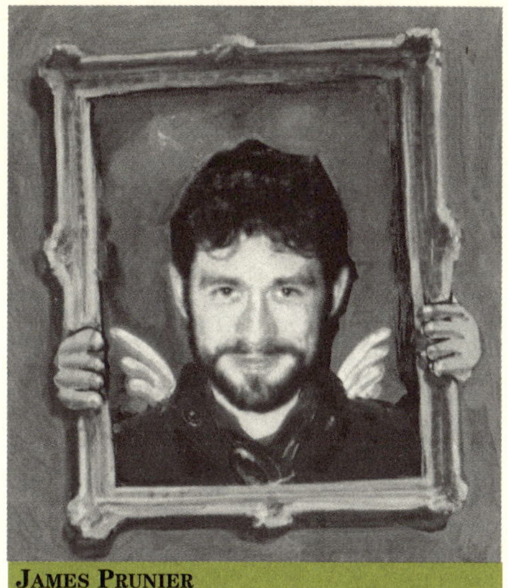

JAMES PRUNIER

Address
10, Boulevard Charles V
54000 Nancy
France

Place and Date of Birth
Oran, 25 April 1959

Art Schools Attended
School of Figurative Arts, Epinal
School of Fine Arts, Nancy

Published Titles
Editions Gallimard:
Une balle perdue
Livre des conquérants de l'espace
Croc blanc
Le fils du loup
l'éléphant
Le dinosaure
Victor victorieux
Le singe
La montre en or
Le tour du monde en 420 jours
Le train
Le manoire aux loups
La vache
Le livre de trains
Histoire de l'aviation
Le Transiberien, Berger Levrault

Techniques
Watercolour, ink, gouache, acrylic, oil

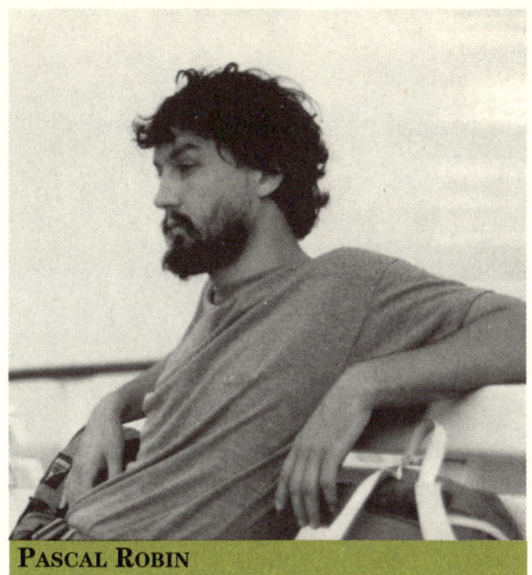

PASCAL ROBIN

Address
9, rue des Souces
92190 Meudon
France

Place and Date of Birth
Versailles, 20 February 1956

Art School Attended
ENSAD, Paris

Published Titles
Les Racines du savoir, Editions Gallimard:
Sur la trace des mammifères
Editions Milan, Carnet de Nature
Poissons de doux
Copains de mer
Copains de montagnes
Editions Fernand Nathan, Animaux Copain
La baleine
Explorons la nature
Grandeur Nature: Les dauphins
Dinosaures de France, BRGM

Techniques
Watercolour

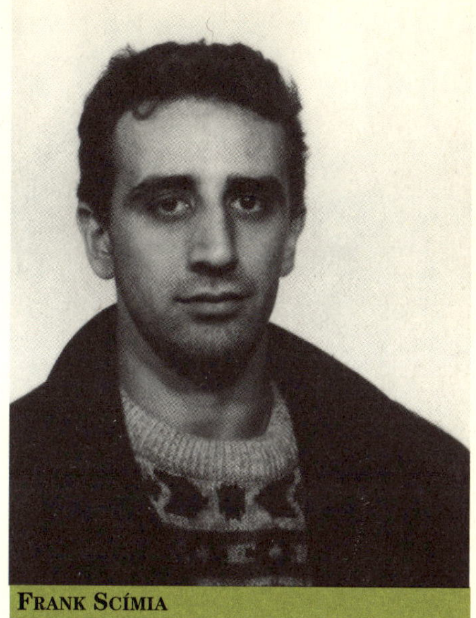

FRANK SCÍMIA

Address
Via del Foro 3
03043 Cassino/Frosinone
Italy

Place and Date of Birth
Moyeuvre Grande, 17 March 1970

Art School Attended
European Institute of Design, Rome

School Director
Francesco Moschini

Coordinator of the Illustration Department
Giovanni Mazzoleni

▲ UNPUBLISHED ▲

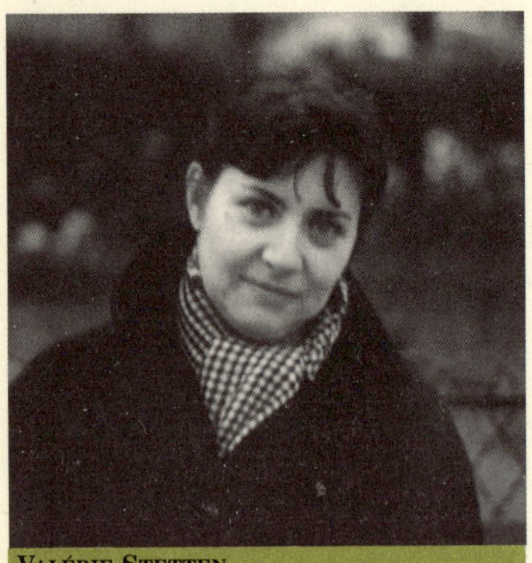

Valérie Stetten

Address
16, Villa Godin
75020 Paris
France

Place and Date of Birth
Paris, 6 July 1956

Art School Attended
University of Paris, Sorbonne

Published Titles
Le livre des chiens, Editions Gallimard
Le livre de la préhistoire, Editions Gallimard
Encyclopédie Découvertes Junior, Larousse S.A.-Editions Gallimard
Ma Première Encyclopédie: L'histoire, Larousse S.A.
Le Monde en poche: La météo, le temps, les saisons, Editions Fernand Nathan
La Bible, Fleurus Presse - Tardy

Being Published Titles
Le règne animal, Marshall Cavendish Books

Techniques
Watercolour, coloured pencil

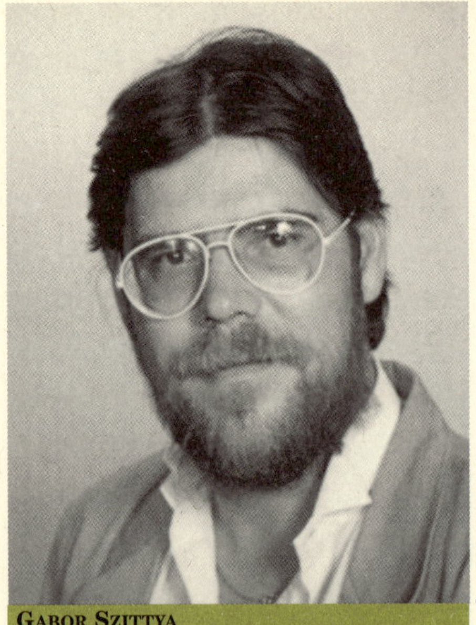

Gabor Szittya

Address
21, Avenue des Amandiers
13600 La Ciotat
France

Place and Date of Birth
Budapest, 29 June 1955

Art School Attended
Academy of Applied Arts, Department of Typography, Budapest

Published Titles
Les Racines du savoir: Les Théatres du monde, Editions Gallimard
Au pays des dinosaures, Editions Fernand Nathan

Technique
Ink

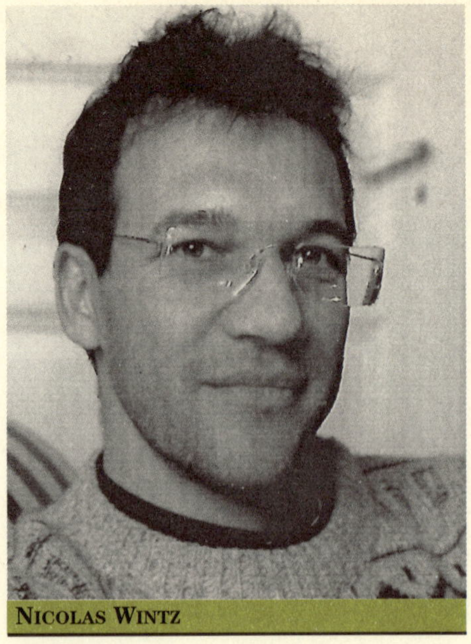

Nicolas Wintz

Address
17, rue Sleidan
67000 Strasbourg
France

Place and Date of Birth
Strasbourg, 26 April 1959

Art School Attended
School of Decorative Arts, Strasbourg

Published Titles
Folio Junior, Editions Gallimard:
L'assassinat du pere Noel
L'invit du ciel
Tristan et Iseut
Le borger qui devint roi
Et Brendan découvrit le paradis
Noel la niut magique
Editions Syros:
J'accuse - Romans temoignages
Les esclaves aujourd'hui
La famine en URSS
La tortureBoire et manger
Souris noire - Roman policier

Techniques
Watercolour

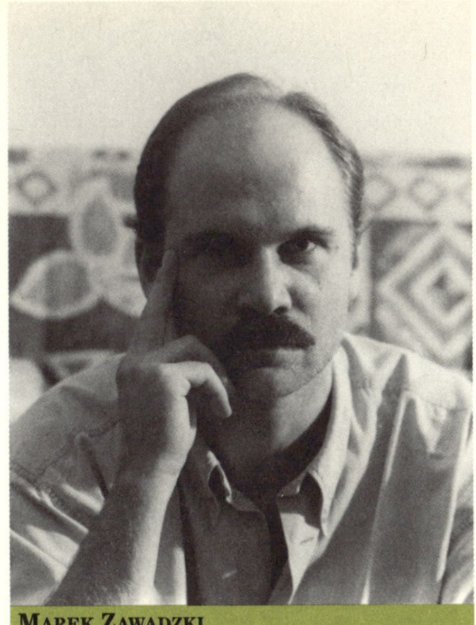

Marek Zawadzki

Address
Scrozberger Strasse 22
70435 Stuttgart
Germany

Place and Date of Birth
Warsaw, 9 March 1958

Art Schools Attended
Academy of Fine Arts, Warsaw and Stuttgart

Published Titles
Ich will Tanzen, Verlag J.F. Schreiber
Das Josephine Baker, Verlag J.F.Schreiber
Bilderbuch, Verlag J.F. Schreiber
Okino und die Wale, Verlag J.F.Schreiber
Ahajute und der Wolkenfresser, Verlag J.F.Schreiber

Technique
Acrylic, coloured pencil and gouache

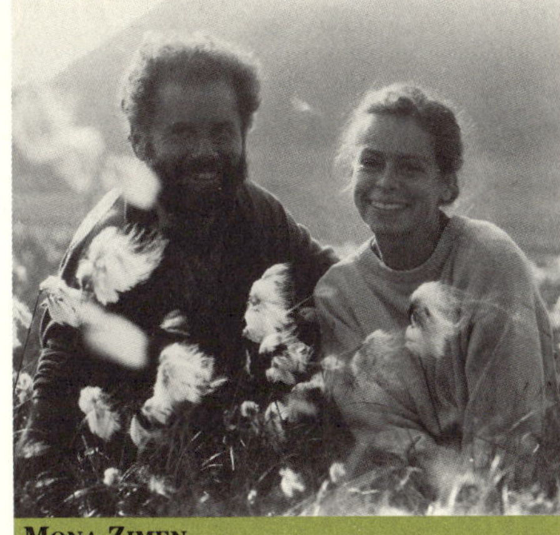

Mona Zimen

Address
Grillenöd
94542 Haarbach
Germany

Place and Date of Birth
Heidenheim, 20 January 1965